One
in Christ™

Student Book

Grade 4

CONCORDIA PUBLISHING HOUSE · SAINT LOUIS

Concordia
Publishing House

Copyright © 2011 Concordia Publishing House
3558 S. Jefferson Avenue, St. Louis, MO 63118-3968
1-800-325-3040 • cph.org

Written by Judy Berg, Neil Boettcher, Glenda Dobbertien, Nicki Dreyer, Jane Fryar, Kris Gaub, Lyla Glaskey, Diane Grebing, Carrie Hartwig, Laura Hildebrandt, Stephenie Hovland, Sharon Kembel, Carrie Kober, Sarah Koehneke, Shirley Koelling, Mary Lou Krause, Jill Otte, Connie Powell, Alfred Renard, Kevin Riemer, Eileen Ritter, Stephen Rockey, Karla Roeglin, John and Elaine Rubel, Lis Schendel, Annette Skibbe, Joan Tietz, Christine Weerts, Barbara Wegener, Debbie Weltmer

Edited by Rodney L. Rathmann

Series editors: Rodney L. Rathmann, Carolyn Bergt, Brenda Trunkhill

Editorial assistant: Amanda G. Lansche

Manufactured in Xochimilco, Mexico/050246/415466

10   11   12   13   14   15   16   17   18   19   30   29   28   27   26   25   24   23   22   21

Table of Contents

Unit 3—Israel in the Promised Land
(Snake on the Pole—David and Goliath)

Unit 4—God's Faithfulness to His People
(David—Elijah)

Unit 5—Looking for the Savior
(Elisha–Coming of the Wise Men)

Unit 6—Jesus Begins His Ministry
(John the Baptist–Jesus Raises Jairus's Daughter)

Unit 7—Jesus Teaches and Performs Miracles
(The Parable of the Sower–Jesus Raises Lazarus)

Unit 8—Jesus' Final Teachings, Death, and Resurrection
(The Parable of the Great Banquet–Jesus Appears to Mary)

Unit 9—Jesus Leaves His Disciples with His Power (Ascension–Timothy)

Creation

Genesis 1:1–2:3

God Created the World

In the beginning, there were no people. Only God was here. Then God went to work. He worked on each of six days of the very first week in the history of the world. We call His work *creation*, which means to make from nothing. On the first three days, God provided the form for what was to follow. On days four, five, and six, God filled out, or completed, what He had made during the first three days. But God made the seventh day to be very different from the others. On the lines below, write what God created on each day of the first week. On the boxes for days four, five, six, and seven use simple drawings so show what God made or did on each day.

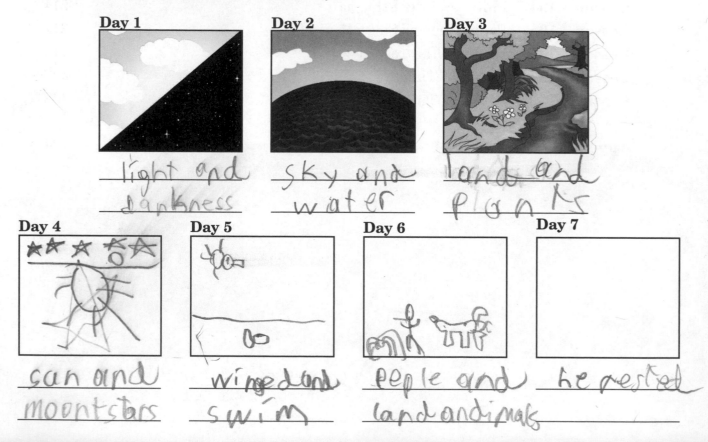

Day 1 — light and darkness

Day 2 — sky and water

Day 3 — land and plants

Day 4 — sun and moon stars

Day 5 — winged and swim

Day 6 — peple and land andimals

Day 7 — he rested

Review

Genesis—"origin"

Creation—coming into being, in the case of the creation of the world, to be made from nothing

Divine attributes of God: (omni—a prefix meaning *all*)

Omnipresent—present everywhere

Omniscient—all knowing

Omnipotent—all powerful

The Creation

Long ago there was no world. There wasn't anything—no sun or moon, no stars, no birds or fish, no flowers or trees, no rivers or mountains—nothing. But God changed that. He made a beautiful world.

Complete the crossword puzzle below to review what you know about the first week in the history of the world.

Across:

3. Present everywhere at the same time
5. First man
6. First woman, wife of Adam
8. Ground adorned with trees, flowers, vegetables, and other plants
9. Animals that live in the water and swim and breath through gills
10. All powerful
11. Flies, has wings and feathers

Down:

1. Because of this, we are able to see things
2. Large plant with woody trunk, branches, and leaves
3. All knowing
4. Name of the garden where Adam and Eve lived
7. Made from nothing

Words to Use:

Adam Eve Omnipotent Omniscient Omnipresent Garden Eden Created Tree Birds Fish Light

Creation and Me

Before God made the world, He knew each of us by name and He chose us to be His people. Because God is all-knowing, He knew sin would enter the world and He knew about each sin we would commit. Because God is loving, He planned even then to send Jesus to be our Savior. Today the beauty and wonder of that week of creation can still be seen and enjoyed around us. God keeps our world going. He continues to bless us with all we are and have, including our bodies and souls, forgiveness and salvation in Jesus, family and friends. Plus He gives meaningful work to do.

What work do you especially enjoy doing?

What makes it enjoyable?

REMEMBER

In the beginning was the Word, and the Word was with God, and the Word was God. **(John 1:1)**

The Fall into Sin

Genesis 3

What Happened?

The peace and happiness Adam and Eve knew in Paradise was not to last. Read Genesis 3:1–24. Then write captions beneath each of the frames below. Then tell what happened in each of the verses.

Genesis 3:1-6

_____

_____

Genesis 3:8-10

_____

_____

Genesis 3:14, 16-19

_____

_____

Genesis 3:15

_____

_____

Romans 5:12 Sin came into the world through one man, and death through sin, and so death spread to all men because all sinned.

Review

Sin—Every thought, desire, word, and deed which is contrary to God's Law.

Original sin—That total corruption of our whole human nature, which we have inherited from Adam through our parents.

Redemption—Salvation from sin through Christ's sacrifice.

Our Sin and Savior

The following Bible verse names a number of sins that continue to trouble our world today as a result of the first sin. But thank God that Jesus came to earn forgiveness for these and all sins. Draw the shape of a cross to "cross out" each of the sins listed in the Bible verse below.

Out of the heart come evil thoughts, murder, adultery, sexual immorality, theft, false witness, slander (Matthew 15:19).

false witness

sexual immorality

evil thoughts

slander

murder

theft

adultery

REMEMBER

For the wages of sin is death, but the _free_ _gift_ of God is _enternel life_ in _jesus christ_ our Lord. **(Romans 6:23)**

11

Cain and Abel

Genesis 4:1–16

The First Murder

Read the story of Cain and Abel in Genesis 4:1–16. Then discuss the following questions. Write answers on the lines below.

1. What did Cain and Abel offer to God as a sacrifice?

_____

_____

2. What was Cain's reaction to God showing favor upon Abel and his sacrifice?

_____

_____

3. One sin leads to another when Cain reacts to God's favor upon Abel's sacrifice. What did God do in order to keep Cain from further sin?_____

_____

4. What did Cain do instead of heeding God's warning about temptation and the sin "crouching at the door"?_____

5. According to the memory verse for today, what is the solution to the problem of all human sins, including the sin of murder?_____

Review

Place a box around every third letter in each of the following, then write the word that matches each definition on the blank following each definition:

TUQXSMGINQUIYWEOTCKBIFSEVCNGHTDO
XMHGPABDTUERQOEIWDR
ZBCKTLYJESMAHTNXGSPGE
IYJPWEMBAGVLIROPTUXCSNVYGK
BRGXCRGTAEYCEWITROQSUNPS

1. A strong dislike of someone

_____

2. To be all knowing

_____

3. Wishing you had what someone else has

_____

4. To clean or remove something bad

_____

5. Showing undeserved kindness, forgiving

_____

Faith for Life

Like Cain, we, too, think jealous thoughts. When we have jealous thoughts, God's Spirit moves us to repent of our sinful thoughts and to ask Jesus for forgiveness. Then the Spirit helps us replace our sinful thoughts with those that honor Him. Read each person's thoughts below and then write a confession of that sin. Finally write a new thought in the empty thought bubble that would take the place of the jealous thought—a thought that God would lead us to think instead, when sin "is crouching at the door."

Confession:

_____

_____

_____

_____

Confession:

_____

_____

_____

_____

REMEMBER

The blood of Jesus His Son cleanses us from all sin. **(1 John 1:7)**

Cain and Abel

Genesis 4:1–16

From Thought to Action

In the story of Cain and Abel, God gives us an example of an evil thought or action of Cain's that leads to another sin in his relationship to Abel. Am I guilty of the same in my relationships? If so, what can I do about it?

What's Next?

Review Genesis 4: 1–16. Then fill in the spaces to place the events of the story in the order in which they occurred.

- [ ] Cain replied to God's question about his brother's whereabouts with, "Am I my brother's keeper?"

- [ ] Cain murdered his brother Abel.

- [ ] God asked Cain why he was so angry that Abel's offering was accepted.

- [ ] Cain and Abel each made an offering to God.

- [ ] God confronted Cain with his sin of murder.

- [ ] God looked with favor on Abel's offering.

- [ ] Cain's jealousy led him to be angry with Abel.

Review

Write the letter of the definition that matches the word in each box below.

- [ ] original sin
- [ ] confession
- [ ] bitterness
- [ ] malice

a. admission of sin and helplessness to God

b. the natural desire to do wrong with which we were born

c. a desire to harm someone

d. a strong feeling of hatred

One Sin Leads to Another

BITTERNESS
LYING MURDER
HATRED

UNREPENTANCE
Jealousy
Self-Love

Why me? What did I do?

Discussing God's Word

1. Cain met Abel in the field. His first sin led him to another. What was that first sin?

_____

_____

2. What was the consequence for Cain because of the sin of which he refused to repent?

_____

3. How did God show love for Cain, even though he complained that his punishment was too much?

_____

_____

Crime and Punishment

After the murder of Abel, God gave Adam and Eve another son. His name was Seth. To Seth's descendants Jesus the Savior was eventually born.

According to God's Word, how does Jesus help us when we have committed sins? Check out Romans 5:8–9. According to these verses, who committed the crime? Who took the punishment? Write your answer in the boxes below.

Faith for Life

How might the forgiveness of Jesus for you move you to respond to others in ways other than those suggested by the statements below?

I will never forgive him!

_____ _____

_____ _____

If I get hit I can hit back!

_____ _____

REMEMBER

Be kind to one another, tenderhearted, forgiving one another, as God in Christ forgave you. **(Ephesians 4:32)**

Tower of Babel

Genesis 11:1–9

Be fruitful and multiply

And fill the earth

Build ourselves a city with a tower that reaches to heaven, and make a name for ourselves

Earth had one language and the same words

Lord confused the language of all the earth...and dispersed the builders of the tower

Review

Pride	Humility
_____	_____
_____	_____
_____	_____

Put these six words under the correct heading above. Three words will be synonyms of pride and three will be synonyms of humility.

insolent   boastful   content   arrogant   gentle   modest

Building Blocks

Look up each verse in the blocks below. If the verse is about sinful pride, color the block red. If the verse is about humility, color the block yellow.

Romans 5:8:_____

_____

Good and upright is the Lord; therefore He instructs sinners in the way. He leads the humble in what is right, and teaches the humble His way. **(Psalm 25:8–9)**

Tower of Babel

Genesis 11:1–9

Babel

In the days after Noah the world was renewed
But sin was still out there; it grew and it grew.
God wanted people, plus the boys and the girls,
To spread out and settle all over the world.
But the people of Babel liked their city a lot
They loved all their buildings, their farms, and their crops.
They wouldn't travel, and they wouldn't grow.
When God said, "Go forth," they all said, "No!"
Instead they decided that they wanted fame;
They wanted the whole world to recognize their name.
So they got together for more than an hour
And finally decided to build a tall tower.
"We'll design it and build it to soar through the skies
But to reach up to heaven it will have to be high!"
Then they started to build and to brag and to boast
That their tower would give them what they wanted most:
"We'll be noticed by everyone; they'll all know our name;
This Tower of Babel will be our claim to fame!"
But the Lord wasn't smiling when He looked down
As the tower went up in the center of town.
"They've sinned by not listening to all My commands;
They want to be greater than I already Am."
"So now I will stop them from building this tower;
I'll confuse all their language and they'll lose all their power."
And suddenly everyone who lived in Babel

Couldn't talk to each other; they were no longer able!
Without the same language, without the same voice
The people of Babel were left with no choice:
They left behind Babel and the places of their birth
Because God spread them out all over the earth.
What then can we learn from that infamous tower?
That God's number One; He's the ultimate power!
He sent down His Son to die on the cross
To forgive all our sins so we wouldn't be lost!
Yes, God's power is great, but His forgiveness is great too;
In any language, God will always love you!

© 2004 Nicole E. Dreyer. Used with permission.

Review

Messiah Christ Emmanuel

The names Messiah, Christ, and Emmanuel are just three of many names for Jesus that describe exactly who He is. Consider the following acrostic. What do each of the names of Jesus tell us about Him?

J ehovah
E verlasting Father
S avior of the World
U nfailing love
S inless Son of God

Praising God's Name

God's Spirit works in those who trust in Jesus the desire to honor Jesus' name. Imagine you are this basketball star. Write the article so that it tells about how the star honors the name of Jesus with his words and actions rather than seeking to glorify himself.

Fourth Grade Basketball Star Breaks All Records.

_____

_____

_____

_____

_____

_____

_____

Reaching to the Heavens

The people of Babel wanted to make a name for themselves by building a tower that reached to the heavens. But God invites His people to reach to the heavens by calling upon His name in their prayers. The rising of incense has long been a symbol of prayer, dating back to the days of the Old Testament. See Psalm 141:2.

REMEMBER

Bless the Lord, O my soul; and all that is within me, bless His holy name.
(Psalm 103:1)

God's Promise to Abram

Genesis 12–13

Good News for Abram

Read Genesis 12:2–3. Fill in the missing words from these verses that tell of seven basic promises from God to Abram.

1) "I will make you a great _nation_ "

2) "I will _bless_ you"

3) "I will make your _name_ great"

4) "you will be a _blessing_ "

5) "I will bless those who _bless_ you"

6) "him who _dishoner_ you I will curse"

7) "in you all the families of the earth shall be _blessed_ ."

God cares about me!

Abram's Problems

Abram found encouragement in God's promises. But still he had problems. Read Genesis 12:10; 12:17–20; and 13:5–7 then list some of Abram's problems on the lines below.

_____

_____

Abram's Assurance

Read Genesis 13:14–18. Summarize God's words to Abram assuring him of His blessings.

_____

_____

God MADE me with	God SUPPORTS me with	God DEFENDS me against
_____	_____	_____
_____	_____	_____

Review

Match each word from the first column with a word in the second column.

Divine	Credit
Merit	Godly
Covenant	Promise

I Don't Feel Very Blessed When. . .

- my dad loses his job.
- I sit on the bench more than I play in the game.
- my friends are not talking to me.
- the tests I take are so difficult.
- my grandma is sick for a long time.
- (add your own)

God never stops loving and caring about you! Still like Abram, you will have problems and troubles. These are because of sin. Because of Jesus, God's people have hope even in the hardest of times. God blesses you each and every day, even when it does not feel like it. God can even bless us *through* our problems.

Blessings You Can Count On

Read the following Bible verses. Find the blessings that God will always provide for you. Fill in the spokes of the circle with those blessings.

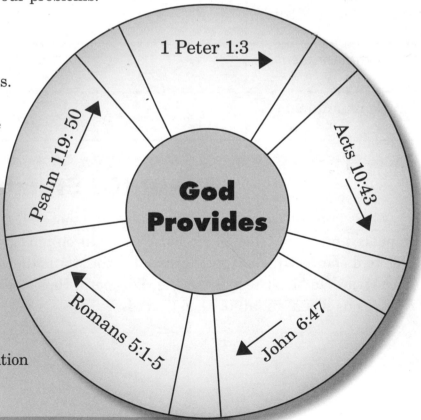

Just Like Abram

- We are given many PROMISES from God.
- We face obstacles and PROBLEMS along the way.
- We have been given the ultimate BLESSING of salvation through Christ our Savior.

REMEMBER

The Lord is faithful in all His words and kind in all His works. (**Psalm 145:13**)

Abram and Lot

Genesis 13

Walking with Our Neighbor

God wants us to walk with our neighbor in peace and love. He shows us how to do this through His Commandments. Fill in the following chart. Write what God commands us not to do to our neighbor. Write what God commands us to do for our neighbor.

Commandment	Do Not	Do
Fourth Commandment		
Fifth Commandment		
Sixth Commandment		
Seventh Commandment		
Eighth Commandment		
Ninth Commandment		
Tenth Commandment		

What if I Stumble?

Wow! That is a lot of "shoulds" and "should nots"! It seems impossible to always walk in peace and love with one another. Put a star on top of the words that tell what you are able to do perfectly. Now put a cross over the words that remain. Jesus is there every step of the way. He helps keep us on the right path. He will pick us up when we stumble. He forgives us when we fail to keep God's Law.

Review

Draw lines to match each word with its meaning.

Neighbor ○   ○ Sinful words, lies
Covet ○   ○ All people
False witness ○   ○ Sinful desire to be or possess
          what belongs to someone else.

Abram Finds a Way Through Conflict

Read about Abram and Lot in Genesis 13. Fill in the details of the story in the path below.

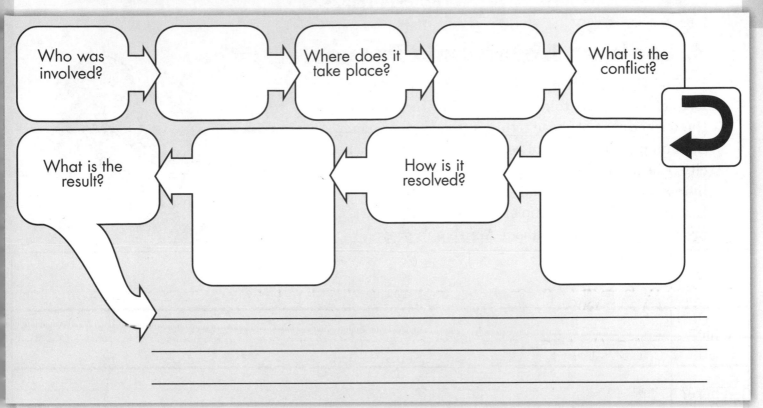

Abram, remembering he is a child of God, put Lot's desires ahead of his own.

Finding Our Way

Consider each of the following situations. What way do you think Jesus would have you go?

Jake and Luke want to play checkers during free time. Owen and Matt want to play checkers too. There is only one game of checkers in the classroom.

Possible Solutions: _____

_____

Emily and Kayla both consider Anna their best friend. They both want her as their field trip partner.

Possible Solutions: _____

_____

Ella and Kendal are not talking. Ella is sure Kendal was spreading rumors about her.

Possible Solutions: _____

_____

REMEMBER

If possible, so far as it depends on you, live peaceably with all. **(Romans 12:18)**

23

Abraham Prays

Genesis 18:22–33

A Look at Abraham's Prayer

God Himself once came to visit Abraham in the form of a man. He told Abraham that He knew of the wickedness of those living in the city of Sodom. Surmising that God had come to destroy the wicked city, Abraham prayed to God on behalf of the people living there, which included Abraham's nephew Lot and his family. Complete the following chart, providing information about Abraham's prayer.

Who?	Abraham and GOD
What?	GAbraham saying to spane the city
Where?	outsine of a tent
When?	
How?	

The Privilege of Prayer

God hears and answers our prayers for Jesus' sake. Because Jesus came to save us from our sins, we can ask God for all things that give glory to God and help ourselves and others.

Review

Complete the following to identify four ways to pray.

C onfestion
(expression of sorrow over sin)

T hankoiving
(gratefulness)

ACTS

A deration
(praise)

S upplication
(requests)

Questions About Prayer

Match each of the following questions about prayer with the best answer in the column at the right.

Question

_____ 1. Who should pray?

_____ 2. What do we pray for?

_____ 3. How do we pray?

_____ 4. Where do we pray?

_____ 5. When do we pray?

_____ 6. Why do we pray?

Answer

a. things that bring glory to God and benefit ourselves and others

b. everywhere, especially when alone, with families, and in church

c. those who believe in Jesus

d. in Jesus' name, with faith in Him as our Redeemer

f. regularly and often, especially when in trouble

e. God desires it and commands us to pray

Those Who Need My Prayers:

_____

_____

_____

_____

_____

REMEMBER

Ask, and it will be given to you; seek, and you will find; knock, and it will be opened to you. For everyone who asks receives, and the one who seeks finds, and to the one who knocks it will be opened. **(Matthew 7:7–8)**

Sodom and Gomorrah

Genesis 19:1–29

God Answers Abraham's Prayer

Remember in the previous lesson, when Abraham interceded for the believers of Sodom and Gomorrah? He pleaded six times that God would spare them. The Lord listened and promised that He would not destroy the cities for the sake of ten believers.

Read Genesis 19:1–23.

Number the following in proper sequence:

_____ The two men (angels) reached out their hands, brought Lot in and blindness struck the men outside.

_____ Lot went out and told the men not to act so wickedly. They pressed hard against Lot and drew near to break the door down.

_____ Lot brought the angels to his house fearing for their safety.

_____ The men (angels) said, to Lot, "The Lord sent us to destroy this place. Have you anyone else here? Bring them out of the place."

_____ Lot gave his two sons-in-law a warning to leave the city.

_____ The angel said he would not do anything until Lot arrived in Zoar. Then when Lot safely arrived, he destroyed the wicked cities.

_____ The angels seized Lot, his wife, and two daughters and said to them, "Escape for your life. Do not look back or stop anywhere in the valley."

Review

merciful   inhabitants   overthrow

Write a sentence about today's story using all three vocabulary words in the sentence.

_____

_____

God Answers Prayer

Read Genesis 19:24–29.

1. How exactly did God answer Abraham's prayer (v. 29)?

_____

2. How many ended up escaping (v. 30)?

_____

3. Why do you think Lot's wife looked back?

_____

_____

4. To what did Jesus compare the destruction of Sodom and Gomorrah in the words He spoke twenty centuries later (Luke 17:28–32)?

_____

_____

5. Why do those who trust in Jesus as their Savior need not fear the coming judgment (Titus 2:13)?

_____

_____

_____

Trust in God

Do you think Abraham knew that God would answer his prayer when he prayed for Sodom? Which of God's qualities do you think Abraham had in mind when he prayed?

_____

_____

_____

REMEMBER

Look up **Titus 2:14**. [Jesus Christ] gave Himself for us to _redeem_ us from all _lawlessness_ and to _purify_ for Himself a people for His own possession who are _zealous_ for good works.

How does this New Testament verse apply to the story of Sodom and Gomorrah?

_____

_____

_____

The Offering of Isaac

Genesis 22:1–19

Abraham Trusts in God

A Call to Sacrifice

Read Genesis 22:1–2.

1. What choice did Abraham have when God asked him to sacrifice his only son?

_____

2. What choice did he make?

_____

3. What do you think he would have rather done?

_____

Read Genesis 22:11–19.

4. How did Abraham show that he trusted in God?

_____

_____

5. How did God show that He trusted Abraham?

_____

_____

Highlight words in the text that indicate that Abraham trusted in God.

Review

Use the words **trust** and **sacrifice** to fill in the blanks below.

When you know someone will do what they promise, you _____ in them.

God required His Old Testament people to make a _____ in order to have their sins forgiven.

When you give up something you love, it is truly a _____ .

We can _____ God completely, because He always keeps His promises.

Whom Can You Trust?

Directions: Read the following stories, each involving followers of Jesus. Think about what is happening in each. Who trusts whom, and why do they trust each other? For what are individuals trusting God in each situation?

1. It's 7:00 in the morning. Rachel needs to get ready for school. She gets clothes out of her closet and gets dressed. Then, she heads down the stairs and into the kitchen for breakfast. After breakfast, she goes out to the bus stop. She gets to school on time and is ready when the first bell rings.

2. It's the day of the big game! Rashad's all dressed and ready to go. His team is cheering and excited. The fans fill the stands. They take the court and get ready to play.

3. Madeline's mom and dad are getting a divorce. She is crying at her desk at school. Mrs. McMichael comes to her and asks what's wrong. Madeline tells her all about the situation at home. Mrs. McMichael suggests that they pray about it.

4. Ian's dog is sick. After school Ian and his parents take the dog to Dr. Wilkins. The vet says he needs to keep the dog overnight for some tests. Ian leaves with his parents. He is worried and doesn't know what to do.

REMEMBER 🩵

Trust in the Lord with all your heart, and do not lean on your own understanding. In all your ways acknowledge Him, and He will make straight your paths.
(Proverbs 3:5–6)

The Offering of Isaac

Genesis 22:1–19

God Provides a Sacrifice

Imagine if the story of Abraham and Isaac happened today. People would really question what this father and son were up to. It might even make the evening news! Read the following play together with your class, and then discuss the questions at the end.

News Reporter: Hello, this is _____ reporting from the scene of a very unusual news story. I'm with a couple of the witnesses; let's see what they have to say.

(Turns to Servant 1, puts microphone to his mouth)

Servant 1: I couldn't believe it! Abraham headed up that mountain, with all the stuff to make a sacrifice, but no animal!

News Reporter: No animal? What was he going to sacrifice? *(Turns to Servant 2)*

Servant 2: That's what we were wondering! He couldn't possibly hurt his son! He loves Isaac WAY too much to do that!

News Reporter: *(Amazed)* What? Sacrifice his own son! Who could possibly do such a thing? *(Looks up the mountain)* Well, it appears that Abraham is on his way back down the mountain right now! Wait! Who is that behind him?

Servant 1: *(Yelling)* Hooray! It's Isaac!

Servant 2: I wonder what they did for a sacrifice?

News Reporter: *(Rushing over to Abraham)* Abraham! Abraham! Can I get a statement from you? What were you doing up on the mountain?

Abraham: Sacrificing to God.

Servant 1: *(Pushes his way into the scene)* But you didn't have an animal!

Abraham: God always provides.

Servant 2: What? That doesn't make any sense!?

Review

"God will provide" Abraham told Isaac when he asked about the lamb for the sacrifice. Complete the chart below writing the meaning to each of the words in the space provided at the right. Choose from among the definitions found beneath the chart.

Word	Meaning
Providence	
Provide	
Provisions	

God's power guiding and caring for humanity.

Things that are needed.

The act of supplying, making available or meeting a need.

Isaac: Sure it does. Dad was all ready to sacrifice me, since that is what God told him to do, but then, a ram appeared, stuck in the bushes by his horns. God even spoke to us.

(Servants and News Reporter look at each other, confused)

News Reporter: Abraham, do you wish to comment further?

Abraham: God provides. Trust Him.

News Reporter: Well, you heard it here first! God provides. Trust Him. I guess that's all for this story—back to you in the studio! *(Points out as if talking to people in the studio)*

1. Did Abraham seem like he was amazed or upset by God's request? Why or why not? Why do you think he felt this way?

   _____

   _____

2. Even though we want to trust God, why do we often try to do things our own way?

   _____

   _____

3. What are some things that God provides to you every day?

   _____

   _____

God Provides for Our Needs

In the story of Abraham's offering, God provided a sacrifice in place of Abraham's son, Isaac. God provides for us, too. Read the following Bible passages together with your class. Discuss what it is that God provides in each passage. Write your answer on the line next to the passage.

Psalm 145:15–15_____

Job 33:4_____

Proverbs 2:6_____

Isaiah 40:29_____

Jeremiah 5:24_____

Matthew 11:28_____

Matthew 6:28–30_____

1 Corinthians 15:56–57_____

REMEMBER

My God will supply every need of yours according to His riches in glory in Christ Jesus. **(Philippians 4:19)**

Jacob Runs Away

Genesis 27:1–46

A Family Struggle

Read the Bible story in Genesis 27. Then draw lines to match each sentence on the left with the correct person on the right.

1. God promised to bless all people through Abraham's descendants by providing a land for them to live in and especially by providing the Messiah through this family. This promise came to him from his father Isaac and his grandfather Abraham (Genesis 26:2–5). ○

Isaac

2. This person ignored God's instruction that the promise should go to the younger of his sons. ○

Rebekah

3. He foolishly traded away his birthright and angrily threatened revenge on his brother. ○

Esau

4. He cooperated in deceiving his father and incited his brother. ○

5. This parent wanted Jacob to receive the blessing. ○

Jacob

REVIEW

Find antonyms for these words that are important in this story. Explain why you choose the antonyms you do.

deceive	blessing
_____	_____
_____	_____
_____	_____
_____	_____

Bringing It Home

Read the following story. Then discuss the questions in Let's Talk about It with your classmates and teacher.

Samantha is happy to see her friend Sydney as she enters the classroom. "Did you finish your science homework? It took me forever!" Panic struck Sydney. She had forgotten to complete her assignment and knew that her teacher would be upset. She made up her mind to tell her teacher that she had gotten sick last night and couldn't finish her homework. Sydney knew her teacher would believe her because she had always completed her assignments. Even though she had a plan, she could not settle her stomach. This was just one assignment, why did being honest matter so much? An A in science would keep her on the honor roll and everyone knew she deserved to be there.

Let's Talk about It

How is Sydney's situation similar to Jacob's? What should Sydney do? What would you do? What promises of God would help you make your decision? Review Genesis 27:41–45. Why does Rebekah want Jacob to flee? How is Jacob like Sydney? Read 1 Peter 2:24 below. Highlight the verse in your Bible. Think about its meaning. Then write a text message to both Sydney and Jacob. What advice would you give them?

REMEMBER

He Himself bore our sins in His body on the tree, that we might die to sin and live to righteousness. By His wounds you have been healed. **(1 Peter 2:24)**

Jacob's Dream

Genesis 28:10–22

Jacob on His Own

Jacob had been forced to run away from home. He had made his brother Esau so angry that he threatened to kill Jacob. But even though Jacob was now on his own, he was not alone. God reminded Jacob in a dream that He was with Him. Read together the story of Jacob's dream in Genesis 28:10–22. Then answer the questions in the space provided on the steps below.

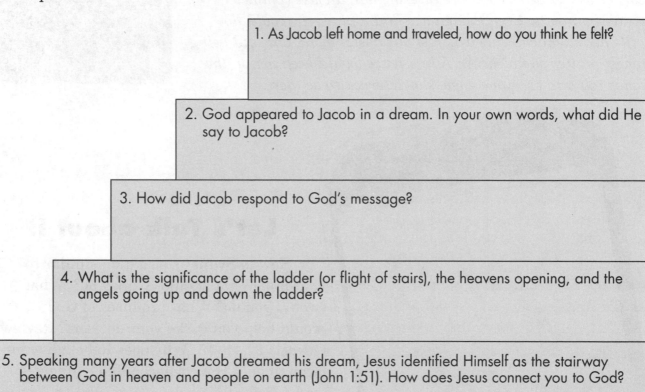

1. As Jacob left home and traveled, how do you think he felt?

2. God appeared to Jacob in a dream. In your own words, what did He say to Jacob?

3. How did Jacob respond to God's message?

4. What is the significance of the ladder (or flight of stairs), the heavens opening, and the angels going up and down the ladder?

5. Speaking many years after Jacob dreamed his dream, Jesus identified Himself as the stairway between God in heaven and people on earth (John 1:51). How does Jesus connect you to God?

REVIEW

dream   offspring

Working with a partner, discuss what the words *dream* and *offspring* mean. Find and highlight them in your Bible, in Genesis 28:10–22. Look the words up in the glossary and read their definitions. Why are these words important in today's story?

When Feeling Alone and Unworthy

Nicholas wanted more than anything to make the basketball team, but tryouts had gone horribly. He could see the coach cringing as he put up brick after brick. Judging by the performance of those around him, he knew he wouldn't have a spot on the team. His friends joked with him and even called him "Brick." He pretended to laugh with them, but he felt ashamed. At home, his mom reminded him of all the things he could do: help around the house, draw well, and make others smile. She suggested he keep practicing and try out for the team again next year. Did she even know that all the cool kids were on the team? That this was the year to start out? He didn't want to be funny or helpful or even an artist. He wanted to be on the team!

When have you felt like Nicholas—alone, apart from the people around you? The story of Jacob is the story of someone who had taken so many wrong turns that he found himself on the outs with his family and traveling alone, sleeping on the cold, hard ground. God came to him in a dream and promised that he would never be alone. God makes that same promise to you. He has given His Son, Jesus, to die for you so that you can have eternal life, and He has given His Holy Spirit to guide you. He reminds us that Jesus is the way, the truth, and the life. What can that mean to Nicholas?

What does it mean to you that Jesus is the way, the truth, and the life? What does it mean to you that Jesus connects us with our Father in heaven?

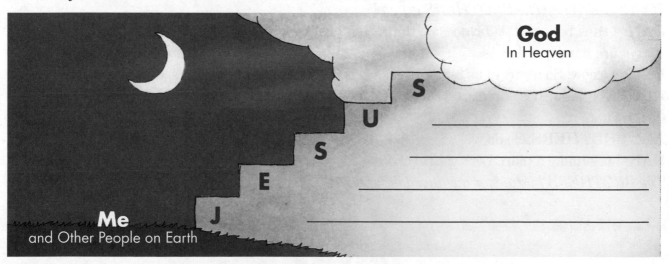

REMEMBER

Jesus said . . . "I am the way, and the truth, and the life. No one comes to the Father except through Me." **(John 14:6)**

Joseph and His Brothers

Genesis 37

Joseph's Bothered Brothers

NARRATOR: Welcome to our story of a boy who gets carried away by his brothers' coveting.

All BROTHERS ENTER.

NARRATOR: A teen named Joseph was minding the family business when his brothers started messing around.

The BROTHERS EXIT. JACOB ENTERS.

JACOB: My son, how's everything going?

JOSEPH whispers in his ear.

JACOB: I'm sorry to hear that. But I have good news. I brought something for you.

JACOB gives JOSEPH a colorful coat. JOSEPH puts it on.

JOSEPH: Oh, Father, it's great. Won't the guys be happy to see my new present?

JACOB EXITS. The BROTHERS ENTER.

JOSEPH: Look what I got! Father just gave it to me.

JOSEPH shows off. The BROTHERS examine their own clothes and look unhappy.

JOSEPH: And guess what else happened? I had two amazing dreams. I think God is trying to tell me something. In one dream, we were tying bunches of wheat. Brothers, your bunches of wheat bowed down to my bunch that was standing up tall. (*The BROTHERS whisper among themselves and look very unhappy.*) Then, there was this other dream. The sun, the moon, and eleven stars bowed down to me. I told Father about it, and he thinks that maybe I'll be powerful some day. Wouldn't that be cool?

BROTHERS: No!

JOSEPH EXITS. The BROTHERS grumble.

DAN: I can't believe it! Who does he think he is? Father gives him a beautiful coat, and all I ever get are hand-me-downs.

LEVI: I know! So many of us brothers get so little of Dad's attention. Joe seems to get it all!

REUBEN: And those dreams! He thinks God is talking to him? Does he think he's that special?

GAD: I hate it!

ALL BROTHERS: So do we!

DAN: Let's make a plan. Let's get rid of Joe—for good!

The BROTHERS huddle for awhile, making plans. Then, they EXIT.

REVIEW

Place the words **favorite** and **jealous** in the appropriate blanks.

To be treated with a special liking is to be the _____.

A _____ person strongly wants something others have, seeing them as rivals.

This isn't the end of the story. Maybe you know the rest, but let's take a break and think about what has happened so far. Joseph and his father, Jacob, clearly love each other and have a great relationship. The other brothers seem to have a problem with that.

Why might the brothers be jealous of how Jacob treats Joseph?

_____

_____

What did the brothers' jealous feelings lead them to plan?

_____

When We Become Jealous

Knowing that Jesus died for every sin we commit, we can be sure that God will help us repent, or turn away from that sin. His forgiveness helps us have a healthy attitude toward others. When you feel jealous of someone else's grades, toys, or family, you can confess that sin to God. You can ask Jesus for forgiveness.

Write a prayer that might help you confess your sin. Complete each line of the prayer by writing on each line, *forgive me, Lord, for Jesus' sake.*

Heavenly Father, You can see in my heart. You know that I covet. You know when I'm jealous. Help me get over those feelings and not hate the other person or want their things.

For the times I have resented others for their good fortune,

_____.

For the evil thoughts I have had about others because they have gotten something I

wanted very much, _____.

For letting my jealous, covetous thoughts lead me to other sins,

_____. Amen.

The devil's temptation to covet what others have is never easy to resist. But God's great love for us in Jesus Christ gives believers the power to resist the devil and to live a new life in Christ. God's Word tells us that we received this power through faith. When we receive faith in Baptism, we put on Christ, a gift we receive from our Father in heaven and can wear just as proudly as Joseph wore the coat he received from Jacob, his earthly father.

REMEMBER

In Christ Jesus you are all sons of God, through faith. For as many of you as were baptized into Christ have put on Christ. **(Galatians 3:26–27)**

Joseph and His Brothers

Genesis 37:25–36

God's Plan Is Greater than Our Plans

The BROTHERS ENTER.

NARRATOR: Later, Jacob sent Joseph to check on his brothers, who were supposed to be working far away from home. He wanted a report on whether or not they were doing their jobs like they were supposed to. Arriving at their camp at Shechem, Joseph walked up to them just as they were planning to hurt him.

(JOSEPH ENTERS and walks up to the BROTHERS. The BROTHERS grab JOSEPH.)

LEVI: Let's kill him!

REUBEN: Wait! I can't live with that. There must be something else we can do. Throw him in this pit while we decide.

NARRATOR: Some time later, slave traders came by. The brothers decided to sell Joseph to them. The traders took him away to Egypt, leaving his colorful coat behind.

(During the above narration, a group of SLAVE TRADERS ENTERS. The BROTHERS take Joseph's coat off and hand JOSEPH to the SLAVE TRADERS. The SLAVE TRADERS give the brothers money and EXIT with JOSEPH.)

NARRATOR: Later, the brothers returned home to Jacob, who noticed that Joseph was missing.

(The BROTHERS ENTER and approach JACOB, who is looking for JOSEPH.)

JACOB: Where is Joseph?

LEVI: He probably was attacked and killed by an animal. All we found was this coat.

(JUDAH hands the coat to JACOB, who cries. ALL EXIT.)

NARRATOR: Joseph's brothers thought they were rid of the person who got the most attention. Jacob thought his favorite son was dead. Joseph was probably afraid of what would happen to him. None of them knew what God had planned for Joseph's amazing future.

REVIEW

When Jesus came, He came as both a slave and a Savior. Write the correct word by the verse that describes each.

_____Whoever would be first among you must be your slave. **Matthew 20:27**

_____Even as the Son of Man came not to be served but to . . . give His life as a ransom for many. **Matthew 20:28**

A Hard Knock Life

Like Annie in the musical *Annie*, at times Joseph lived a "hard knock life." Jesus came to earth to live a "hard knock life" too. He did it willingly, so that we might be forgiven and saved. At times, we, too, live a "hard luck life" because of sin in our own lives and in the lives of those around us. But Jesus knows. He understands and He gives us His help. Read the Bible verse at the bottom of this page. Then complete the following sentences.

Jesus gave His life for me because

_____

_____

_____

When I experience a "hard knock" life,

_____

_____

_____

Prayer

Pray together: Jesus, our Savior, thank You for suffering and dying on the cross for me. When You rose from the dead, You showed power over all sins, even mine. Heal my family and me when we hurt one another. Thank You for saving me. In Your name I pray. Amen.

REMEMBER

We know that this is indeed the Savior of the world. **(John 4:42)**

39

Job

Job (especially chapters 1, 2, and 42)

A Very Bad Day

I will trust in God!

Sometimes you might want a "do over" for the beginning of your day because so many things went wrong. Maybe you woke up late, missed breakfast, couldn't find what you wanted to wear, left some homework at home, and missed your ride to school. That isn't a successful beginning for a day. Will your day improve? Will a bad start affect your attitude for the rest of the day? Who gets the blame when you have a bad day? Why do bad things happen? That is the question Job struggled with. It is a question all of us face. In Job's struggle, God provides an answer.

Job's Very Bad Days (Job 1–42)

Characters: God; Satan; Job; Angel/Messengers 1, 2, 3; Eliphaz; Bildad; Zophar; Job's Wife.

Scene 1   Setting: Heavenly places

God: Welcome to our meeting. You angels are doing well at your jobs. (*Satan joins the group.*) Well, Satan, where have you been lately?

Satan: Oh, I've been wandering to and fro across the face of the earth.

God: Did you happen to notice My servant Job? He has great integrity in My eyes. He worships Me faithfully.

Satan: Yes, I know about Job. But why would he not worship You? He has everything a person could want.

God: True. I have blessed him.

Satan: Give me a chance with him, and I will turn him from You. He's only faithful because he has it so easy.

God: Go ahead and try. Only you may not touch his body.

REVIEW

Write a definition for each of the two words in this box. Consult the glossary and the sentence after each word to help develop your definition.

Consecrate—Job made sacrifices to consecrate his children when he was afraid they had sinned (Job 1:5).

_____

_____

Integrity—The integrity of Job was known to those who lived around him (Job 2:3; Proverbs 11:3).

_____

Scene 2   **Setting: The land of Uz, during a birthday party for Job's oldest son**

Messenger 1 (*entering*): Job! Job! I have bad news. Some of your enemies have killed all your servants and animals in the fields.

Messenger 2: Job! Enemies of yours have just slain all your servants and animals that you use for trading with others.

Messenger 3: Job! A huge tornado just hit the house of your oldest son and killed everyone—all your children.

Job (*tearing his clothes*): Oh, no! I came into the world with nothing, and that's the way I'll leave. But I can't blame God. He gives, and He takes away. Blessed be the name of the Lord.

Scene 3   **Setting: Heavenly places**

God: Satan, you came to our meeting again. Have you noticed My servant Job?

Satan (*grouchy*): Yes, and I know he hasn't turned away from You. He's only faithful because he hasn't been hurt. If I could hurt him, he'd soon curse You.

God: Okay. You may injure his body in any way you like, but you may not take his life.

Satan: Huh! He's going to be hurting from head to toe!

Scene 4   **Setting: In the land of Uz**

Job: I hate all these horrible sores on my body. They hurt. I wish I hadn't been born.

Job's Wife: Many people have heard of your bad fortune. Three of your friends are here to help you feel better.

Eliphaz: Job, don't you know that God helps the good prosper? You must have done something bad to turn God against you.

Job: I don't think so. I even consecrate my children so they will be free of guilt.

Bildad: Maybe you did some sin you know nothing about. Repent before God.

Job: I have nothing to repent. Please, God, tell me why all this is happening.

Zophar: You don't really fear God. The proof is in your misery.

Job: Where is God? Why won't He answer me?

Job's Wife: You have driven your friends away. I agree with them. It's something you did, and God is punishing you for it.

Job: God, I do not deserve this. Please tell me why all this is happening.

God: Job, My son. Did you create the earth and all its creatures? the universe? Do you understand how it all operates on its own?

Job (*in a very small voice*): No.

God: I am in charge. I am God.

Job (*in sorrow*): I am Your creature, and I was acting like I was perfect. Only You are perfect, my Lord.

God: I had a greater purpose than you can ever know.

Job: I'm sorry for doubting You, God. I am sorry for all my sins. I know that my Redeemer lives.

God: You are forgiven. Now, since you did not curse Me or turn from My ways, you will be doubly blessed.

Job: Thank You, Lord. Make me strong enough to trust You always. I know that my Redeemer lives and that You rule all things and will continue to do so forever.

REMEMBER

I know that my Redeemer lives, and at the last He will stand upon the earth. **(Job 19:25)**

Baby Moses

Exodus 1:1–2:10

Adoption

Directions: Fill in the information in the certificate on the left with facts you learned from your teacher. If you don't know the information, put N/A in the blank. Then read the story of another adopted child in Exodus 2:1–10. Use the information in this Bible story to complete the certificate on the right.

Adopted Baby 1

Name of child: Sammy

Age: couple mouths old

Male or female: male

Race or tribe: ?

Names of birth parents: ?

Names of adoptive parents: Kirt Amy

Adoption approved by: CPS

OFFICIAL ADOPTION SEAL

Adopted Baby 2

Name of child: Moses

Age: a year old

Male or female: male

Race or tribe: Hebrew

Names of birth parents: (Exodus 6:20) A and J

Names of adoptive parents: Pharaohs daughter

Adoption approved by: God

OFFICIAL ADOPTION SEAL

Many people are eager to adopt children. Their reasons could be that they can't give birth to children on their own or that they love children so much they want to share their home with other children. Adoption is usually a very good thing. Both the child and the family adopting the child are happier. Through adoption, God provides loving parents who will care for and nurture children who have no parents to guide them. God works through adoption at times too, to see that His will is done on earth, as He did in the case of Moses.

REVIEW

Look up the following words in the dictionary in the back of your book. Write a short meaning beside each word.

adoption—

bulrushes—

God's Plan for Moses

In the following story, unscramble the words. Then read the story.

God had a special plan for SOSEM _____ even before he was born. First, he was hidden and DVSAE _____ from being killed by the HOARAHP _____ . Next, the princess found Moses in the ELIN _____ and saved him. The princess gave him the name *Moses* because she drew him out of the water. When his RISSET _____said she knew someone who could ENRSU _____ the baby, God was providing a way for MEOSS _____ to learn who the true ODG _____ is. Moses' own parents TTHUAG _____ him the story of the people of Israel. Moses' NTSPARE _____ loved him; they knew Moses had KROW _____ to do for God. They let the CNREISPS _____ adopt Moses. In the palace, Moses received a good CEDUANITO _____ and learned Egyptian ways. This prepared him for the work God wanted him to do.

God's Plan for Me

You were saved by water just as Moses was. Did you know that? You have also been adopted. Through Baptism, God has adopted you to be His own child. He wants you to be His child in all that you do. You may not know yet what career path you will follow, but you can serve Him in many vocations. Look at the list below, and put a smiley face on the line in front of any activity you enjoy or think you may enjoy.

_____ singing
_____ playing a sport
_____ helping younger kids
_____ drawing
_____ playing an instrument
_____ scuba diving
_____ writing stories

_____ being with many people
_____ making people laugh
_____ doing big projects
_____ building things
_____ making money
_____ being a hermit
_____ using the computer

Now circle one of your smiley faces above. Write about that item from the list and tell how you can use this activity to serve God as His adopted child. Thank God for this blessing and for your Baptism.

_____

_____

REMEMBER 💜

But when the fullness of time had come, God sent forth His Son, born of woman, born under the law, to redeem those who were under the law, so that we might receive adoption as sons. **(Galatians 4:4–5)**

The Plagues

Exodus 7–11

The Family of God's People

Long after Joseph and his brothers had died, their families continued to live in Egypt. Here, God blessed them and they became many in number. With the passing of time, the rulers made them slaves. But God remembered His people. He raised among them a leader named Moses. Moses told Pharaoh, the king of Egypt, "The LORD, the God of the Hebrews, sent me to you, saying, 'Let My people go, that they may serve Me in the wilderness' " (Exodus 7:16). He warned Pharaoh that terrible things would happen if Pharaoh disobeyed God. When the king ignored God, God displayed His power to show that He was not to be ignored and was more powerful than the gods the Egyptians worshiped.

The Ten Plagues of Egypt

Directions: Read through Exodus 7–11. Find and highlight Bible verses that name the ten plagues God sent to Egypt. When you have read about a plague, place a number in the box to indicate the order in which the plagues occurred.

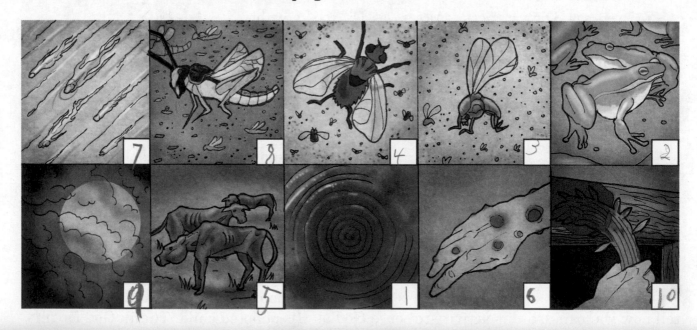

REVIEW

God sent the ten _____ to convince _____ to permit the people of Israel to

leave Egypt and to show that He was more powerful than the gods of the Egyptians. When

_____ continued to ignore God, God sent more _____ , but the _____

did not affect the lives and property of the Israelites living in Goshen.

God Cares

At times, all of us, like the Israelites, find ourselves in bad and hurtful situations. How can this happen to people of God? God's nature is to love. So how do you know God loves and cares for people? Look at the three Old Testament stories below; read the account and then note how God helped each person. Then find other Bible stories in which Christ rescues people. Briefly describe these rescues on the lines provided.

Genesis 14:12–16 _____

_____

Esther 8:3–11 _____

_____

Jonah 1:17 _____

_____

_____   _____   _____

_____   _____   _____

_____   _____   _____

_____   _____   _____

REMEMBER

Our soul waits for the LORD; He is our help and our shield. **(Psalm 33:20)**

Passover

Exodus 12

God Delivers His People from Harm

Look at the picture to the right. What is the most important item in the picture? Asked another way, What is the key to the Israelites being released from slavery in Egypt?

The Last Plague and the Passover

Read together the story of the last plague God delivered on the Egyptians in Exodus 12. Then answer the following questions.

1. Why did the children of Israel want to leave Egypt? there were living in slavery.

2. What would have happened if the Israelites had not put lamb's blood over their doors? any first born in thier faimly would die.

3. How is the Passover a picture of how God saves us? The lamb was sacrificed to save israelites. Jesus was our lamb that was sacrificed for our salvation.

REVIEW

Draw lines to match each of the following words with its definition on the right.

Passover

Seder

Matzo

A flat unleavened bread Jews ate while they were slaves in Egypt; they took this type of bread with them when they fled the land of Egypt.

The religious celebration commemorating God saving the firstborn in Israelite families by passing over their homes, which had the blood of a lamb painted on their doorposts.

The term refers both to the service commemorating God's saving of His people during the night of the death of the firstborn in Egypt and to the meal eaten in remembrance of the event, which follows a prescribed order for serving the items in the meal.

Our Deliverance Meal

On Thursday of Holy Week, Jesus and His disciples went to a home in Jerusalem to celebrate the Passover meal (Matthew 26:17–29). As He celebrated the Passover, however, Jesus changed this meal forever. As He ate and shared the bread with His disciples, He said, "Take, eat; this is My body" (Matthew 26:26). Later, as He drank and shared the wine, He said, "Drink of it, all of you, for this is My blood of the covenant, which is poured out for many for the forgiveness of sins" (Matthew 26:27–28). What do believers receive when they drink wine and eat bread in the Lord's Supper? Circle each correct group of words that tells of something believers receive in the Lord's Supper. Draw a line through each group of words that indicates something believers do not receive when they receive the Lord's Supper.

Christ's body and blood received in a mysterious way

Healing from disease

Escape from death for the firstborn in the family

Forgiveness of sins

Eternal life and salvation

Victory over sin and hell

Strength for the new life in Him

REMEMBER

Christ, our Passover lamb, has been sacrificed. **(1 Corinthians 5:7)**

The Exodus

Exodus 13:17–14:31

Identifying Key Points

Form a team with three to five classmates. Then work together to list the things that happened in today's Bible story. Have your Bibles open to Exodus 13:17–14:31 and look back at it so you don't forget anything important. You should have at least eight to ten items on your list. (Hint: It may help you to keep items in the right order if you put verse numbers behind each item. For example, *Pharaoh let the people go—13:17*.)

Now go through the list and cross off numerals until only the five most important parts of the story are left. Talk it through until everyone on your team agrees. Write those five parts on the second notepad below in the correct order. Then get your teacher's approval.

When you're ready, begin to plan a six-part presentation for your class. Your presentation will tell what God did for His people in the exodus. Base the first five parts on the five key points your team has identified. The sixth part should tell everyone who watches your presentation why the exodus matters to kids your age today.

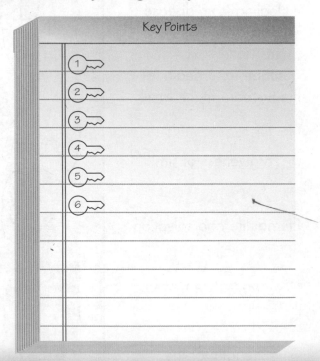

What Happened in the Exodus
1
2
3
4
5
6
7
8
9
10

Key Points
1.
2.
3.
4.
5.
6.

REVIEW

Use the words *exodus*, *chariots*, and *pillar* to fill the blanks in the sentence below.

After the __exodus__, or leaving, of Egypt, Pharaoh and his army pursued them in two-wheeled horse-drawn carts known as __chariots__; but God directed and protected His people, traveling with them in a __pillar__ of cloud by day and a __pillar__ of fire by night.

Truth or Lie?

Did you notice how fearful the people of Israel became during God's rescue? Did you hear their grumbling words? We know that God noticed. We know He heard. God is *omniscient* (om-**nish**-uhnt); He knows everything. Still, despite their unbelief and grumbling, God protected His people. He saved them from their enemies.

There's often a big difference between what God is doing to help us and what we think He's doing. We sometimes grow suspicious, wondering if He really plans to do what's best for us. Satan fuels these doubts. He lies to us, just as he lied to the people of Israel. Then we grow fearful. We may even grumble.

For example, Israel thought God was letting Pharaoh's army thunder down on them to kill them. Really, though, God knew all along that He would provide safe passage through the middle of the Red Sea!

• Think about a time something happened in your life—something you worried or grumbled about. How did it come out? Looking back, what can you say about how God was really there for you, helping you? What people did He use? What events? Share your story with your class.

• Think about something that worries or upsets you right now. Take a few minutes and talk silently to Jesus about it. Ask Him to teach you to trust Him, no matter what. Ask Him to give you comfort and courage. He will!

Today's Key Learning

Read the question below, and take sixty seconds to think about it quietly. Then talk with your class about it.

What one main thing do I want to remember from our time together with Jesus today?

REMEMBER

May those who love Your salvation say evermore, "God is great!" **(Psalm 70:4b)**

Songs of Moses and Miriam

Exodus 15:1–21

A Song of Celebration

Every year, God's people celebrated Passover. They observed it just as God had commanded. During Passover, everyone remembered what God had done to rescue them from slavery in Egypt.

Pretend someone has given you a ticket on a time machine. The dials are set to transport you back in time to the east bank of the Red Sea. Pharaoh's army has just drowned. God's people are free—and safe.

You'll get to stay for a few days with an Israelite family. They have come out of slavery. Every so often, someone in the family begins to sing a song you've never heard before. Then everyone else in the family joins in. Sometimes people in neighboring tents do, too!

Work with a friend to read some of the lyrics of their song from Exodus 15:1–21. On the lines below, list at least three phrases that clue you in that the song is about God's victory in the exodus. Put the verse number behind each phrase.

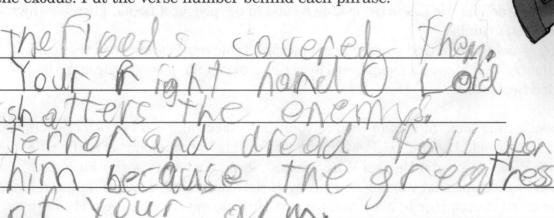

the floods covered them.
Your Right hand O Lord
shatters the enemy.
terror and dread fall upon
him because the greatness
of your arm.

REVIEW

Triumph
1. the act, fact, or condition of being victorious;
2. a noteworthy or remarkable success;
3. the feeling of joy victory brings.

Glorious
1. wonderful, exciting, delightful;
2. full of glory;
3. spectacularly beautiful or splendid.

I Will Sing to the LORD . . .

Now, get back into your time machine. You'll leave the desert near the Red Sea and soon find yourself near the Sea of Galilee. It's just one year after Jesus died on the cross, rose from the dead, and ascended into heaven. You will live for a few days with a Christian family. They are celebrating Easter. But surprisingly enough, they are singing words you recognize—words from Exodus 15!

Again, working with your friend, study Exodus 15:1–21. On the lines below, list at least three phrases that make the words of this song a fitting celebration for Jesus' Easter victory over sin, Satan, and death. Put the verse number behind each phrase.

_____

_____

_____

_____

_____

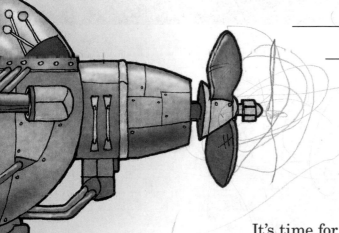

The Song of Moses— and of the Lamb

It's time for one last time machine voyage. But now, you will travel forward, not backward, in time. When you step out, you find yourself in eternity—with God's people in heaven. Some of them are singing about God's glorious triumph. The song sounds familiar. Read it from Revelation 15:3. The words aren't exactly the same, so how do we know it's the same song as the one you read in Exodus 15?

The lord is great and amazing

REMEMBER 💙

Let the word of Christ dwell in you richly, teaching and admonishing one another in all wisdom, singing psalms and hymns and spiritual songs, with thankfulness in your hearts to God. **(Colossians 3:16)**

God Appears on Mount Sinai

Exodus 19:1–25

At the Foot of Mount Sinai

Imagine that you are an Israelite reporter. You have witnessed many amazing events in the past months. You crossed the Red Sea; you drank refreshing water that had been bitter; you have been eating manna that you receive fresh each morning. Now, after three months of traveling, you find yourself at the foot of Mount Sinai. Read Exodus 19:1–25; use the chart below to record your reflections about all of these experiences in the light of what you see at Mount Sinai.

See	Hear	Touch or Smell	My Reactions
Thick cloud lighting smoke	thunder very loud trumpet blast Moses speaking	rock plant smoke felt the mountain tremble	That God is true.

REVIEW

Write letters on the lines to match the following words with their definitions:

_b___ Covenant

_c___ Priesthood

_a___ Consecrate

a. Set apart for serving Yahweh (God)

b. Statement describing the relationship between two people or parties

c. People dedicated to serving God

God's Promise to the Israelites

1. How does God remind the Israelites of His love for them (Exodus 19:4–6)?

they crossethe read sea. He drowned theirenmies. Heresue them from slavery

2. What does God want the Israelites to do (Exodus 19:5–6)?

Obey his voice. keepmy covent, they will be a holy nation belonging to god

3. How do the Israelites respond to the promise (Exodus 19:8)?

All that the lord will do.

4. How have the Israelites responded to God's care in the past (Exodus 15:22–24; 16:1–3)?

they grumble about having no water they grumbled about having no food. Manna

5. What does this covenant reveal about how God feels about the Israelites?

He loved then and cared foathem.

How are we like the Israelites?

God's Assurances

As God forgave the people of Israel, He forgives us with the forgiveness Jesus earned for us. And what does that mean for us? Rewrite the Bible verse for today in your own words as an answer to that question.

REMEMBER 💙

But you are a chosen race, a royal priesthood, a holy nation, a people for His own possession, that you may proclaim the excellencies of Him who called you out of darkness into His marvelous light. **(1 Peter 2:9)**

The Ten Commandments

Exodus 20:1–26

God's Will for Us

God presented Moses with the Ten Commandments thousands of years ago. The Commandments given in Exodus 20 are to guide our actions so that we can do what is right in the eyes of God. Read the situations described in each box. In the tiny box in the upper left hand corner, write the number of the commandment that was broken in each example. Refer to a list of the Commandments as you work.

4 **a.** Jimmy's mom asked him to clean his room. He chose to watch TV instead.	6 **b.** Josh became friends with the new student, but he wouldn't let him play with anyone else at recess.	2 **c.** Ramon was tagged out at third base, so he angrily yelled at the umpire.	6 **d.** LaVon looked at a Web site with many suggestive pictures.	3 **e.** TaKeisha wanted to skip church and Sunday School because she stayed up too late the night before.
1 **f.** Ed says he loves his new bike more than anything else.	9 **g.** Brian was mad at his friend, so he said mean things about him to classmates.	10 **h.** Sarah felt bad because she didn't have an Xbox like Jamie's.	5 **i.** Gloria's little brother took her favorite toy, so she hit him.	7 **j.** Ruth forgot to finish her homework, so she copied a classmate's answers.

REVIEW

Match each of the following words to its meaning.

_____ commandment

_____ idol

_____ neighbor

a. a false and powerless object of worship and devotion

b. anyone we may know or relate to in any way

c. an order or expectation

Two Great Commandments

Look back at the Ten Commandments in Exodus 20. Which commandments do you think are the most important?

_____

Why?

_____

In Matthew 22:36–40, Jesus answers this same question by narrowing the list to two commandments. What are these?

_____

_____

A Free Gift

Read the following statements. Circle the letter in the True column if the statement is true. Circle the letter in the False column if it is false.

	True	False
1) It is easy to keep all the Commandments perfectly.	E	T
2) The only person who kept the Law perfectly was Christ.	S	M
3) Christ took our sins as a substitute for us.	I	L
4) Christ gave us His holiness and took on Himself our sinfulness.	R	A
5) Being made righteous gives us full forgiveness and eternal life.	H	D
6) We should not share this joy of forgiveness with others.	N	C

Now write the letters you circled on the corresponding numbered line below to complete the sentence.

The only way to heaven is through C h r i s t
                                  (6) (5) (4) (3) (2) (1)

By ourselves, we cannot keep the Ten Commandments perfectly. But through Christ's death and resurrection, we obtain full forgiveness and salvation. Rejoice that you are a fully redeemed child of God. Now go back to the ten boxes on the previous page. In each box, write a response to each situation that would better bring praise to God for the salvation He gives through Jesus.

REMEMBER

For our sake He made Him to be sin who knew no sin, so that in Him we might become the righteousness of God. (2 Corinthians 5:21)

Just about There

The journey to the Promised Land was continuing. Finally they drew near its borders. But what would they find there? In Numbers 13:1–2, God told Moses to send spies into the land. Read the report the spies gave after they returned (Numbers 13:25–33). Then complete the following matching exercise.

_____ 1. What was the land like? See verse 27.

_____ 2. Ten of the spies were afraid to enter the land. Why? See verse 28.

_____ 3. Read Numbers 14:20–30. How did God punish the people for failing to trust in Him?

_____ 4. Besides food, how did God provide other daily bread? Read Deuteronomy 29:5–6 to find another way God provided for them during all these years.

_____ 5. Read Revelation 2:10. What is God's promise to all who remain faithful?

a. He will give us a crown of life.

b. Clothes and shoes never wore out, even after 40 years.

c. It flowed with milk and honey.

d. None of the adults except Caleb and Joshua would enter the Promised Land.

e. The people were strong, and the cities were fortified.

FINISH

REVIEW

Write each word on the blank in the correct sentence definition.

Rebellion   Repentance   Restoration

1. The children of Israel committed an act of_____ when they constantly complained about their daily bread and spoke against God.

2. The people realized their sin when they were bitten by the fiery serpents and asked Moses to say a prayer of _____ to the Lord.

3. God heard their prayer and poured out His grace on His faithful people in an unconditional act of _____ via the snake on the pole.

Our Promised Land

Find questions 190 and 191 in *Luther's Small Catechism with Explanation.*

HEAVEN

At the Last Day, both _____ and

_____ will begin the full enjoyment of being

with Christ forever.

At the time of death, the soul of a believer is immediately

_____.

God gives eternal life to

_____.

Eternal life is a _____
possession.

Believing in Jesus Christ as my Savior, I (can/cannot) be sure that I have eternal life. This is true because of (my effort/God's grace in Christ).

Let's Review

1. How are you like one of the Israelites wandering in the wilderness?

_____

_____

2. How are you rescued by God each day?

_____

_____

3. Why will we see one another in heaven?

_____

_____

REMEMBER

For by grace you have been saved through faith. And this is not your own doing; it is the gift of God, not a result of works, so that no one may boast. **(Ephesians 2:8–9)**

Snake on the Pole

Numbers 21:4–10

Saved

A. Fill in the blanks with the words from Numbers 21:4–10.

1. The people went around the Land of __ __ __ __ .

2. The people spoke against God and _m o s e s_ .
   6   4   12

3. "There is no _f o o d_ or water."
   7

4. "We loathe this __ __ __ __ __ __ __ __ food."
   9

5. The Lord sent fiery __ __ __ __ __ __ __ __ among the people.
   13

6. Many people of Israel__ __ __ __ .
   11

7. The people __ __ __ __ to Moses.
   1

8. "We have _S i n n e d_ against the Lord."
   5

9. "_P r a y_ to the Lord for us."
   2

10. Moses made a _b r o n z e_ serpent.
    10

11. He set it on a __ __ __ __ .
    3

12. The people set out and__ __ __ __ __ __ in Oboth.
    8

B. Write the letter that appears over each number in the correct space at the bottom.

What Saves Us?

The __ __ __ __ __ __ __ __ __ __ __ __ __
    1 2 3 4 5   6 7   8 9 10 11 12 13

REVIEW

Match each word on the left with its definition on the right.

_____ 1. Rely   a. to trust, depend, or count on someone keeping a promise

_____ 2. Reject   b. to save or deliver from harm and danger

_____ 3. Rescue   c. to turn away, to say no more, to cancel a promise

Our Daily Bread
The Fourth Petition

Give us this day our daily bread.

What does this mean? God certainly gives daily bread to everyone without our prayers, even to all evil people, but we pray in this petition that God would lead us to realize this and to receive our daily bread with thanksgiving.

Daily bread includes everything that has to do with the support and needs of the body. Draw a line through each of the following that does not fit with the others.

worry   health   goods   drink   house   self-control   shoes   a devout husband or wife   pain   good friends   enemies   home   money   grumbling   land   devout and faithful rulers   devout workers   food   faithful neighbors   sin   peace   clothing   good reputation   animals   devout children   good weather   good government

Let's Review

1. How are we often like the children of Israel in this story?

_____

_____

2. What is meant by daily bread?

_____

_____

3. What are some of the "fiery serpents" in your life?

_____

_____

REMEMBER

The eyes of all look to You, and You give them their food in due season. You open Your hand; You satisfy the desire of every living thing. (**Psalm 145:15–16**)

Israel Crosses the Jordan

Joshua 3–4

Israel's Journey to the Promised Land

Open your Bible to the Book of Exodus. Starting at chapter 1, page through Exodus and put the following events in order. (The last event occurs in Joshua 4.) Number the events 1–10.

_____ The Passover
_____ Water from the Rock
_____ Moses and the Burning Bush
_____ Crossing the Red Sea
_____ The Birth of Moses
_____ The Golden Calf
_____ The Building of the Tabernacle
_____ Ten Plagues of Egypt
_____ Joshua and the Israelites Cross the Jordan
_____ The Ten Commandments

Pretend that you are a father or a mother who just learned that tomorrow you will travel into the Promised Land. You know how God has led your nation during the past forty years. But you also see that you must cross the Jordan River in order to get into the Promised Land. What would you tell your son or daughter about what is about to happen?

REVIEW

Look up the following Bible passages. Then write the definition in your own words.

Repent (Acts 3:19) _____

Trust (Psalm 56:4) _____

Obey (1 John 5:2) _____

Israel Crosses the Jordan

We Follow God Today

Praise be to God who has promised to forgive our sins and give us eternal life with Him. The Israelites followed God into the Promised Land. But how do Christians today follow God?

We follow God by obeying His commands, trusting in His Word, and sharing the Gospel with others. Thankfully, we are not left on our own to follow God. The Holy Spirit will guide and lead us on our spiritual journey. God promises that He is with us always, even to the end of the age (Matthew 28:20).

Read the following. Give examples of how a Christian could follow God in each situation.

1. You forgot to study for your science test. You always do well and know how disappointed your parents will be if you get a bad grade. The girl sitting next to you is a good student. You are tempted to cheat. What should you do?

_____

_____

2. Justin is a new student. He hasn't made any friends yet and is very quiet. Between classes, he drops his books in the hallway and everyone around laughs at him. What should you do?

_____

_____

3. A new family moves into your neighborhood. They have a boy your age. You notice they never go to church. What should you do?

_____

_____

REMEMBER 💙

Have I not commanded you? Be strong and courageous. Do not be frightened, and do not be dismayed, for the LORD your God is with you wherever you go. **(Joshua 1:9)**

Israel Crosses the Jor an

Joshua 3–4

Mercy on the Israelites

Review Joshua 4:2–3, 7. Fill in the blanks in the paragraphs below.

God showed mercy on a sinful nation. He forgave their sins, fulfilled His promise, and safely led His people across the Jordan River. What an amazing, powerful God! God did not want this miracle to be forgotten. He told Joshua, "Take _____ men from the people, from each tribe a man, and command them, saying, 'Take _____ _____ from here out of the midst of the Jordan, from the very place where the priests' feet stood firmly, and bring them over with you and lay them down in the place where you lodge tonight.'" Joshua said, "So these _____ shall be to the people of Israel a _____ forever."

Why did God do this? Our lesson today answers that question in Joshua 4:24: He did this "so that all the peoples of the earth may know that the hand of the LORD is _____, that you may fear the LORD your God forever." Indeed, we have a powerful God!

We don't want to forget how powerful God is in our lives today. On the picture of the stone, write a powerful attribute of God that comes to your mind.

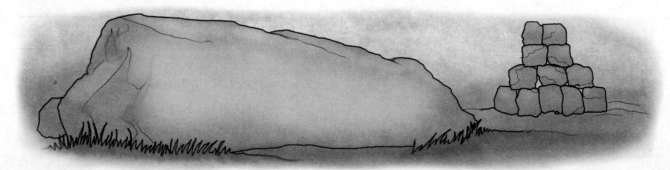

REVIEW

Grace is receiving something you *don't* deserve.
Mercy is *not* receiving something that you *do* deserve.
Look up the following verses. Decide if they describe God's mercy or God's grace. Write the word *mercy* or *grace* for the appropriate verse.

Ephesians 2:8 _____

1 Peter 1:3 _____

Mercy—Again and Again!

We call the Israelites "God's chosen people." But they didn't always act that way! In fact, they often failed to trust in God, and many times they did not follow His commands. However, God is faithful. He kept His promise and led the Israelites into the Promised Land. He showed great mercy to the Israelites, just as He shows mercy to us today.

Look up the following passages. Discuss together how God showed mercy to His people.

1. Exodus 12:12–13

_____

_____

2. Exodus 14:19–25

_____

_____

3. Exodus 16:11–12

_____

_____

4. And in today's lesson . . .
Joshua 4:23–24

_____

_____

REMEMBER

> As a father shows compassion to his children, so the LORD shows compassion to those who fear Him. **(Psalm 103:13)**

63

Gideon Leads God's People

Judges 6:11–16, 36–40

God Calls Gideon

Again and again, God showed kindness to His people. Yet they often forgot about God's love and His rules. Many times after the Israelites began to disobey God or even worship other gods, problems followed. Special leaders called "judges" were sent to deliver the Israelites from their enemies. Read the story of how God chose one of the judges, Gideon, in Judges 6:11–16, 36–40. Then, put the events of his story listed below in the correct order by numbering them 1–5.

☐ Gideon questions whether God is still helping the Israelites.

☐ Dew falls only on the fleece as a sign from God.

☐ Gideon hides from the Midianites as he works.

☐ Dew falls only on the ground as a sign from God.

☐ The angel of the LORD calls Gideon a "mighty man of valor."

Called to Be a Savior

Gideon was not sure that it was really God who was calling him to do this special task of being a judge to deliver Israel. He needed God to show him—more than once. The New Testament is also filled with signs about the special task that Jesus was called to carry out. However, God did not give these signs to convince Jesus. No, these signs show *us* that He is our Savior. Fill in the blanks to correctly explain these prophecies that Jesus fulfilled.

Jesus would be born in the town of _____ (Matthew 2:4–5).

Jesus would be a descendant of King _____ (Matthew 1:6, 16).

As a baby, Jesus was taken to _____ (Matthew 2:13–15) to stay safe from King Herod.

Jesus would ride into Jerusalem on a _____ (Matthew 21:5).

Jesus would be betrayed for 30 pieces of _____ (Matthew 26:14–16).

REVIEW

Draw a line from each word on the left to the matching definition on the right.

Prophet	A leader whom God chose to deliver His people from their enemies
Judge	A person who was with Jesus and preached the Gospel
Apostle	A person chosen to speak for God, especially about the future

God Calls Us Too

Did you know that you are also called to do work in God's kingdom? God called you and gave you faith through His Word. Now He moves you and other Christians to respond by living God-pleasing lives. Think of Christians in the world around you who are called to serve God in the following ways.

Care for people who are sick or suffering

_____

Teach people about God and His Word

_____

Keep people safe

_____

Provide food for other people

_____

Make wise decisions to help others

_____

Share God's love by being honest, hardworking, and forgiving

_____

Power to Fulfill Our Calling

Dear Heavenly Father,

Thank You for calling me to be Your child. I know that I don't deserve the forgiveness that Jesus earned for me. Please send Your Holy Spirit to help me

_____

_____

_____

so I can live the life that You are calling me to live. Amen.

REMEMBER

You . . . are called to belong to Jesus Christ. **(Romans 1:6)**

Gideon Leads God's People

Judges 7:1–8, 16–23

The Battle Belongs to the Lord

_____   _____

_____   _____

_____   _____

What are some of the ways that this story shows that God's power won the battle and not the power of the Israelites?

_____

_____

_____

What are some things in life that we need God's power to accomplish?

_____

_____

_____

REVIEW

A _____ is a "trumpet" of the Old Testament that was made from a ram's horn and has important uses to the people of Israel.

God Delivers

We know that it was really the power of God that rescued the Israelites in the story of Gideon. In the New Testament, God rescued all people in an even more important way. Fill in each of the blanks in the chart below to compare these great rescues.

Gideon	Jesus
Gideon's closest followers were three hundred_____ .	Jesus' closest followers were the twelve _____ .
Gideon delivered the Israelites from the people of _____ .	Jesus delivered us from our _____ .
Gideon's unusual battle plan included playing _____ and breaking _____ .	Jesus' unusual battle plan included dying on a _____ .
Gideon got his power from _____ .	Jesus got His power because He is true _____ .
The deliverance Gideon gave the Israelites lasted only a _____ time.	The deliverance that Jesus gives to us will last through _____ .

Our Battles

We also fight against the devil, the world, and our sinful nature to try to do what God has called us to do. Think about different parts of your life and the things that you need God's help to do. Write these things on the jars below. Remember to ask God for help in winning these battles as you seek to follow Jesus.

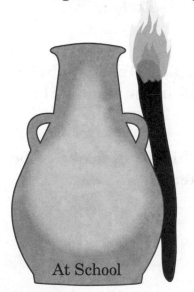
At School

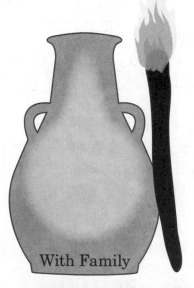
With Family

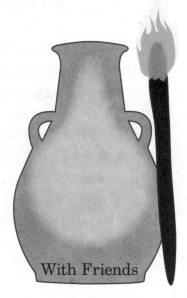
With Friends

REMEMBER

Fight the good fight of the faith. Take hold of the eternal life to which you were called and about which you made the good confession in the presence of many witnesses. **(1 Timothy 6:12)**

God Chooses Samson

Judges 13:1–5, 24–25; 14

Who Was Samson?

Read about Samson in Judges 13:1–5, 24–25. Then draw lines to the words on the right to finish each of the following sentences.

1. The Lord gave Israel into the hands of the Philistines because (v. 1) ☐   ☐ **great physical strength.**

2. Samson was a Nazirite. He was to (v. 5) ☐   ☐ **save Israel from the hand of the Philistines.**

Now read about Samson in Judges 14.

☐ **strike down thirty men in the town of Ashkelon.**

3. God gave Samson (vv. 5–6) ☐

4. Samson was not always obedient. He showed disrespect for his parents when he demanded they (v. 2) ☐   ☐ **the people of Israel did what was evil in the sight of the Lord.**

5. God delivered Samson from trouble when the Spirit of the Lord gave Samson the strength to kill a young lion and when the Spirit of the Lord gave him the strength to (v. 19) ☐   ☐ **get a Philistine woman to be his wife.**

REVIEW

Nazirite: _____ Spirit of the Lord: _____

Judge:_____

What Is God's Plan?

Do each of the following.

1. Underline the words in the Remember verse at the bottom of the page that tell God's will for all people.

2. Underline the words in the verse below that tell how God has called us.
   "He called you through our gospel, so that you may obtain the glory of our Lord Jesus Christ." 2 Thessalonians 2:14

3. Underline and then draw a light bulb above the words in the verse below that tell what we as God's people are to shine as lights to those around us so they will see them and give glory to our heavenly Father.
   "Let your light shine before others, so that they may see your good works and give glory to your Father who is in heaven." Matthew 5:16

4. Circle the words in the verse below that tell how God would have us use the gifts He has given us.
   "As each has received a gift, use it to serve one another, as good stewards of God's varied grace." 1 Peter 4:10

5. Circle the words in the following verse that tell why Jesus came.
   "I came that they may have life and have it abundantly." John 10:10

God's Goals for My Life

God the Father created me with His plans in mind.

God in Christ redeems me from my sins of disobedience.

God the Holy Spirit shows me the gift of salvation and how to use my gifts to serve God and others.

(your gifts and talents)

(name)

REMEMBER

[God our Savior] desires all people to be saved and to come to the knowledge of the truth. (1 Timothy 2:4)

Samson Sins and Repents

Judges 16:4–31

What Is Repentance?

_____
_____

_____
_____

Repentance in Samson's Life

Judges 16:4–12

_____
_____

Judges 16:13–17

_____
_____

Repentance in My Life

_____
_____

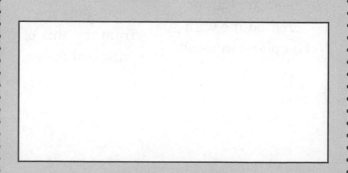

_____
_____

REVIEW

Repent: _____

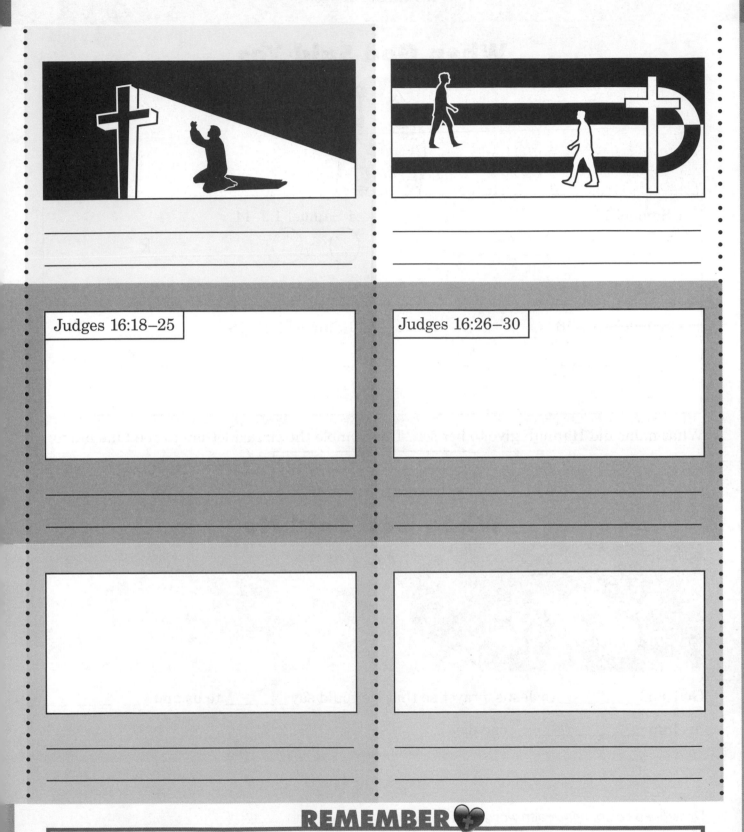

Judges 16:18–25

Judges 16:26–30

Go Gives Hanna a Son

1 Samuel 1:1–28

When God Said Yes

1 Samuel 1:3–8	1 Samuel 1:9–14
P ___ ___ ___ ○ ___ ___ ___	○ ___ ○ ___ ___ ___ ___ R – ___ ___ ___ ___ ___
1 Samuel 1:15–16	1 Samuel 1:17–18
Ⓐ ___ ___ ___ ○ ___ ___ ___ ___ ___ ___ ___	___ ___ ○ ___ ___ ___ ___ Y

What name did Hannah give to her son? Unscramble the circled letters to spell his name.

When God Said No

God said _____ to Jesus' prayer so that He could say _____ to us and _____

us into _____ one day.

REVIEW

Draw lines to connect each word with its definition.

Supplication   Speaking to God in words and thoughts

Prayer   God's desire or purpose

God's Will   A humble and earnest request

God Answers Our Prayers—
Yes, No, Wait, or Something Better

_____ "What you have asked for is good for you, and I will give it to you." Example: Hannah's prayer for a son	_____ "What you have asked for is not good for you, and I will not give it to you because it will harm you or your faith or others and their faith." Example: Jesus in the Garden of Gethsemane
_____ "What you have asked for is good for you, but it's not the right time yet." Example: Mary and Martha when their brother Lazarus was sick and died	_____ "What you have asked for is good, but I have something even better for you." Example: Zacchaeus wanted to see Jesus, and Jesus went to his house.

Directions: Decide how God is answering each of the following prayers. Write Yes, No, Wait, or Something Better in the blank in front of the prayer.

_____I prayed that my mom would quit smoking, and she did.

_____I prayed about a spelling test. The next day, I got them all right.

_____I had a basketball game, and I prayed that we would get at least 10 points. We got 17.

_____I prayed that I would get Lego building blocks for Christmas, but I didn't.

_____When I was 8, I prayed that I would get a dirt bike. I didn't get it until I was 12.

_____I prayed that George would live. He died the next day.

_____I prayed that God would be with me during the storm.

_____I prayed for my dad to find a million dollars. He didn't.

_____I prayed for forgiveness after getting mad at my mom.

REMEMBER

Do not be anxious about anything, but in everything by prayer and supplication with thanksgiving let your requests be made known to God. (Philippians 4:6)

God Gives Israel Its First King

1 Samuel 10:20–24; 11:12–15; 15

Hey You! Over There in the Baggage!

_____

_____

_____

Samuel was looking for Saul because he had been chosen to be
_____. But Saul did not step up
proudly to take on his new role. To be a good king, he would need to trust
in God and follow His commands. But did he?

The Tale of Two Battles

	1 Samuel 11:1–15	1 Samuel 15
Against whom did Saul and the Israelites fight?	Ammonites	Verse 3
What was Saul told to do?	Rescue the Israelites at Jabesh-gilead	Verse 3
What did Saul do?	Rescued the Israelites from Jabesh-gilead	Verses 8–9
To whom did Saul give the credit for the victory?	Verse 13	Verse 13
What was the result?	Verse 15	Verse 23

REVIEW

Idolatry _____

Confession _____

Have I Been Like Saul?

Directions: Put a dot inside the box when you think of something in your own life that matches what Saul did.

☐ Think about a time when you were told to do something; you did part of the task, but you didn't complete it.

☐ Think about a time when you lied to someone—either about something that you did or about something you didn't do—so that you wouldn't get in trouble.

☐ Think about a time when you tried to make an excuse for what you did by making it seem like the thing you did would help someone.

☐ Think about a time when you blamed someone else for something that you did wrong.

☐ Think about a time when you said you were sorry but didn't really mean it. "Take heart, My son; your sins are forgiven" (Matthew 9:2).

How Great Thou Art

Do this activity together, as a class.

Find the hymn "How Great Thou Art" in your hymnal (*LSB* 801). After everyone has found it, sit quietly and think about the sins you just talked about. Remember Jesus' words: "Your sins are forgiven."

End your quiet time by singing stanza 3 of "How Great Thou Art."

Next, think about what Jesus' gift on the cross means to you. Write or draw your thoughts in the box to the right.

REMEMBER

If we say we have no sin, we deceive ourselves, and the truth is not in us. If we confess our sins, He is faithful and just to forgive us our sins and to cleanse us from all unrighteousness. **(1 John 1:8–9)**

Goliath Threatens Israel

1 Samuel 17

Who Can Help?

Narrative Part 1

Narrator: (Background) Things have not changed in Israel. The Philistines have begun another war with King Saul and the Israelites. This time, they are encamped near Socoh, about 15 miles from Bethlehem, south of Jerusalem. Three of David's brothers are with the army. Remember, there are no "action news reporters" for TV or radio. David's father wants news of the battle and wants to know how his sons are doing. So he calls David in from watching the sheep and gives him food for his sons and cheeses for the commander. When David arrives at the battle site, he watches as Goliath comes from the Philistine side and issues a challenge to the Israelites. They respond by running like frightened sheep.

Goliath: Why should your whole army battle with us? I am a Philistine. Choose one of your men to fight me. If I kill him, you will be our servants. If he kills me, we will be your servants.

Narrator: This challenge is repeated every morning and evening. David hears the challenge.

David: What can this mean?

Soldier: Have you noticed what a giant he is? If a man kills Goliath, the king will give him riches and let him marry his daughter. King Saul has promised to pay all the debts of the man's father.

REVIEW

Fill in the blanks with the correct words. See 1 Samuel 17:5–7.

Goliath stood about 9 feet tall. He wore a bronze helmet and was armed with a

_____ ____ _____ . His bronze _____ was slung between

his shoulders. His _____—_____ went before him. Goliath's coat of armor

weighed about 125 pounds.

David: Why should we allow this Philistine to bother us? I will kill him.

Narrator: David repeats this to other soldiers. Then his brother hears his boast.

Eliab (angry): Why are you here? Who's taking care of the sheep? Are you here just to watch?

David: Why are you angry with me?

Narrator: A messenger arrives from the king, who has heard of David's boast.

Messenger: David, King Saul wishes to speak to you.

Saul: Why, you are just a boy! You cannot fight this giant. You don't have any experience as a soldier.

David: Oh, King! I have taken care of my father's sheep. I have protected them from a lion and a bear. When the lion or bear took one of the sheep, I rescued the sheep and killed the wild animal. The Philistine giant is just like one of those wild animals. The Lord who helped me protect the sheep will help me defeat this Philistine.

Saul: Go, and the Lord be with you.

Narrator: David is wearing shepherd's clothing.

Saul: I want you to wear my armor for your battle with the giant Goliath.

Narrator: David tries to wear the king's armor.

David: I cannot wear these. I am not used to them—and they are too big for me.

The Lord Provides

God gives good things to my family and me. He forgives us our sins in Jesus. He gives us many other good things as well.

Under "Name," write some names from your family and extended family.

Under "Examples of How the Lord Provides," write one way God has helped each family member.

Include your own name.

Name   **Examples of How the Lord Provides**

_____   _____

_____   _____

_____   _____

_____   _____

_____   _____

_____   _____

REMEMBER

The LORD is my strength and my song; He has become my salvation. **(Psalm 118:14)**

David Slays Goliath

1 Samuel 17

The Sling Is Mightier Than the Sword

Narrator: David has tried King Saul's armor, but he finds it impossible to fight the giant unless he wears the clothing he wears as a shepherd. Now he approaches the giant. On his way to meet the giant, David stops to pick up several smooth stones at a brook. He puts them in the bag he wears with the supplies needed for a shepherd.

Goliath (surprised): What? Am I a dog that you come to fight me with a stick? I will tear you to pieces and feed your body to the birds.

David: You come to fight me with a sword, spear, and shield, but I come to fight you in the name of the Lord God of hosts. You have made fun of the Lord, and today He will deliver you into my hand. All the earth will know there is a Lord God in Israel. Those watching today will know that the Lord does not give the victory with the sword and spear. The Lord will help us win this battle.

Narrator: Goliath, with his heavy armor, moves toward David slowly. David picks a stone from his bag and runs toward Goliath. David releases the stone from his sling, striking Goliath in the forehead and knocking him down. David then runs forward, grabs Goliath's sword, and removes the giant's head. The armies of the Philistines flee, while the Israelites give chase to secure the victory.

REVIEW

Look up these two words in your glossary and discuss them as a class. Also look up Judges 20:16. Next, draw a picture of each on David and write a few words about how David used these tools and how he may have been trained to use them.

Sling— _____

_____

_____

Staff— _____

_____

_____

Call Upon the Lord

Find the Second Commandment and its meaning in the Catechism. Write the words that are missing below.

We should _____ and _____ God so that we do not _____, swear, use satanic arts, _____, or _____ by His name,

but _____ _____ ____ ____ _____ _____, _____, _____, and _____ _____.

Stand Up for the Lord

Mark an X in each box by situations where God and/or His name is being attacked.

What's happening in each of these pictures?

1. _____

2. _____

3. _____

REMEMBER

Make haste, O God, to deliver me! O LORD, make haste to help me! **(Psalm 70:1)**

Jonat an Warns Davi

1 Samuel 20

The Friendship of David and Jonathan

David, a shepherd, and Jonathan, King Saul's son, were close friends. Their friendship began soon after David killed Goliath. Their faith in God guided their lives. Although Jonathan was the king's son and heir to the throne, the people of Israel considered David to be a hero and wanted him to be their next king. When King Saul became jealous of David's popularity with the people, he threatened to kill David. Jonathan courageously defended his friend, even though it meant opposing his father, endangering his own life, and losing the crown. First Samuel 20 tells their story. To review the account, match each of the following questions with the letter of its answer from the column on the right. Note: you will not use all of the items found in the right-hand column.

_____ 1. What did King Saul expect David to attend (1 Samuel 20:24–27)?

_____ 2. How did King Saul show anger to Jonathan when he defended David (1 Samuel 20:28–33)?

_____ 3. How did Jonathan send a warning message to his friend (1 Samuel 20:18–23; 34–40)?

_____ 4. What did David and Jonathan promise each other in their farewell (1 Samuel 20:41–42)?

a. He shot arrows according to a prearranged signal.

b. To never give up on Saul.

c. To remain friends and care for each other's families.

d. He tied a red ribbon to the shade of his window.

e. Jonathan's birthday party.

f. He threatened to disown him.

g. He threw a spear at him.

h. The new moon festival.

REVIEW

Friend_____

Friendship_____

What Are My Qualities as a Friend?

What kind of a friend are you? What gifts has God given you to be a person who cares about your classmates? To find out, ask your classmates to write the gifts you show in the body shape. You will need to exchange your books with classmates to complete this activity.

friendly

caring

musical

smiley

happy

good student

athletic

creative

writer

singer

artist

funny

How Can I Be a Friend to Others?

Name people you know who need a friend. Fill in each box with the name of a new friend and an idea about how to begin being a friend.

_____ _____

_____ _____

_____ _____

REMEMBER

Beloved, let us love one another, for love is from God, and whoever loves has been born of God and knows God. Anyone who does not love does not know God, because God is love. **(1 John 4:7–8)**

Jonathan Warns David

1 Samuel 20

Jesus Is Our Best Friend

David and Jonathan had a special friendship that included loving and trusting God. But there came a time when David had to hide from Saul. At that time, David and Jonathan shared a blessing. The blessing David and Jonathan shared is a blessing you can also share with your friends. Answer each of the questions on the left by drawing a line to its answer on the right.

1. What blessing of God did Jonathan share with David at their farewell (1 Samuel 20:42)?

2. Like David and Jonathan, we share our love of Jesus with our friends and those we meet. What was the most loving thing Jesus did for all of us (2 Corinthians 5:15)?

3. Why did Jesus do this (Galatians 2:20)?

4. Read Matthew 28:19–20. What does Jesus want us to share with our friends?

5. In this Great Commission, what promise does Jesus give us, His friends?

"Go therefore and make disciples of all nations, baptizing them in the name of the Father and of the Son and of the Holy Spirit, teaching them to observe all that I have commanded you."

"The Son of God . . . loved me and gave Himself for me."

"The Lord shall be between me and you, and between my offspring and your offspring, forever."

"And behold, I am with you always, to the end of the age."

"He died for all."

6. How can we follow the example of David and Jonathan in our friendships with others?

_____

_____

_____

REVIEW

| blessing | griefs | solace |

Although we often suffer _____ of various kinds, we can find relief, or _____ ,

in the _____ of the friendship we have in Jesus.

Jesus Is with You Always

Jesus promises to be with you all the time. When you were baptized, God made you His child. He has been with you every day of your life. He loves and cares for you. Scripture assures us of God's love. Read each passage below and summarize the assurance it gives us.

1. Psalm 23 _____

_____

2. Luke 12:20–24 _____

_____

3. Acts 2:38 _____

_____

_____

4. Write about a time when you were able to tell or show a friend what Jesus is like or what He has done for him or her. _____

_____

Jesus, My Friends, and Me

Where do you take Jesus in your life? List as many places as you can around the box on this page. Inside the box, draw a detailed picture of you and Jesus with your friends. Examples of places you might picture include the school lunchroom, a game, your home, the school bus, or a park.

Jesus is with me when I _____.

REMEMBER

Go therefore and make disciples of all nations, baptizing them in the name of the Father and of the Son and of the Holy Spirit, teaching them to observe all that I have commanded you. And behold, I am with you always, to the end of the age. **(Matthew 28:19–20)**

David and Saul

1 Samuel 17:55–18:30; 24; 26

Jealousy in Action

Saul was an <u>arrogant</u> man, and now he was angry. He had just won a hard-fought battle against the Philistines. But it seemed that David, who had conquered Goliath, was being given the greater honor. People were chanting, "Saul has struck down his thousands, and David his ten thousands" (1 Samuel 18:7). Hearing this chant, Saul became angry. After all, he was the king! People should be praising him, not some lowly shepherd boy who just happened to get lucky. Saul thought, "Next thing you know, David will want to be king!" Saul let his <u>jealous</u> anger take control. He decided he had to kill David!

Over the next few years, Saul tried several times to kill David, and David had his chances to get back at Saul. Once David was so close to Saul that he was able to cut off a part of Saul's clothing without Saul knowing it. Another time, David crept into Saul's camp while everyone was sleeping and took Saul's spear and water jug. Both times, David could have killed Saul, but he refused. David said, "I will not put out my hand against my lord, for he is the LORD's <u>anointed</u>" (1 Samuel 24:10, emphasis added). Another time, David's own soldiers asked him to give them orders to kill Saul, but David told them, "Do not destroy him, for who can put out his hand against the LORD's anointed and be guiltless?" (1 Samuel 26:9). David knew that Saul's life was in God's hands, not his. For David, it was more important that he let God solve the problem rather than take matters into his own hands.

REVIEW

Directions: Look at each of the numbered words below and see how it is used in the story above. Then check the best definition.

1. **Arrogant**
_____ always fighting for what you want
_____ telling lies about someone else
_____ believing you are better than others

2. **Jealous**
_____ wanting things your own way
_____ resenting a person because he or she has something you want
_____ hating another person because of your own failures

3. **Anointed**
_____ specially chosen by God
_____ elected by the people
_____ winner of a race

Checking Your Jealousy Meter

Do you get jealous sometimes? Check your "jealousy meter" by thinking about the following situations. Mark your responses by using this scale:

The Situation: A new student has joined your class.

| 4 = This would make me insanely jealous |
| 3 = I'd be pretty jealous about this |
| 2 = This would make me jealous |
| 1 = I might be a little bit jealous |
| 0 = I wouldn't be at all jealous |

_____ 1. Everyone wants to sit by this new student.

_____ 2. The new student can do math really well and is also a great writer.

_____ 3. The new student chooses your best friend to be friends with.

_____ 4. It was your turn to do something in class, but the new student got to do it instead.

_____ 5. The new student gets straight A's.

_____ 6. The new student lives in a fabulous new house.

_____ 7. The new student wins your seat in band tryouts.

Solving the Problem

Jealousy is a problem. Because of our sinful nature, we have a desire to be more important than others. What problems cause jealousy? What problems result because of jealousy? What does God want us to do? How do we get rid of our jealousy? As you think about these questions, summarize the main idea in each of the following Bible passages. Discuss your answers with others.

1. Now may our Lord Jesus Christ Himself, and God our Father, who loved us and gave us eternal comfort and good hope through grace, comfort your hearts and establish them in every good work and word. 2 Thessalonians 2:16–17

_____

_____

2. If we live by the Spirit, let us also walk by the Spirit. Let us not become conceited, provoking one another, envying one another. Galatians 5:25–26

_____

3. Love is patient and kind; love does not envy or boast; it is not arrogant or rude. It does not insist on its own way; it is not irritable or resentful; it does not rejoice at wrongdoing, but rejoices with the truth. Love bears all things, believes all things, hopes all things, endures all things. 1 Corinthians 13:4–7

_____

_____

REMEMBER 💙

Above all, keep loving one another earnestly, since love covers a multitude of sins. **(1 Peter 4:8)**

David Becomes King

2 Samuel 1:1–6:23

Whether in the classroom, on the playground, or even in a large country, leaders are people others want to follow. What qualities do you think a good leader should have? Share your ideas with your classmates.

God chose David to be king of Israel; he was anointed when he was rather young. In fact, Saul was still king at the time, but God rejected Saul because he had disobeyed God. David did not <u>usurp</u> Saul's authority, but waited for God to fulfill His promise. David's struggles during this time helped to prepare him for the great responsibilities he would have. God had chosen him to lead His people Israel in spite of his youth and inexperience.

The following Bible passages from 2 Samuel 1–6 tell about David's activities at the beginning of his rule. As you read the passages, match them with the letter that describes what is happening with David.

_____ 1. 2 Samuel 1:19, 23   a. Takes Jerusalem and makes it the capital of Israel

_____ 2. 2 Samuel 2:1   b. Is made king over Judah

_____ 3. 2 Samuel 2:4   c. Brings the ark of God to Jerusalem

_____ 4. 2 Samuel 4:11–12a   d. Defeats and drives the Philistines from Israel

_____ 5. 2 Samuel 5:3   e. Honors Saul and Jonathan after their deaths

_____ 6. 2 Samuel 5:6–7   f. Punishes men who had killed Ish-bosheth, Saul's son

_____ 7. 2 Samuel 5:17–25   g. Is made king over Israel

_____ 8. 2 Samuel 6:12–15   h. Inquires of the Lord what he is to do

Qualities of a King

David was a great king, chosen by God. But even then, activities in the kingdom weren't always done in God-pleasing ways. Some of the <u>treachery</u> in Israel included a <u>conspiracy</u> against David, division of the kingdom, and betrayal by people he trusted to be good leaders. What qualities do you see in David that make him a great leader?

_____

_____

Where did David get these qualities (2 Samuel 5:10–12)?

_____

_____

REVIEW

Choose the correct definition for each word; write the letter for that definition on the line.

_____ 1. Usurp   _____ 2. Treachery   _____ 3. Conspiracy

A. Surrender, give in to   A. Evil behavior   A. Bringing together
B. Take a liking to something B. Playing make-believe   B. Plan to take over
C. Take over by force   C. Hatred   C. Way of using the army

The Kingdom of God

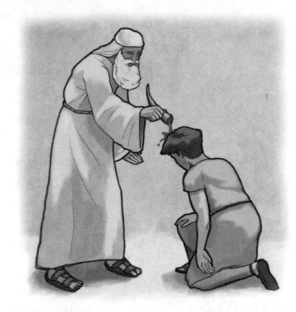

What is the kingdom of God? Most people will say it is heaven. That's true, but for those who know and believe in Jesus as their Savior, the kingdom can also be here, right now! Your classroom is a "mini-kingdom of God." Each believer in Christ is a citizen of God's kingdom (Philippians 3:20; Colossians 1:13–14). What is this kingdom like? Work with some members of your class in a group to complete one of the following projects and share your work with your class. Other class members will work on the other projects.

PROJECT 1: Jesus Is Our King. What kind of ruler is He? Use information from these Scripture passages to find out: Revelation 1:5b; John 21:17; Jeremiah 23:24; Deuteronomy 32:4; Leviticus 19:2; Psalm 145:8–9. Make a list of the qualities described in the passages. Then create a poster with the title "Jesus Is Our King." On the poster display the qualities you found.

PROJECT 2: Responsibilities of Citizens. What are the responsibilities of citizens in God's kingdom? These passages will help you list these responsibilities: 1 John 5:3a; Philippians 4:8; Matthew 22:37, 39; Colossians 3:12–15; 1 Timothy 4:12. First make a note of the responsibilities of citizens; then create a document with the title "Responsibilities of Citizens in the Kingdom of God" for everyone to sign as a member of His kingdom.

PROJECT 3: Rights and Privileges of Citizens. What rights do we have as members of the kingdom of God? What are our privileges? These Bible passages provide that information: Matthew 22:39; Psalm 103:3–5; 1 Thessalonians 5:17; 1 Timothy 4:13; 1 John 4:15. Write the rights and privileges you identify in a list. Then make a "Certificate of Citizenship" that lists these rights and privileges; ask your teacher to make a copy for everyone in the class.

REMEMBER

To Him who loves us and has freed us from our sins by His blood and made us a kingdom, . . . to Him be glory and dominion forever and ever. Amen. **(Revelation 1:5b–6)**

David and Bathsheba

2 Samuel 11–12

Choices, Choices

People have to make many choices each day. Some are easy to make; some are hard: what to wear? to accept one friend's invitation or another's? to get home on time or stay out a little longer with friends? If you care to, tell about a tough choice you know someone had to make.

After you have discussed some tough choices, read the tragic story of King David—the King David who was a man after God's own heart (1 Samuel 13:14)—who had to make some tough choices and made all sinful ones. The story of this sad part of his life is in 2 Samuel 11. As you read the story, list the sinful choices David made on the notebook paper below.

2 Samuel 11:2

2 Samuel 11:4

2 Samuel 11:8–12

2 Samuel 11:14–16

REVIEW

Look up each word in the glossary. Then write the definition of the word. Next, write an antonym (opposite) for each word.

Content _____

Sin _____

Kill _____

Adultery _____

_____

Guidance for Choices

Directions. Look up the Bible passage listed near each symbol below. Then write about the help God gives us to make wise choices when we have to make decisions.

Hebrews 4:13

John 19:1–3

Romans 3:20

Hebrews 6:19

REMEMBER

Out of the heart come evil thoughts, murder, adultery, sexual immorality, theft, false witness, slander. (Matthew 15:19)

David and Bathsheba

2 Samuel 11–12

God's Bone

I have a bone to pick with you.

God did not abandon David because of his sin with Bathsheba. Read what God did about David's sin in 2 Samuel 12:1–6. On the lines below, write what God did about David's sin.

_____

_____

_____

It wasn't Nathan who had a bone to pick with David; it was God. What was the "bone" God had to pick with David? (See 2 Samuel 12:9.)

_____

_____

_____

Review 2 Samuel 12. Match David's sins with the commandment broken. See Luther's Small Catechism for help.

_____ 1. He despised God's Word.

_____ 2. He lusted after Bathsheba and committed adultery with her.

_____ 3. He had Uriah killed.

_____ 4. He conspired with others to have Uriah killed.

_____ 5. He misused his authority while failing to yield to the authority of God.

a. Commandments 1 and 3

b. Commandment 4

c. Commandment 5

d. Commandments 6 and 10

e. Commandment 8

REVIEW

Draw a line to match the words with the sentence that best fits the meaning.

Lie ☐   ☐ Rahna said she hated reading the Bible and praying.

Accuse ☐   ☐ When Carrie couldn't find her cell phone, she told her mom her brother had taken it.

Despise ☐   ☐ His teammates told De'Shaun he was not playing by the rules.

David's Response

With Nathan's accusation, "You are the man!" David confessed that he had sinned against the Lord. Printed below is portion of Psalm 51. In this prayer, David asked God for forgiveness in many different ways, similar to what we do when we beg our parents for something we really want.

⁷Purge me with hyssop, and I shall be clean;
wash me, and I shall be whiter than snow.
⁸Let me hear joy and gladness;
let the bones that You have broken rejoice.
⁹Hide Your face from my sins,
and blot out all my iniquities.
¹⁰Create in me a clean heart, O God,
and renew a right spirit within me.
¹¹Cast me not away from Your presence,
and take not Your Holy Spirit from me.
¹²Restore to me the joy of Your salvation,
and uphold me with a willing spirit.
¹³Then I will teach transgressors Your ways,
and sinners will return to You.
¹⁴Deliver me from bloodguiltiness, O God,
O God of my salvation,
and my tongue will sing aloud of Your righteousness.
¹⁵O Lord, open my lips,
and my mouth will declare Your praise.
¹⁶For You will not delight in sacrifice, or I would give it;
You will not be pleased with a burnt offering.
¹⁷The sacrifices of God are a broken spirit;
a broken and contrite heart, O God, You will not despise.

1. Underline the phrases in the psalm that show David's trust in God to forgive him.
2. If God restores to him the joy of salvation, David promises he will do something (Psalm 51:13–15). Write in the boxes the three things David says he will do in verses 13–15.

v. 13	v. 14	v. 15

Write the beginning of a confession you might make when you commit a sin. Leave room at the end so you can complete the confession by naming the sin you need to confess. You might use David's psalm as a model.

_____

REMEMBER

Create in me a clean heart, O God, and renew a right spirit within me. **(Psalm 51:10)**

Solomon Builds a Temple

1 Kings 5–8

God Comes to His People in Worship

After Moses led the people of Israel out of Egypt, God continued to demonstrate His presence, power, and protection in their lives. During the reign of King Solomon, many people worked to build a magnificent temple so the people could worship God there in response to His faithfulness. The temple was a constant reminder that God was with His people.

REVIEW

Each frame below contains a word and its definition. Make a picture definition of the word in each box.

worship—anything a person does to show love and respect. Solomon built the temple to worship the one true God.

incense—a mixture of spices from plants; when burned, it makes a sweet smell. Incense was burned on the golden altar to worship God.

ark of the covenant—a special wooden chest that was covered with gold. The ark showed the people that God was with them. The ark was placed in the Most Holy Place in the temple.

Solomon Builds a Temple

Although King David completed many of the preparations for the building of the temple, God designated King Solomon to build the temple in His honor. Solomon gathered many workers to build the temple and artists to decorate it.

1. Why didn't King David build the temple (1 Kings 5:3)?

_____

_____

2. Why did King Solomon want to build the temple (1 Kings 5:5 and 1 Chronicles 22:19)?

_____

_____

3. Name some of the art designs the artists used in the temple (1 Kings 6:18, 29; 7:17, 18).

_____

_____

4. What separated the two rooms of the temple (2 Chronicles 3:14)?

_____

_____

5. What promise did God make to Solomon when the temple was being built (1 Kings 6:11–13)?

_____

_____

6. Name some of the temple furnishings (1 Kings 7:43–44; 48–50).

_____

_____

7. How did God show He was pleased with the temple (1 Kings 8:10–13)?

_____

_____

8. Referring to His body as a temple, Jesus once made a statement describing His death and resurrection. What was that statement (John 2:19)?

_____

_____

REMEMBER

Oh come, let us worship and bow down; let us kneel before the LORD, our Maker! **(Psalm 95:6)**

Solomon Builds a Temple

1 Kings 5–8

A Response to God's Faithfulness

Do you remember how many years it took to build the temple? It was a seven-year project. In our lesson today we will use the number 7 to review the story of the building of the temple. Today we watch as Solomon and the people respond to God's faithfulness.

REVIEW

First review three words that are important in this story. Connect the dots to make three words from individual letters. Begin each letter with a 7 and then proceed by counting either forward or backward according to the direction indicated by the arrow. Draw a line from the word to its definition. Be careful. There is an extra definition.

☐ An agreement between God and His people

☐ A gift or offering given to God

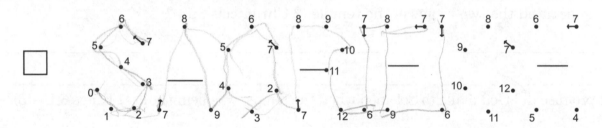

☐ A payment that is deserved

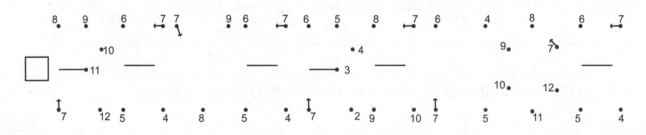

☐ A feeling of deep love and respect

Solomon Builds a Temple

When the work Solomon had done to build the temple of the Lord was finished, Solomon asked the priests to bring the ark of the covenant into the temple. Filled with reverence for God, the priests led a joyful procession to the temple. Read about this procession in 1 Kings 8:2–11.

At the dedication, the people offered sacrifices to God. Their offering was so large that Solomon had to use a special area in front of the temple for their sacrifices. Then the people joined together to give praise and thanks to God. They sang songs and played instruments: cymbals, harps, lyres, and trumpets. With one voice they sang our memory words for today. You can read about this celebration in 2 Chronicles 7:3–6.

Solomon's Prayer of Dedication

During the dedication festivities, Solomon prayed a model prayer. He stood in front of the temple altar and thanked God for keeping His promises to the people of Israel. He spoke of God's faithfulness to the people. He also asked God to take care of the people forever. Solomon had seven prayer requests. You can read Solomon's prayer in 1 Kings 8:22–53. God listened to Solomon's prayer (1 Kings 9:3). Solomon concluded the dedication service with a benediction (1 Kings 8:54–61). Work with a partner to identify the seven things for which Solomon prayed and to complete the following matching exercise.

_____ 1. 1 Kings 8:28–30

_____ 2. 1 Kings 8:31–32

_____ 3. 1 Kings 8:33–34

_____ 4. 1 Kings 8:35–40

_____ 5. 1 Kings 8:41–43

_____ 6. 1 Kings 8: 44–45

_____ 7. 1 Kings 8:46–53

a. Justice in settling disputes

b. Victory in future battles

c. Help in times of drought, famine, sickness, and other calamities

d. God's continued presence, forgiveness, and protection

e. Forgiveness for the nation when it is captured and taken into exile

f. Help for strangers and foreigners (Gentiles)

g. Israel's deliverance from defeat by their enemy upon confession of sin

REMEMBER

[God] is good; His love endures forever. **(2 Chronicles 7:3b NIV)**

Elijah and the Prophets of Baal

1 Kings 18

Elijah's Journey of Faith

Read the story of God's prophet Elijah, who was fired up and ready for a mission from God, in 1 Kings 18:1–19. Then supply the missing dialogue to complete the story map below.

God told Elijah (v. 1):

Then Elijah met Obadiah the prophet. He sent Obadiah to tell King Ahab where Elijah was. Obadiah didn't want to go.

He was afraid that (vv. 9–12)

Obadiah told Elijah that he had hidden one hundred of the Lord's prophets in a cave. He hid them because (v. 13)

When Ahab saw Elijah, Ahab said to him (v. 17),

Elijah answered (v. 18),

REVIEW

Use the words from the word list to complete the following sentences about Elijah.

prophet	mission	repentance	judgment

Elijah was a _____, a man sent by God to pronounce _____ against sin and to call God's people to _____ . Elijah boldly spoke out against evil in defense of God and His Word. Elijah was a man on a _____ .

Choices, Choices . . . Launching a Response

How could you respond to campaigns like these that are frequently in the news? Pick a partner or two. Briefly discuss one of the placards. Then choose a cause of interest to you and prepare a presentation for your class including a sign, a short speech, and a message or verse telling what God's Word says about the issue. Pray for the Holy Spirit's help. Be BOLD!

Speak this Rhythmic Word Walk prayer thoughtfully as you walk or step in place.

> Lord, lead us today,
> Teach us to pray,
> Help us to follow Your way,
> Help us to know,
> Which way to go,
> Help us obey
> Whatever You say,
> Lord, lead us today!

emPOWERED by God's Spirit

Try this: Make a 1-inch clay cube launching pad. Tuck the end of a 6-inch piece of yarn into the top of the clay cube. Make the yarn stand straight up. Let go. What happens? Now poke a pencil into the clay and tape the free end of the yarn to the pencil. What happens when you let go? Like limp yarn, by ourselves we are weak and scared. The strength of God's Spirit gives us boldness to take a stand on God's Word and witness to others.

REMEMBER

Let him who has My word speak My word faithfully. **(Jeremiah 23:28)**

Elijah and the Prophets of Baal

1 Kings 18:20–46

Elijah Trusts God

Elijah fearlessly followed God when it seemed that everyone was against him. Read the story of Elijah and the prophets of Baal in 1 Kings 18:20–46. Write the missing words in the plot graph below to diagram what happened in this amazing story.

Elijah challenges the prophets of Baal to show whose God can send fire.

Baal does not answer, but God sends fire to burn up the sacrifice, altar, and water.

All the people say, "The LORD is God!"

All the prophets of Baal are killed. God sends rain!

There is a drought in the land because the people have forsaken God.

The people are worshiping Baal.

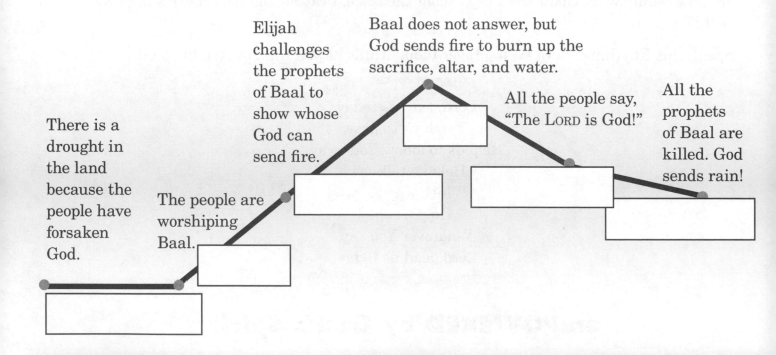

REVIEW

Some of the words below describe Elijah; others do not. Circle those that describe Elijah.

limp unwavering hesitating determined

fluctuating resolute vacillating fickle unswerving

98

Whom Will You Serve?

Choosing Baal

Choosing God

God's First Commandment says, "You shall have no other gods before Me" (Exodus 20:3). But things get complicated as the devil tempts us to sin and follow evil ways. In today's story, for example, everyone was worshiping and praying. But Elijah was worshiping and praying to God, while others were worshiping and praying to Baal. The devil uses peer pressure, crowd behavior, and the excuse that "everybody's doing it" to lure us to forget God and His Word. Take turns reading situation game cards your teacher will give you. Give an example of when each situation would be "Choosing Baal" and an example of when each situation would be "Choosing God." On the stones above, list choices (both good and bad) that you have made in your own life.

Create in me a clean heart, O God!
Signed,

_____

Inside-Out Clean

Try this: Put dry coffee grounds into a white coffee filter. This represents a heart filled with the "crud" of sin. Now hold the filter over a sack and turn it inside out to remove every speck. When we as God's people turn to Him for cleansing from sin, God answers our prayer. Because of Jesus' sacrifice on the cross, God forgives us and cleans our hearts of every speck of sin from the inside out! God turns our hearts back to follow Him and His ways. God invites you to come to Him to receive forgiveness for your sins of weakness. He will make you strong and courageous to follow His way at all times.

REMEMBER

You shall worship the Lord your God and Him only shall you serve. (**Matthew 4:10**)

Elijah Goes to Heaven

2 Kings 2:1–14

What Happens When Believers Die?

All living things on earth have set life spans. Houseflies live an average of three to four weeks. The average life span of a chicken is eight to ten years. A lion may live about fifteen years in the wild, and African elephants live an average of forty to fifty years. The average life span of the Galapagos tortoise is more than one hundred years. But eventually, all living things die.

Today the average life span of a human being is between seventy-five and eighty years. But human beings are different from animals in a very important way. Human beings were created by God in His own image and given souls that live on after death.

When we confess our faith in the words of the Apostles' Creed, we say, "I believe . . . in the resurrection of the body, and the life everlasting." In his explanation of the Third Article, Martin Luther wrote, "On the Last Day He will raise me and all the dead, and give eternal life to me and all believers in Christ" (Luther's Small Catechism). At the time of death, the soul of a believer is immediately with Christ in heaven. On the Last Day, the believers will begin the full enjoyment of being with Christ forever in both body and soul.

REVIEW

eternal

anoint

_____   _____

Elijah's Story

"I am Elijah, the Tishbite, the prophet of the most-high God. I have followed God my whole life, speaking for Him whenever He directed me. My life has not been easy. Sometimes God used me to show His power over His enemies, like when He sent fire to consume my offering in front of the prophets of Baal. But often He sent me to tell the king news he didn't want to hear. Then I had to run from the king and hide wherever I could. God gave me a helper named Elisha. God told me to anoint Elisha to be prophet in my place.

"I knew that it was time for God to take me to heaven. Elisha and I went to see the prophets at Gilgal. I was going to go on to visit the prophets at Bethel. I told Elisha to stay at Gilgal, but he refused. When I was ready to leave Bethel and go to the prophets at Jericho, I told Elisha to stay at Bethel. Again he refused and came with me.

"Then I told Elisha, 'Stay here, for the Lord has sent me to the Jordan River.' But Elisha insisted on coming with me. Fifty of the prophets followed us and watched from a distance. When we reached the river, I rolled up my cloak and struck the water. The water parted so Elisha and I could cross on dry ground. I asked Elisha what I could do for him. He answered, 'Please let there be a double portion of your spirit on me.'

"As Elisha and I spoke, chariots of fire and horses of fire came between us, and a whirlwind carried me up to heaven."

My Story

Like Elijah's life, my time on earth will also end some day. This may happen when I am young or when I am very old. But because I believe in Jesus as my Savior from sin, death, and the devil, I know that my death will not be the end of my story.

Discuss the following situations. Use Bible verses to help you decide what you would say to the people in each of the situations.

"I'm afraid to die because I don't know what will happen to me after death." (John 3:16)

_____

"Will everyone go to heaven when they die?" (John 3:36)

_____

_____

"Does your soul go to heaven right away when you die, or do you have to wait somewhere else first?" (Luke 23:43)

_____

"If our souls go to be with Jesus right away when we die, what happens to our bodies?" (1 Thessalonians 4:16)

_____

REMEMBER ♥

Jesus said to her, "I am the resurrection and the life. Whoever believes in Me, though he die, yet shall he live, and everyone who lives and believes in Me shall never die." **(John 11:25–26)**

Elijah Goes to Heaven

2 Kings 2:1–14

What Happens When Loved Ones Die?

Have you ever experienced the death of someone you love? Maybe a friend or a member of your family has died. How did you feel when you first heard the news? What questions did you have? How did people try to help you and your family? What do you do to remember the person who died?

When a Christian dies, we know that his soul goes to live with Jesus forever and his body will be raised on the Last Day. In the Apostles' Creed, we confess that we believe in "the resurrection of the body, and the life everlasting." Martin Luther explained those words this way: "On the Last Day He will raise me and all the dead, and give eternal life to me and all believers in Christ" (Luther's Small Catechism). *All believers* includes your Christian friend or family member who has died, and it includes you. You can look forward to spending eternity together with Jesus.

We receive the promise of eternal life through Baptism. In writing about the blessings of Baptism, Martin Luther explained, "It [Baptism] works forgiveness of sins, rescues from death and the devil, and gives eternal salvation to all who believe this, as the words and promises of God declare." What words and promises did Martin Luther mean? Read Romans 6:3 and 5: "Do you not know that all of us who have been baptized into Christ Jesus were baptized into His death? . . . If we have been united with Him in a death like His, we shall certainly be united with Him in a resurrection like His." Through Baptism we share Jesus' death to sin; through Baptism we share His resurrection to eternal life.

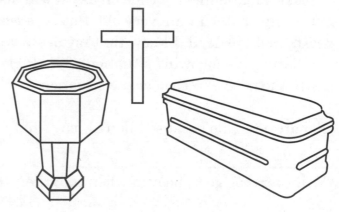

We know that, for our Christian friend or family member and for us, death is not the end of life. Because Jesus died and rose again, we will begin a new life with Him after we die. And this new life will never end.

REVIEW

Read the definition of each term in your glossary. Then mark the meaning that best fits the way the word is used in this lesson.

Prophet

_____ A person who can foretell the future.

_____ A person who spoke for God in Old Testament times.

_____ Money you make when you sell something.

Successor

_____ Someone who is very successful in business.

_____ The person who continues your work after you.

_____ Someone who had your job before you had it.

Elisha's Story

"My name, *Elisha*, means 'God is salvation,' and God chose me to bring the news that God is salvation to His people in Israel. One day when I was plowing my family's fields with twelve pair of oxen, the prophet Elijah came and threw his cloak over my shoulders. I knew that meant God wanted me to be Elijah's successor. I killed my oxen, cooked the meat, and gave it to the people. Then I followed Elijah and helped him in his ministry.

"Elijah knew God was about to take him to heaven. He told me to stay at Gilgal, but I would not leave him. We went on to Bethel, where Elijah told me to stay with the prophets. But I would not leave him. Then we traveled on to Jericho. Again Elijah told me to stay at Jericho with the prophets. But I insisted on going with him to the Jordan River.

"When we reached the river, Elijah rolled up his cloak and struck the water. The waters separated, and Elijah and I crossed on dry land. Elijah asked what he could do for me before he was taken away. I replied, 'Please let there be a double portion of your spirit on me.' Elijah told me that if I could see him as he was being taken up to heaven, I would receive what I had asked. As we were talking, chariots of fire and horses of fire came between us, and I saw Elijah being taken up to heaven in a whirlwind. I cried, 'My father, my father! The chariots of Israel and its horsemen!' (2 Kings 2:12). And then I saw him no more.

"My grief at losing Elijah was so great that I tore my clothes in two pieces. Then I picked up Elijah's cloak and walked back to the Jordan River. I struck the water with the cloak as Elijah had done, and the water parted for me to walk through. The prophets from Jericho who had watched from the other side of the river said, 'The spirit of Elijah rests on Elisha' (v. 15), and they bowed to the ground before me. God had shown them that I would be the prophet to carry on Elijah's work."

My Story

Like Elisha, you may have experienced the loss of a friend or family member. Like Elisha, your grief may have made you want to tear your clothes or scream or throw things. You may have cried when you heard the news or when you went to the funeral home or funeral. That's normal—even Jesus cried when His friend Lazarus died (John 11:35).

Knowing what Elisha did in his time of grief may help you when you are separated from a loved one by death. Elisha knew where Elijah had gone; he had seen him taken into heaven in the whirlwind. You know where your Christian loved one has gone too. Jesus has promised believers that they would spend eternity with Him in heaven. Elisha picked up Elijah's cloak, parted the waters of the river, and went on to do Elijah's work. We can continue the work of a Christian friend or family member by staying close to Jesus in worship and Bible study, by telling others the Good News of salvation, and by sharing His love through Christian service.

REMEMBER

And we know that for those who love God all things work together for good, for those who are called according to His purpose. **(Romans 8:28)**

Naaman and Elisha

2 Kings 5:1–16

The Cast of Characters

How does God use ordinary people to further His kingdom? Read today's Bible story. Draw expressions on the faces of the people from the story to show something about them. Then talk with your classmates, explaining why you drew the faces the way you did.

King of Aram

King of Israel

Naaman

servant girl

Elisha

REVIEW

Unscramble the following words. Then place each in the appropriate blank.

lceeasn	mmcoadnre	ylepros	eeorstr

_____ 1. a leader who is in charge of a military unit

_____ 2. a skin disease

_____ 3. to bring back to the original

_____ 4. to make clean

Faith for Life

Together with your name, the following words can be used to fill in the blanks below.

servant girl   Naaman   God   Holy Spirit   Jesus

MYSELF—_____ How can God use me to be a witness for Him?

By the power of the Holy Spirit, I can _____

_____.

In today's story God used a _____ _____ to witness her faith,

which led an army commander named _____ to experience the miraculous

healing power of the true _____ ! Today God can use_____ to witness

faith by the power of the _____ _____ to lead others to know the

power and salvation through _____ !

REMEMBER 💙

> But you will receive power when the Holy Spirit has come upon you, and you will be my witnesses in Jerusalem and in all Judea and Samaria, and to the end of the earth. **(Acts 1:8)**

Naaman and Elisha

2 Kings 5:1–16

God Heals Diseases

God uses His healing power to bring people to faith in Him. After God healed Naaman, Naaman proclaimed, "Behold, I know that there is no God in all the earth but in Israel" (2 Kings 5:15). By God's grace, someday we will meet Naaman at the throne of Jesus, for as a believer in the one true God, Naaman also received the spiritual healing available only through Jesus.

Naaman received physical healing by God's grace as he washed in the waters of the Jordan River. People today receive spiritual healing through washing in the waters of Holy Baptism.

Both the physical healing of Naaman and the spiritual healing offered through Baptism are received in connection with God's Word. Naaman's healing through the waters of the Jordan only happened because God told him to wash there and Naaman obeyed. Spiritual healing happens through the waters of Holy Baptism as God brings spiritual healing through the words of Baptism, which name the only true God.

1. Use a blue marker or crayon to draw water in each illustration below.
2. Complete the words of Baptism in the speech bubble on the right.

REVIEW

These words refer to medical healing, but can also refer to spiritual healing. Use one of these words to complete each of the sentences below.

restore—to bring back to a former condition **regenerate**—to revive and to produce anew
renew—to restore, replenish, and reestablish **repair**—to restore to good condition after decay or damage

1. The family worked to _____ an old house.

2. The starfish is able to _____ its arms.

3. Andy was able to _____ his bicycle tire after he ran over a nail.

4. After working hard in school, the students thought of spring break as a chance to _____ themselves.

Clean Hearts

The Offertory is the part of the worship service that is often sung after the sermon and before the taking of the offering. The words of the Offertory come from Psalm 51:10–12. They remind us of the healing, forgiveness, and new beginning God in Christ provides.

Dead in Sin   **Clean and Renewed in Jesus**

Write sins on the heart above.

Color the heart above red as a reminder that Jesus shed His blood to cleanse and heal us.

Write the words of the Offertory on the cross.

REMEMBER

Bless the LORD, O my soul, and forget not all His benefits, who forgives all your iniquity, who heals all your diseases. (**Psalm 103:2–3**)

Jonah

Jonah 1:1–3:3

A Job for Me?

You have been asked to pack a bag to travel to a remote island on the other side of the world. The people of the island are not Christian. They conquer other people and make them their slaves. They worship false gods and do not like outsiders. You will leave immediately.
Would you take the job?

YES   NO

Which Way to Go?

NINEVEH

Jonah was given a similar task by God. He had two choices: to obey or disobey. As you read the first chapter of Jonah, imagine all the thoughts he was having. Below are a list of emotions. Circle any that you think Jonah was feeling:

NERVOUSNESS   Sadness   HOPE   Love

FRUSTRATION

FEAR   EXCITEMENT   JOY   ANGER

REVIEW

Write the definitions for the following:

Casting lots—_____

Sheol—_____

Pagan—_____

Action/Reaction

Jonah was given a choice. He chose to rebel against God. When we rebel against God, there are consequences for our actions. As you review the first chapter of Jonah, tell what happened in response to each of the situations that happened due to Jonah's chosen action of disobeying God.

Jonah boarded a ship headed for Tarshish.

When Jonah was identified as the cause of the storm, the sailor asked him what to do. Jonah told them to throw him into the sea.

Jonah was in the sea. Under normal circumstance he would have drowned.

REMEMBER

Where shall I go from Your Spirit? Or where shall I flee from Your presence? **(Psalm 139:7)**

Jonah

Jonah 3:3–4:11

Uniquely You

God made each of us special. Think of the things that you do best. Are you a fast runner, a good speller, or a great builder? We all have special talents and abilities that make us unique. Look around the classroom; think about people you know or have met. On the left lens in the glasses below, write characteristics that make us unique. Listed items may include things you can see in others (hair color, eye color) or the things you can see others doing (design creative artwork, read well).

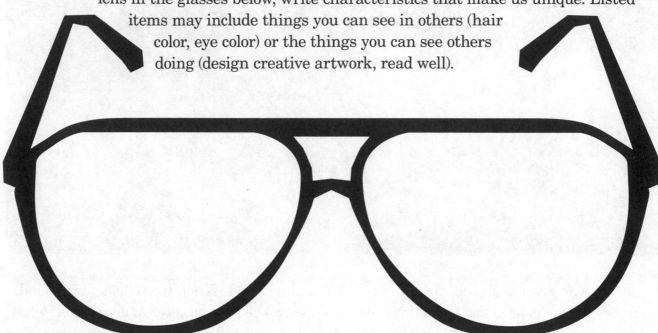

As you learned in our previous lesson, the people of Nineveh were different from Jonah and the people of God. Though Jonah tried to escape, eventually God's will was done. Today, Jonah meets the people of Nineveh.

REVIEW

Grace   Mercy

Write each of the words above in the blank below where it fits best.

Filled with compassion for the people of Nineveh, God relented of the disaster He said He would do to them. God is a God of _____ ; because of Jesus, He does not give us the punishment we deserve.

God is a God of _____ ; because of Jesus, He blesses us with blessings we do not deserve.

Meeting the Ninevites

1) What did God ask Jonah to do (Jonah 1:2)?

_____

2) Jonah has now arrived in the city. What message does Jonah proclaim (Jonah 3:4)?

_____

3) Though Jonah does not tell them what to do, how do the people of Nineveh respond (Jonah 3:5)?

_____

4) How is God's response different than Jonah's (Jonah 3:10–4:1)?

_____

5) Jonah shows his displeasure with the way God forgave the people of Nineveh by leaving the city. How does God show compassion to Jonah (Jonah 4:6)?

_____

6) What does this tell us about God?

_____

7) What is the best evidence we have of God's love and compassion?

_____

The More We Are Different, the More We Are the Same

Jonah obviously was not happy that God spared the Ninevites. Sometimes we, too, can sin and judge others based on the way they look and act. Thankfully, God is a compassionate, kind God. He sent His Son to be our Savior because He loves all people. Where do you see God's grace and forgiveness shown to Jonah?

_____

_____

Look back at the Jonah story. God doesn't see things the way we do. Consider each of the following statements, which tell of thoughts and attitudes we may have at times. What perspective does God have about each?

She is different from me.
I don't have to be nice to him because he was mean to me.
She doesn't need to hear about Jesus because she has her own religion.

Now go back to your "Uniquely You" glasses. In the lens at the right side of the glass write several ways you are similar to everyone else.

REMEMBER

He died for all. **(2 Corinthians 5:15)**

Three Men in the Fiery Furnace

Daniel 3

Courage in the Face of Temptation

Shadrach, Meshach, and Abednego are three young men of Israel taken from their homes and families to Babylon, where they were held captive and ordered to study and work for King Nebuchadnezzar.

Read Daniel 3:1–7. Then fill in the blanks below to review the story.

King Nebuchadnezzar set up a _____ of gold. It was sixty cubits in height and the breadth was six cubits (approximately nine feet in diameter and ninety feet high). Nebuchadnezzar had it built on the plain of Dura. The king had all the officials of the provinces of _____ come together for a _____ of this image.

At this ceremony, the King's herald announced: "You are _____ , O peoples, nations and languages, that when you hear the sound of the horn, pipe, lyre, trigon, harp, bagpipe, and every kind of music, you are to fall down and _____ the golden image that King Nebuchadnezzar has set up" (vv. 4–5).

The herald continued: "Whoever does not fall down and worship shall immediately be cast into a burning fiery _____"
(v. 6).

REVIEW

Draw lines to match each of the following words with its correct meaning.

Image   another name for Babylonians

Herald   an official who announces important information

Chaldeans   a form designed to represent an object or person

Faith Questioned, Faith Confessed

Read Daniel 3:8–18.
Indicate T or F for the following statements:

_____ 1. King Nebuchadnezzar asks Shadrach, Meshach, and Abednego if they have refused to obey the decree.

_____ 2. King Nebuchadnezzar does not give the three men a second chance.

_____ 3. King Nebuchadnezzar wants to know what god will be able to rescue them.

_____ 4. Shadrach, Meshach, and Abednego respond with a strong confession of faith in the one true God.

_____ 5. Shadrach, Meshach, and Abednego apologize and promise to obey the king from now on.

_____ 6. Three people were cast into the fire and joined there by a fourth person.

_____ 7. Nebuchadnezzar referred to the deliverer as "like a son of the gods."

Faithful Followers

As God's Spirit enabled them, Shadrach, Meshach, and Abednego remained faithful followers of the one true God. Similarly, as God's Spirit works through God's Word today, He enables believers to stand firm in their faith. Write a prayer asking God to help you to remain faithful to your God and Savior just as Shadrach, Meshach, and Abednego did.

_____

_____

_____

_____

REMEMBER 💙

Be faithful unto death, and I will give you the crown of life. **(Revelation 2:10)**

Three Men in the Fiery Furnace

Daniel 3

Cause and Effect: The Savior in a Furnace

As we study this account from Daniel 3, we shall learn how God enabled the three men, when confronted with a sinful ultimatum, to remain confident that the one true God would deliver them from evil.

Daniel 3:13–18

Is it true that you will not serve my gods or worship the image I have set up? Who is the god who will deliver you out of my hands? If you do not worship, you will be cast into a fiery furnace.

Cause

God gave Shadrach, Meshach, and Abednego faith through His Word.

Effect

Daniel 3:19–23

Cause

The king commanded that all obey his command or be punished.

Effect

REVIEW

Faithfulness—_____

Worship—_____

Daniel 3:24–25

The king was astonished and rose up in haste. He was amazed by what he saw in the funance.

Cause

God looks with mercy upon His faithful people.

Effect

Danicl 3:26–28

Blessed be the God of Shadrach, Meshach, and Abednego who has sent His angel and delivered His servants, who trust in Him and yielded up their bodies rather than to worship any god other than their own God.

Cause

The king recognizes that God had saved the three men.

Effect

REMEMBER

He saved us, not because of works done by us in righteousness, but according to His own mercy. **(Titus 3:5)**

Daniel in the Lions' Den

Daniel 6

Daring Daniel

King Darius *Form a crown on your head with your hands*

Put Daniel in charge of part of his kingdom. *Palm up, arm straight, sweep arm from one side to the other.*

The other leaders were very jealous. *Squint your eyes and cross your arms.*

They tried to find something wrong with him. *Put hands on hips.*

But he followed all the rules. *Pretend to have a checklist and check things off.*

So, the jealous men made a plan. *Wring hands, smile, and nod your head.*

They told King Darius to write a law: *Pretend to write on your hand.*

No one can pray or worship anyone except King Darius. *Fold hands in prayer.*

Anyone who broke the law would be thrown into a den of lions. *Roar like a lion and claw the air with your hands.*

Everyone kept the law except for Daniel, who prayed to the true God. *Kneel and fold hands.*

The king loved Daniel and didn't want to punish him. *Cover face with hands and pretend to cry.*

But the law couldn't be changed. So, Daniel went to the lions. *Roar like a lion and claw the air with your hands.*

The king was so worried about Daniel, he didn't sleep or eat all night. *Wring hands and look worried.*

The next day, King Darius went to the lions' den, looking for Daniel. *Yell, "Daniel!"*

Daniel was alive! He answered the King: *Say, "My God sent His angel. The lions never hurt me."*

King Darius was surprised. He let Daniel out and put the jealous men in the lions' den. The lions killed them immediately.

REVIEW

Deliver + er = _____

Redeem + er = _____

Save - e + ior = _____

_____

Daniel's Lions

Daniel faced some difficult things in his life. On the lions' manes, list some of the difficult things Daniel had to deal with. On Daniel's clothing, write one or more words identifying the God-given qualities that enabled Daniel to face the lions. When you are finished, lightly color the scene with colored pencils.

God Rescues His People

God gave Daniel faith and courage to face his lions—his challenges. God sent His Son, Jesus, to save Daniel from his sins.

Daniel was good, but he wasn't perfect. Neither are we. God sent Jesus to save us from sin. We can be like Daniel, because God sends His Holy Spirit to us when we were baptized. The Holy Spirit lives with us every day, growing our faith and giving us courage to face our lions—our challenges.

In what ways does God help you in face your challenges each day? Circle the words **deliver, redeems,** and **save** as you find them in each of the following Bible verses. Then underline the words that tell what God will rescue us from.

And lead us not into temptation, but deliver us from evil. Matthew 6:13

From the deceitful and unjust man deliver me! Psalm 43:1

My savior; You save me from violence. 2 Samuel 22:3

He redeems my soul in safety from the battle that I wage. Psalm 55:18

REMEMBER 💙✝

Even though I walk through the valley of the shadow of death, I will fear no evil, for You are with me. **(Psalm 23:4)**

Daniel in the Lions' Den

Daniel 6

Be sober-minded; be watchful. Your adversary the devil prowls around like a roaring lion, seeking someone to devour. 1 Peter 5:8

Daniel's Adversaries

Prowl: Like lions that prowl, searching for their next meal, Daniel's enemies were on the **prowl**, searching for a way to be more powerful. They did not care who got hurt in the process. (Read Daniel 6:1–2.)

Seek: Like hungry lions that spot an animal they want to hunt, the men began to **seek** ways to bring Daniel down. (Read Daniel 6:4–5.)

Roar: Like lions that **roar** to keep other lions out of their territory, the men complained to the king, then convinced him to sign a law that would force others to practice their religion somewhere else. (Read Daniel 6:6–9.)

Devour: Like lions that **devour**, or eat, those they attack, the men made sure Daniel would be eaten by lions. (Read Daniel 6:10–17.)

The Result?

Read Daniel 6:10.

Did Daniel panic when he heard about the new law?

Did Daniel give up his religion when the law told him to?

Did Daniel change how he worshiped God?

Did he hide it?

Daniel knew God's Word; he trusted God. God gave Daniel the faith and courage he needed to continue serving Him in faithful worship.

REVIEW

Write the following words in the blanks to complete the sentence.

adversary	adversity

Wanting God's followers to fall away from God, our _____ , the devil, brings all

manner of _____ into the life of the believer.

God's Grace in Adversity

Working through God's Word, God kept Daniel faithful, even in the face of death. God sent an angel and saved Daniel from death. God also sends His angels to watch over us, but He doesn't promise that we will never die. Daniel did die eventually. Now, he is getting the ultimate reward from God—eternal life in heaven! Such is the final home of all who trust in Jesus as their Savior. Jesus made heaven possible for us because He endured great adversity, living a sinless life for us, and then faced and defeated our great adversary, the devil, in our place.

Though defeated, the devil still has power. He still works to trouble God's people just as he did Daniel. He wants us to give up on the God who did not give us on us. Instead, God keeps on working good, even through our adversity—just as He did during the life and times of Daniel.

Match each of the following with events from the Daniel account.

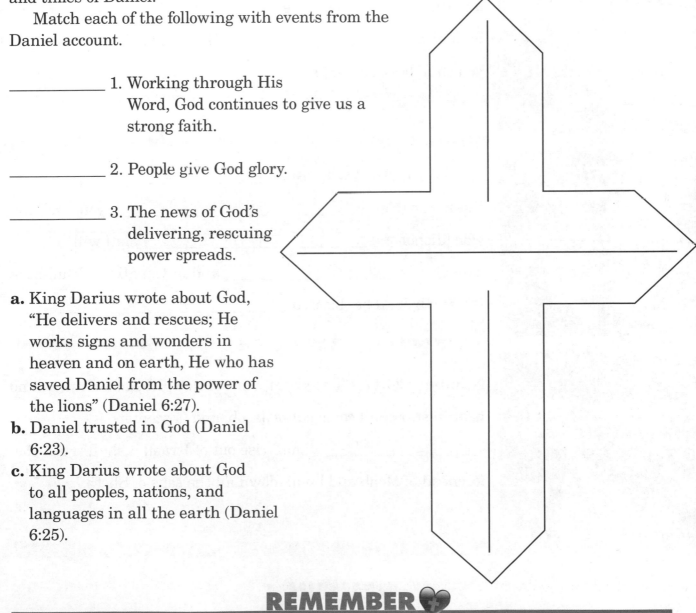

_____ 1. Working through His Word, God continues to give us a strong faith.

_____ 2. People give God glory.

_____ 3. The news of God's delivering, rescuing power spreads.

a. King Darius wrote about God, "He delivers and rescues; He works signs and wonders in heaven and on earth, He who has saved Daniel from the power of the lions" (Daniel 6:27).

b. Daniel trusted in God (Daniel 6:23).

c. King Darius wrote about God to all peoples, nations, and languages in all the earth (Daniel 6:25).

REMEMBER

The Lord will rescue me from every evil deed and bring me safely into His heavenly kingdom. To Him be the glory forever and ever. Amen. **(2 Timothy 4:18)**

Prophets Tell of the Savior

Genesis 3:15; Genesis 12:3; Numbers 24:17

Promises

For thousands of years before the time came, God's Old Testament people trusted in God's promises and awaited the Savior's coming. Let's study some of the promises in which God's faithful people of long ago placed their trust.

Read these verses and substitute synonyms for the words in parentheses.

Genesis 3:15—"I will put (enmity) _____ between you and the woman, and between your (offspring) _____ and her (offspring) _____ ; He shall bruise your head, and you shall bruise His heel."

Genesis 12:3—"I will (bless) _____ those who (bless) _____ you, and him who (dishonors) _____ you I will (curse) _____ , and in you all the families of the earth shall be (blessed) _____ ."

Numbers 24:17—"I see Him, but not now; I behold Him, but not near: a star shall come out of Jacob, and (a scepter) _____ shall rise out of Israel; it shall crush the forehead of Moab and break down all the sons of Sheth."

REVIEW

enmity _____   bless _____   curse _____

offspring _____   dishonor _____   scepter _____

Dig Deeper

At the beginning of human history, our first parents committed the first sin. Because of sin, all of creation was thrown into chaos. Death and violence, hardship and trouble came into existence. Then Adam and Eve heard these words.

Who is speaking in these words? _____

Who is the special offspring of Eve? _____

Who will do the head crushing? _____

Many years after Adam and Eve, God called Abraham to be the father of a mighty nation of followers God would claim as His very own.
What does God promise to those who follow Him?

_____

Does God force people to follow Him?

_____

What is the blessing that Abraham's family gives to your family?

_____

Long after the time of Abraham, the Israelites were traveling to their home in the land God had promised them. A man named Balaam was called by enemies to curse God's people. Instead, he blessed them with these words.
What would rise out of Jacob (also called Israel), the grandson of Abraham?

_____

What would the scepter do to Moab and Sheth, enemies of God's people?

_____

_____

Who is the star and scepter?

_____

REMEMBER

Christ died for our sins in accordance with the Scriptures. **(1 Corinthians 15:3)**

121

Prophets Tell of the Savior

2 Samuel 7:16; Psalm 22; Isaiah 7:14; 60; Micah 5:2–5

Jesus—Prophecy Fulfilled

Psalm 22 Echo

Group 1: In Psalm 22, David wrote, "My God, my God, why have You forsaken me?"

Group 2: In Mark 15, Jesus said, "My God, my God, why have You forsaken Me?" when He was dying on the cross.

Group 1: Psalm 22 says, "In You they trusted and were not put to shame."

Group 2: Apostle Paul told the Romans, "Whoever believes in Him will not be put to shame."

Group 1: Psalm 22 says, "All who see me mock me."

Group 2: Luke tells us that the soldiers also mocked Jesus.

Group 1: Psalm 22 says, "They divide my garments among them, and for my clothing they cast lots."

Group 2: Matthew wrote that when the people crucified Jesus, they divided His garments among them by casting lots.

All: Why are there so many echoes in the Bible?

Group 1: The echoes are prophecies fulfilled in Jesus Christ.

Group 2: Jesus came to save us from the sin all around us.

Group 1: In the beginning was the Word, and the Word was with God, and the Word was God.

Group 2: And the Word became flesh and dwelt among us.

All: Jesus is God's Word sent down to live with us. Jesus is God's Word sent down to save us!

REVIEW

Draw a straight line from the word to the definition.

prophecy (noun)   to breathe, to fill with a message

fulfill (verb)   to tell about the future

inspire (verb)   to carry out or finish something

Sounds great, but can I be sure the Bible is true? Did God really inspire the whole Bible?

God's Word for Us

Do you think people from thousands of years ago could write over one hundred predictions that all came true hundreds of years later? Could one person be born and just happen to fulfill all the prophecies? Or is it more likely that God planned each event to happen just as it did?

After His resurrection from the dead, Jesus met up and began walking with two of His disciples who were traveling from Jerusalem to their home in Emmaus. Jesus talked with them and "beginning with Moses and all the Prophets, He interpreted to them in all the Scriptures the things concerning Himself" (Luke 24:27). What do you think Jesus told them?

_____

_____

_____

God's Word is for you. Its central message is about Jesus. What does the central message about Jesus mean to you? Write your answer on the lines below.

_____

_____

_____

REMEMBER

These are written so that you may believe that Jesus is the Christ, the Son of God, and that by believing you may have life in His name. **(John 20:31)**

Jesus Is Born

Luke 2:1–40

"Fear not, for behold, I bring you good news of great _____ that will be for all the people. For unto you is born this day in the city of David a Savior, who is Christ the Lord."

"Glory to God in the highest, and on earth _____ among those with whom He is pleased!"

Jesus Brings Peace and Joy

Often we hear people talk about peace. They say things such as, "I wish for world peace" or "I just need some peace and quiet!" Long before Jesus was born, the prophet Isaiah wrote about Jesus. Isaiah called Him "Prince of Peace" (Isaiah 9:6). Jesus earned this title, not because He came to bring peace between people and other people, but because He came to bring peace between God and man. With the peace Jesus brings also comes joy. We can have joy knowing that Jesus earned forgiveness for our sins and an eternal home for us in heaven.

REVIEW

Draw a line to connect the word with the phrase that best fits.

reconcile   the opposite of peace

conflict   to bring peace between God and man

barrier   sin created this between God and man

Jesus Is Born

Jesus has brought great joy to us through His birth, life, death, and resurrection. Read how He brought great joy to many people that first Christmas.

Scene 1

Joseph: We're almost there.

Mary: Good! I need a soft place to lie.

Joseph: The bad news is that the only place I could find is a small barn, but it has plenty of hay!

Mary: The baby is coming.

Mary and Joseph: Joy, joy, joy! Baby born in a lowly stable bare, to show the world His great loving care!

Scene 2

Shepherd 1: I got stuck with the night shift again!

Shepherd 2: It's not so bad. The stars are bright tonight.

Shepherd 1: Oh, my! That's not a star!

Angel: "Fear not, for behold, I bring you good news of great joy that will be for all the people. For unto you is born this day in the city of David a Savior, who is Christ the Lord" (Luke 2:10–11).

Angel Chorus: "Glory to God in the highest, and on earth peace among those with whom He is pleased!" (Luke 2:14).

Shepherd 2: Let's go check this out!

Shepherd 1: This is amazing! Boy, I am so glad I was on night shift tonight!

Shepherds 1 and 2: Joy! Joy! Joy! A miracle to see! A tiny baby boy came for you and for me!

Scene 3

Priest: Simeon, so you are back to the temple courts again.

Simeon: The Spirit of the Lord has led me here. He has promised that I will not die until I see the Lord's Christ. I am waiting, waiting on the Lord.

Priest: Well, I think you'll be waiting quite a while.

Simeon: I'll do whatever it takes. I trust the Lord's promises.

Joseph: (*Walking up to the priest*) We are here to present our child to the Lord.

Simeon: (*Taking Jesus into his arms*) Praise God! It is the Christ! "Lord, now You are letting Your servant depart in peace, according to Your Word; for my eyes have seen Your salvation that You have prepared in the presence of all peoples, a light for revelation to the Gentiles, and for glory to Your people Israel" (Luke 2:29–32).

Mary: What you have said is amazing! All of this about my child!

Simeon: May the Lord bless you.

Priest: (In another area in the temple) Anna, you are still here too!

Anna: You know I am here to worship, fast, and pray night and day.

Priest: You may want to go see what your friend Simeon is up to.

Anna: (*Walking up to Simeon, Mary, Joseph, and Jesus*) Thanks be to God! It is the Christ! He will save us all from sin, death, and the devil. Our redemption is finally here!

Simeon and Anna: Joy! Joy! Joy! Waiting patiently for the promised one. Finally, we have seen God's very own Son!

All: Joy, Joy, Joy! We have seen Christ the Lord! Peace! Peace! Peace! He has come to bring us salvation! Love! Love! Love! He has shown His great love for us!

REMEMBER

> May the God of hope fill you with all joy and peace in believing, so that by the power of the Holy Spirit you may abound in hope. **(Romans 15:13)**

LESSON 60

The Coming of the Wise Men and the Flight to Egypt

Matthew 2

Two Voices Worship the One

Matthew 2:1–18 shows us that Jesus came for both the Jews and the Gentiles. He came to offer salvation freely to all, and His Spirit enables all to worship Him. Read the following worship chant with a partner or in two groups. Listen as the two voices, Jews and Gentiles, come together to worship the one king, Jesus.

Jews	Gentiles
Waiting	(silent)
(silent)	Waiting
We are Jews	(silent)
Waiting so long	Waiting (silent)
For the King	For the King
(silent)	Searching
Searching	(silent)
(silent)	We are Gentiles
Searching (silent)	Searching all over
For the King	For the King
Bowing	(silent)
(silent)	Bowing
We are believers	(silent)
Bowing our knees	Bowing (silent)
To the King	To the King
(silent)	Bringing
Bringing	(silent)
(silent)	We are worshipers
Bringing (silent)	Bringing our praise
To the King	To the King

Jews	Gentiles
Needing	(silent)
(silent)	Needing
We are sinners	(silent)
Needing forgiveness	Needing (silent)
From the King	From the King
(silent)	Rejoicing
Rejoicing	(silent)
(silent)	We are God's children
Rejoicing (silent)	Rejoicing for the gift
Of a King	Of a King
Living	(silent)
(silent)	Living
We are redeemed	(silent)
Living our best	Living (silent)
For the King	For the King

REVIEW

Define the following.

Magi—_____

worship—_____

126

Jesus Came for All People

Epiphany is sometimes called the season of light because Jesus is the light of the world—the entire world. Read about each person below. Decide if the person is more like the Wise Men, seeking the light of Jesus and who He is, or if the person is more like Herod, lost in the darkness of sin. Label each as either "seeker of the light" or "lost in darkness."

1. Bradley wants to know about the true God. His Muslim friends at school are telling him that he should worship Allah. A Christian friend in his neighborhood recently told him that Jesus died for his sins and He is Lord of all.

   _____

2. Mrs. Bleakly, a high school teacher, is teaching about evolution. She tells her students that the world came about over time, gradually. She says that the Bible is just a fairy tale and a lie.

   _____

3. On "Oliver," a popular talk show, the host talks about spirituality a lot. He tells the audience that as long as you believe something, you will be okay. He told a Christian guest that to say Jesus is the only way is closed-minded and wrong.

   _____

4. Emma knows that there is someone out there who created everything and is in control of the universe, but she wants to know more. She asks her Christian neighbor about Jesus. Who is He? What should she know about Him? Why should she believe in Him?

   _____

5. Jack's friend asks whether he can go with Jack to his church. Jack's friend is of a different race and culture than Jack, but he wants to go with Jack to learn more about Jesus.

   _____

Jesus came for all sinners. He came to save those who seek Him, and He came to save those who don't know or care about knowing Him. God's gift of salvation is for all people. Just as King Herod tried to destroy Jesus, enemies of God and His Church continue in the world today. But God remains true to His promises. He will continue to work through His Word to change people and bring them to faith in Jesus. He will strengthen His people in the face of persecution and danger until the threat has passed and He brings us home to live with Him in heaven.

REMEMBER

My eyes have seen Your salvation that You have prepared in the presence of all peoples, a light for revelation to the Gentiles, and for glory to Your people Israel. (**Luke 2:30–32**)

John the Baptist Prepares the Way

(Luke 3:1–20)

John the Baptist—Forerunner of Jesus

A forerunner is _____

_____

John's Message

Directions: To figure out John's message to the people who heard him preach in the wilderness, write the letter that comes before the given letter in the alphabet. (For example, B = A; N = M)

<u>r</u> <u>e</u> <u>p</u> <u>e</u> <u>m</u> ___ and ___ ___ ___ ___ ___ ___
S F Q F O U   D I B O H F

How Did They Repent?

Repent does NOT mean
* being sorry that I got caught.
* being sorry that I got in trouble.
* being "fake sorry" to avoid getting in trouble.
* being sorry for doing something today, but planning on doing it again tomorrow too.

Repent means _____

_____

REVIEW

Circle the correct definition of each word.

Forerunner	Repent
* a person who runs four miles a day * a person who goes before someone to prepare the way	* be truly sorry for the wrong things we have done * be sorry that we got caught doing something wrong

_____, Forerunner of Jesus

Write your name on the line.

God Helps Us to Repent!

Read 2 Timothy 1:9 and fill in the missing words.

"Not because ____ _____ _____, but because of His own

purpose and grace."

God Helps Us to Change

If John the Baptist were talking to a group of fourth graders in the wilderness and they asked him the question in Luke 3:10, "What should we do then?" what would he say

to the child who disobeys his or her parents? _____

to the cheating student? _____

to the fighting friends? _____

to the person who uses bad language? _____

    Writing the correct answers on these lines was the easy part. Following God's will in our everyday life can be difficult as we face temptations, but we can draw strength from the words of Philippians 4:13. Write them on these blanks.

___ _____ ___ _____ _____ _____ _____

_____ ____ _____ ___ ___

To Think and Pray About

    Think about someone in your life for whom God might be calling you to be a John the Baptist. Who in your life does God want you to prepare for the coming of Christ? Pray for that person! Share God's love with them!

REMEMBER

I can do all things through Him who strengthens me. **(Philippians 4:13)**

The Temptation of Jesus

(Luke 4:1–13)

Without the Power?

We face challenges in our lives when we are not spiritually charged with God's Word. Our spiritual batteries get weak. The devil came to tempt Jesus after He spent forty days in the wilderness. The devil was hoping that Jesus would not draw on the power of His heavenly Father's Word. Wrong idea, Satan! Jesus depended on the power of God's Word to fight off the devil's temptations. Doing so, He shows us how to face temptations today.

Satan Tried . . . Jesus Used

1   **Temptation #1**—Luke 4:1–4: Satan tried to appeal to Jesus' desire for _____.

Jesus used _____ _____ to fight the temptation.

2   **Temptation #2**—Luke 4:5–8: Satan tried to appeal to Jesus' desire to _____ _____ _____ _____ _____.

Jesus used _____ _____ to fight the temptation.

3   **Temptation #3**—Luke 4:9–12: Satan tried to appeal to Jesus' desire for _____ , _____ , and _____.

Jesus used _____ _____ to fight the temptation.

REVIEW

Write the definition of the word *temptation* from the glossary in the back of the book.

_____

_____

Now Satan Tries to Tempt Us

Satan often offers the same temptations to us that he offered to Jesus.
Temptation 1: Satan tries to appeal to our desire for physical things.

God's Word says in Philippians 4:11:_____

_____

Temptation 2: Satan tries to appeal to our desire to take the easy way out.

God's Word says in Colossians 3:23: _____

_____

Temptation 3: Satan tries to appeal to our desire to have adventure, popularity and fame.

God's Word says in Matthew 6:33: _____

_____

Satan tries to appeal to my need to_____

_____

God's Word and prayer: the best weapons against Satan's temptations.

HELP!

With the power of God's Word, we can fight against the temptations of Satan. But unlike Jesus, there will be times that we give in and fall into sin. That's when the message of forgiveness through Jesus' death on the cross is so powerful!

Romans 5:8: "God shows His love for us in that while we were still sinners, Christ died for us."

1 John 1:9: "If we confess our sins, He is faithful and just to forgive us our sins and to cleanse us from all unrighteousness."

On a note card, write a short prayer. Thank God for earning forgiveness for your sin and pray for strength to resist Satan's temptations. Pray this prayer each day for several days.

REMEMBER

Thanks be to God, who gives us the victory through our Lord Jesus Christ.
(1 Corinthians 15:57)

Jesus Goes to a Wedding

(John 2:1–11)

Their Problem . . . God's Solution

After Jesus called His disciples, they stayed with Him and went wherever He went. In John 2, we find Jesus and His disciples at a wedding with Mary, the mother of Jesus. Read John 2:1–11. Write the letter of each answer given below next to its matching question on the stone jars.

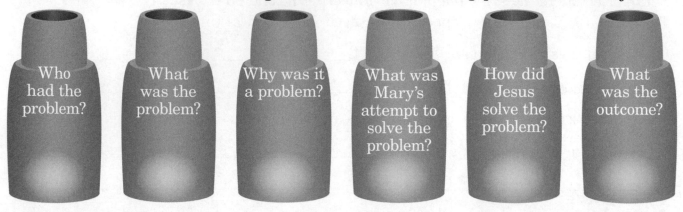

Who had the problem?

What was the problem?

Why was it a problem?

What was Mary's attempt to solve the problem?

How did Jesus solve the problem?

What was the outcome?

a. She told Jesus about it.

b. He told the servants to fill the jars with water and turned the water into wine.

c. They were running out of wine.

d. The bride and groom and their families had a problem.

e. It was the best wine at the banquet.

f. It would be a social embarrassment.

Jesus Gave His Very Best

John 2:10 says that the wine Jesus made was the best wine of the whole banquet. God always gives us His very best. This was the first of Jesus' miracles. Toward the end of His earthly ministry, Jesus took care of our greatest problem—sin. Jesus' sacrificial gift on the cross gives us the certainty of eternal life in heaven. And that's the best for us!

REVIEW

Fill in the blanks with definitions of these words.

| Miracle | Ceremonial washing | Glory |

Jesus did His first *supernatural act* (_____) at a wedding in Cana.

He told the servants to fill jars used for *washing required by Old Testament laws* (_____

_____) with water.

He then turned the water into wine. This showed His *divine power* (_____) to

the disciples, and they put their trust in Him.

My Problem . . . God's Solution

Today most of us will not face the problem of running out of wine at a wedding. However, we face problems of our own. God, in His great mercy and love, cares for us and wants to help us face those problems. Some of the problems we face today are listed on the jars below. Match one of the Bible verses with each jar to show how God lovingly provides a solution for each of our problems.

a. Matthew 28:20b   **c.** Philippians 4:12–13   **e.** Psalm 145:16
b. Psalm 50:15   **d.** Proverbs 3:5–6   **f.** John 14:27

God Gives Us His Very Best

God knows what is best for us, and He knows what we need and the right time to give it to us. The words of Romans 8:28 remind us that God is working all things together for our good—even things that may appear to be a problem for us. Write the words of that verse on the lines below.

_____

_____

REMEMBER

We have seen His glory, glory as of the only Son from the Father, full of grace and truth. **(John 1:14)**

Jesus Goes to a Wedding

(John 2:1–11)

Reporting from Cana

Reporter: Hello! This is Mike Waters, reporting for W-I-N-E radio station here in the city of Cana, where an amazing thing took place today. The hosts of a wedding party were faced with what could have been a terrible situation—no wine. But one of the guests, a Jesus of Nazareth, saved the day by turning water into wine. Yes, folks, you heard me correctly—water into wine.

Who is this man who did such an amazing thing? We talked to a few of His friends at the wedding banquet, and this is what they had to say.

Andrew: We were with John the Baptist the other day, and he told us that Jesus is the Lamb of God who has come to take away the sins of the world. I hurried off then to get my brother Peter.

Peter: Andrew came and told me that he had found the Messiah. We've been waiting for Him to come.

Philip: Jesus invited me to follow Him, so I did.

Nathanael: He knew who I was before I even met Him. He is truly the Son of God.

Peter: We've been with Him now for a few days. He told us we would see amazing things. And today we did. We couldn't believe it when Jesus told the servants to fill the jars with water. Water wouldn't satisfy the guests, but when the master of the banquet said it was the best wine he had ever tasted, we knew why. Jesus is great and powerful. Only the Son of God could do such amazing things.

Andrew: Yeah! I trust Jesus more and more each day, knowing that He is God's Son. We'll be following Him from now on! I can't wait to see what miraculous things He will do next.

REVIEW

Jesus' _____ _____ is everything about Him that is like God.

Jesus' _____ _____ is everything about Him that is like you and me.

Omni means "all," so

Omniscient means _____ knowing.

Omnipresent means _____ present—always here and everywhere.

Omnipotent means _____ powerful.

MIRACLES TO HELP PEOPLE

ETERNAL LIFE

We Trust in Jesus

"Now Jesus did many other signs in the presence of the disciples, which are not written in this book; but these are written so that you may believe that Jesus is the Christ, the Son of God, and that by believing you may have life in His name" (John 20:30–31).

What is your reaction to God's greatest miracle? How does it make you feel to think God performed that miracle because He wants you to spend eternity with Him in heaven?

_____

_____

Jesus Helps Me Every Day

* My heart beats more than a hundred thousand times every day!
* I breathe more than seventeen thousand times a day.
* My blood clots when I cut myself.
* I have food to eat and clothes to wear.
* I am kept safe.

_____

_____

What things will Jesus
do in my life today?
tomorrow?
next week?
next year?
I can't wait to find out.
I'm following Jesus!

REMEMBER

Therefore, as you received Christ Jesus the Lord, so walk in Him. (Colossians 2:6)

Nicodemus Visits Jesus

(John 3:1–21)

HAPPY REBIRTHDAY!

Happy Rebirthday!

When are you born of water and the Spirit? Are you thinking of Baptism? In Baptism, we celebrate our rebirthday. Look up the Bible passages to see what gifts we receive in our Baptism. Write each answer on one of the gifts in the picture.

Acts 2:38

Colossians 1:13–14

Titus 3:5

REVIEW

These words will appear in today's Bible reading. Read the definitions and fill in each blank with the correct word.

condemn—to find guilty and deserving of punishment

marvel—to wonder at with a sense of awe

perished—died

1. The stray dog would have _____ if our neighbors hadn't fed him.

2. The judge decided to _____ the man to fifty years in prison.

3. I _____ at the beauty of the Grand Canyon.

An Undercover Investigation

Find this account in John 3:1–21.

Nicodemus visited Jesus after dark because he didn't want the other Pharisees to see him. He also wanted Jesus all to himself while he asked some serious questions. Nicodemus went to investigate Jesus, but Jesus had a surprise for him. Jesus uncovered some important things about Nicodemus instead!

Report # JN3/1–21

Jerusalem Investigations
Licensed Private investigators
JI · JI
DETECTIVE NOTES

Office 4
★ ★ ★ ★

Persons Observed:
_____

Time of Incident:
_____

Nicodemus Questions Jesus
Q: How can man be born again?

A: _____

_____

Q: How can this be?

A: _____

_____

_____

Jesus Questions Nicodemus
Are you a teacher of Israel and yet you do not understand these things?
Q: How can man be born again?

A: _____

_____

_____

_____

_____

CASE SOLVED

Q: How is a person saved?

A: _____

Problem: _____

_____

Solution: _____

_____

_____

_____

_____

A Reason to Celebrate

Have you been born of water and the Spirit? Has the Holy Spirit put faith in your heart to believe that Jesus is your Savior? Celebrate!

REMEMBER

Jesus answered, "Truly, truly, I say to you, unless one is born of water and the Spirit, he cannot enter the kingdom of God." **(John 3:5)**

LESSON 66

Nicodemus Visits Jesus

(John 3:1–21)

One God, Three Persons

We often use the word *Trinity* when we talk about the one true God. Father, Son, and Holy Spirit are not three gods, but one God. This is hard to understand, isn't it? God's ways are higher than our ways. He tells us about Himself in the Bible, but we can never completely understand who He is while we are still on earth.

We can use a math problem to help us understand a little better.

$$1 + 1 + 1 \text{ does not} = 1.$$
$$1 \times 1 \times 1 \text{ does} = 1!$$

Just like multiplication is a higher form of math than addition, so are God's ways higher than ours. God doesn't ask us to understand the Trinity. He asks us to trust Him and leave the details to Him.

REVIEW

Match the words with the correct definition.

1. Sanctified

2. Justified

A. Made righteous by Jesus' death on the cross

B. Changed by the Holy Spirit so our lives are pleasing to God

The Wind and the Holy Spirit

"The wind blows where it wishes, and you hear its sound, but you do not know where it comes from or where it goes. So it is with everyone who is born of the Spirit" (John 3:8).

What does wind look like?
How do you know when it is windy?
What can wind do?

Nicodemus had a hard time understanding the work of the Holy Spirit. Nicodemus wanted to believe what he could see. Jesus pointed out to him that, like the wind, the Holy Spirit is often unseen but very powerful.

What does the Holy Spirit do?

1._____

_____

2._____

_____

3._____

_____

REMEMBER

God did not send His Son into the world to condemn the world, but in order that the world might be saved through Him. **(John 3:17)**

Jesus Heals the Official's Son

John 4:46–54

No More!

The power of sin and death affects all of our lives. Sadness, loneliness, sickness, and pain can happen to anyone. Our loving God sent us rescue from the power of sin, death, and the devil. In Jesus, God says, "No more!"

Jesus Has the Power to Heal!

Narrator 1: (*Jesus and disciples come into room from hallway, or from back of room to front. Narrator 1 stands to the side.*) Jesus left Samaria and came back to Cana, the town where He had turned water into wine—His first miracle!

Narrator 2: (*Narrator 2 stands to the other side. Official and crowd enter.*) An official from down in Galilee heard that Jesus was back. His son was dying, so he hurried to find Jesus.

Official: (*Running to Jesus*) Please, come down to Galilee with me. My son is at the point of death!

Jesus: (*Looking around at the crowd of onlookers*) Unless you see signs and wonders, you will not believe.

Official: (*Getting down on his knees*) Sir, come down before my child dies.

Jesus: Go; your son will live. (*Official turns and runs back the way he came.*)

Narrator 3: (*Crowd and disciples exit. Narrator 3, who was part of the crowd, remains

REVIEW

The definitions of these words are scrambled next to them. Unscramble them to find the meaning.

redeemed   BGOTUH CKBA

_____

reigns   LESUR OEVR

_____

standing. Waits for crowd to clear.) The man believed the word that Jesus spoke to him and went on his way. As he was going down, his servants met him. *(Official enters. Servants enter from other direction to meet official. Narrator 4 waits to the side.)*

Servant 1: Your son! He is recovering!

Official: At what hour did he begin to get better?

Servant 2: Yesterday at the seventh hour, the fever left him. *(Official and servants exit excitedly.)*

Narrator 4: The father knew that was the hour when Jesus had said to him, "Your son will live." And he himself believed, and all his household.

Encouraging Others

People who are hurting or ill need encouragement that Jesus loves and cares for them. Create a card with a Bible verse and a prayer that reminds someone of God's love and care for him or her.

My Verse to Share:

_____

_____

REMEMBER

He is the true God and eternal life. **(1 John 5:20b)**

Jesus Heals the Official's Son

(John 4:46–54)

Trusting Jesus

In today's story, the official shows his trust in Jesus in several ways. Fill in each of the thermometers below to describe how much trust you think he showed.

Traveled from Capernaum to Cana to see Jesus
Asked Jesus to heal his son
Asked Jesus a second time to heal his son
Went home and believed that his son was healed

How much do you need to trust Jesus to

--go to church and worship?

--stand up to a friend who is doing something wrong?

--read the Bible regularly?

--believe that Jesus forgives sins so you can go to heaven?

Promises to Trust

The Bible has many promises for God's people. Look up the following verses and write down what God has promised in each of these verses.

Genesis 9:13–15 _____

Romans 8:28 _____

_____

Acts 2:38 _____

REVIEW

Judea—_____ part of Israel; it includes the cities of _____

Samaria—_____ part of Israel; it includes the city of_____

Galilee—_____ part of Israel; it includes the cities of _____

More than Just Healing

Read each of the Bible verses listed below and describe the healing that happened by writing on the lines inside the cross.

1. Matthew 20:29–34

_____

_____

_____

2. Mark 2:1–12

_____

_____

3. Luke 17:11–19

_____

_____

_____

4. John 19:28—20:8

_____

_____

_____

REMEMBER

If then you have been raised with Christ, seek the things that are above.
(Colossians 3:1)

Jesus Preaches at Nazareth

(Luke 4:14–30)

Prophecies Fulfilled

The Old Testament contains many messages about what Jesus would do. We call those messages *prophecies*. Read each of the Bible passages listed below and draw a line to the picture that shows each promise being fulfilled by Jesus.

Zechariah 9:9   **Isaiah 53:3**   **Hosea 11:1**

What Happened?

A great change took place among the people listening to Jesus as He taught in His hometown of Nazareth. Fill in the blanks of the Bible verses that describe how the mood changed.

Luke 4:22: "All spoke _____ of Him and _____ at the gracious _____ that were coming from His mouth. And they said, 'Is this not Joseph's _____ ?'"

Luke 4:28–29: "When they heard these things, all in the _____ were filled with _____ . And they rose up and drove Him out of the _____ and brought Him to the brow of the _____ on which their town was _____ , so that they could _____ Him down the _____ ."

REVIEW

Synagogue _____

What Do I Do?

Jesus came to fulfill the Old Testament prophecies; He came to save us. And He gives us His Holy Spirit to help us live our lives in ways that God wants. In the three situations below, describe how you might respond without Jesus' presence in your life. Then write how your response is different because you know that Jesus is present in your life.

You see other students teasing one of your classmates before class.

_____

_____

You are not allowed to use the computer when you are home alone, but you are bored and want to get online.

_____

_____

You can't remember several answers for the test you studied for, but you know the student next to you probably has the right answers.

_____

_____

REMEMBER

Christ Jesus came into the world to save sinners. **(1 Timothy 1:15)**

Jesus Preaches at Nazareth

(Luke 4:14–30)

Jesus Tells the People about Himself

Read Luke 4:14–30. Recall that Jesus had stopped at Nazareth. This is the town where He grew up, learned carpentry, and studied in the local synagogue. Follow along as we read these verses again. Then finish the paragraph below by filling in the consonants.

The hometown of Jesus was __ A __ A __ E __ __.

In the __ I __ A __ O __ U E at Nazareth, Jesus was

asked to __ E A __ __ a lesson. He read from the book

of the prophet I __ A I A __. The prophet was talking

about the __ O __ __ Jesus was sent to do on earth.

Next, Jesus explained the message to the

__ E O __ __ E. They were amazed at how much

__ E __ U __ knew about the Scriptures. Then Jesus said, "The prophecy is talking about Me."

Jesus also told them about E __ I __ A __ and E __ I __ __ A, who were teachers of both

Jews and Gentiles. Now the people became very A __ __ __ __. They did not want to believe

that God loved the Gentiles. They did not believe that Jesus is __ O __.

But Jesus saw that the people were too proud to recognize Him for who He is. They

remembered when Jesus was a little boy in their __ I __ __ A __ E. He was just a person.

He couldn't be __ O __! The people wanted Jesus to do a __ I __ A __ __ E for them. Jesus

saw that the people of His __ O __ __ were unwilling to recognize Him as God. So Jesus

refused to do any miracles among them and __ A __ __ E __ through the crowd and out of town.

REVIEW

Circle the correct answer.

A scroll is   a. a headband.   b. a handkerchief.   c. a roll for writing a document.

A Messiah is   a. one who saves.   b. the name of a town.   c. a tool used in farming.

Who Jesus Is and What He Came to Do

The people in Nazareth believed that Jesus could do miracles. But they missed the most important point in His message: He is the promised Messiah.

Jesus did everything that the Old Testament said the Son of God would do. He demonstrated His power. He told people to repent of their sins, because their salvation was near. He was truly God, born in Bethlehem, as promised. He taught in the synagogues, showing how the Old Testament prophecies pointed to Him as the promised Messiah. Later, He would die and rise from the dead to take away all of their sins. Those were the facts that His hometown people could not believe. They were too focused on themselves to see what was right before their eyes. Perhaps they were too proud to see themselves as sinners and Jesus, who had grown up in their community, as their God and Savior.

The Big I

Am **I** too focused on myself to admit that **I** have sinned? Have **I** become my own god by failing to recognize my need for Jesus as my Savior? If **I** am honest, **I** will say Yes!

Jesus already knows about my self-centeredness. He has taken away this and all the rest of my sins! Draw a big **I** through the middle of the box on the right. Then write S**I**N in the first blank, using the big **I** as part of the word. Talk about your sin with Jesus. He will forgive you.

Now that I am forgiven, I can cross out the word S**I**N. Finish the other words, because now I am FORG**I**VEN, REJO**I**CING, and THANK**I**NG.

Why is it wrong to be too focused on myself? It makes me look at myself, not at Jesus, who took away all my sins. Jesus loves me, a sinner.

REMEMBER

We have our hope set on the living God, who is the Savior of all people. **(1 Timothy 4:10)**

'e u ai e Jairu ' aughter

(Mark 5:22–24, 35–43.)

Twelve-Year-Old Raised from the Dead

Carefully read today's story in Mark 5:22–24, 35–43. Be ready to be one of the people interviewed by the news reporter when your class finishes reading. Your teacher has the questions for the interview.

In the boxes below, write two emotions that this person must have felt on this day.

Jairus

Wailer

Mother

Disciples

Jesus

Young Girl

REVIEW

Look this word up in the glossary. Then write its meaning.

Resurrection _____

Feelings about Death

Read the statements below and decide which heading you will put them under. Then place the number in front of the statement under the heading where you think it belongs. Not all the blanks will be filled in.

Yes, this is true.	I really don't know.	This is not true.
__ __ __ __	__ __ __ __	__ __ __ __
__ __ __ __	__ __ __ __	__ __ __ __

1. I am afraid to die.
2. Only old people die.
3. It hurts to die.
4. Jesus leaves you when you die.
5. When someone dies, that's the end of everything for him or her.
6. After I die, I will come back to earth as someone else.
7. I'm afraid my parents will die and I'll be alone.
8. Bad people go to hell and good people go to heaven when they die.
9. I know I'll go to heaven when I die.
10. I will sleep a long time after I die, waiting for enough people to pray that I can go into heaven.
11. Angels will guide believers to heaven when they die.

What Does This Mean?

Now I can live a happy, faith-filled life because Jesus took away all my worries about what will happen to me when and after I die. He did all the work, and I get all the benefits. Isn't that great?

In the puzzle below, use the bouncing ball to skip over all the letters Q, X, and Z. Let the ball land on the other letters of the alphabet. Copy those letters on the lines below, and divide the letters into words. These words will tell what this lesson means to me.

QXIXWZQILXZLQZGXOQZXTOZHQXEXZAQVEZNQZWX

HZQEZNXIQDZQIXEZXQBEXCZXAQZUQXSZEXIZQBXQEQLZI

EQZVXEZJQZEXSXZUQSXQTOZOKXAQWZAYXAZLXLMZYZSQ

IZXNXSQANZXDQXMZQXAZDXQEQMZXEZQHXQOZLQYZ.

__ ____ __ __ _____ ____ _ __ _____ _ _____

_____ ___ ____ ____ __ ___ ___ __ ____

REMEMBER

Do not fear, only believe. **(Mark 5:36b)**

149

Jesus Raises Jairus's Daughter

(Matthew 9:18–19, 23–26)

Life Cycles

Label the parts of the life cycles below.

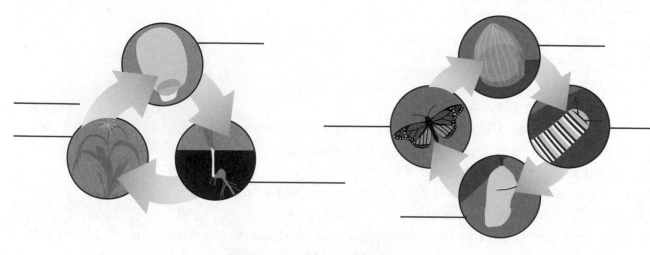

CORN LIFE CYCLE

BUTTERFLY LIFE CYCLE

An Unusual Event

To discover another cycle, review the Bible story from your last lesson. Matthew, Mark, and Luke all include this miracle in their Gospels. Today, read Matthew's account in Matthew 9:18–19, 23–26. The daughter of Jairus seemed to be finished with her life, but by God's strength, she returned to life.

What about us? Do we also have a life cycle? The section on the top of the next page shows how God planned our lives before the devil spoiled the design. It was the greatest life plan ever!

REVIEW

Cycle: Something that repeats itself or goes around

Use the vocabulary word to complete the words below. Then tell what each means.

bi _____   tri _____   uni _____

God's natural laws are examples of _____.

God's Perfect Design

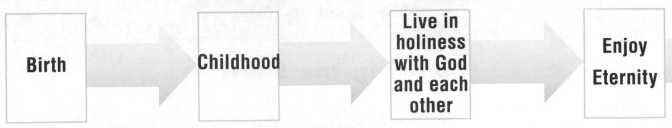

Birth → Childhood → Live in holiness with God and each other → Enjoy Eternity →

This perfect design was messed up when Adam and Eve fell into sin, which they passed on to us. Now we inherit their sin and do plenty of sinning on our own. The devil started this bad design and wants to keep it going.

Sin and Its Consequences

See if you can identify the effects of sin on God's perfect design.

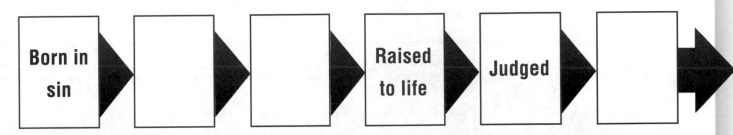

Born in sin → → → Raised to life → Judged → →

Sin really messed up the world. That's exactly why God wanted to do something about it. He sent His Son Jesus to suffer the punishment for all sin, so we won't end up in hell. That was quite a job, but He did it because He loves us. Now we have a new life design because of what Jesus did.

My New Life in Christ

Guess these parts of the plan that include God's disruption of sin and its consequences.

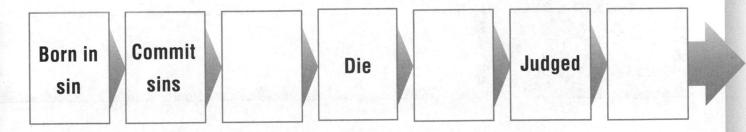

Born in sin → Commit sins → → Die → → Judged → →

The Good News of eternal life ends our suspense. Yes, we will live in heaven with God forever because of our faith that Jesus erased all our sins. We may even get to meet the daughter of Jairus in our heavenly home.

REMEMBER

Jesus said, . . . "I am the resurrection and the life. Whoever believes in Me, though he die, yet shall he live." **(John 11:25)**

The Parable of the Sower

(Matthew 13:1–30)

Sowing the Seed

Jesus shared parables to teach biblical truths. Many times, the objects in the parables were symbolic for something else. Read Matthew 13:18–23 to discover what each type of soil symbolized in the parable:

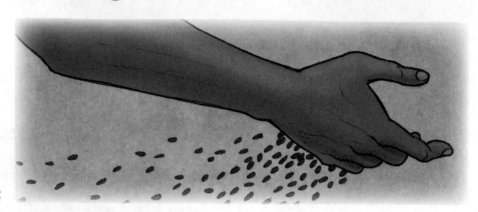

Soil	Meaning
The Path	
Rocky Soil	
Thorny Soil	
Good Soil	

REVIEW

Define the following two words:

sower:_____

parable:_____

A Chance to Sprout and Grow

God wants us all to be like the seeds that fell in the good soil. He wants us to learn more and more about God and share Him with others. But often we fail. We may even act as if we are rocky or thorny soil to look cool around our friends.

God sent Jesus to be our Savior. Through Jesus' death and resurrection, God offers us full forgiveness. We cannot earn that forgiveness; it is a free gift to be shared. God sends us His Holy Spirit to nurture and grow us strong in the faith. That's great news—the kind God would have us share with others.

Whom will you share it with? _____

_____

_____

Lifestyle Choice

Living Your Life

Each of these seeds is symbolic of a lifestyle choice we may or may not make. Match the choice with the correct seed and soil combination. Put the correct letter in the column at the left:

a. Receive Jesus' Word and share it with others

b. Do not believe in God and refuse to learn about Him

c. Think things are more important than God

d. Fear what others will think of us if we admit we believe in Jesus

REMEMBER

Fill in the missing vowels. Use the symbols below the lines to find the correct vowel.

| A=△ | E=□ | O=♡ | U=☆ |

B☆t bl□ss□d △r□ y♡☆r □y□s, f♡r th□y s□□, △nd y♡☆r □△rs, f♡r th□y h□△r. M△tth□w 13:16

153

Jesus Is Transfigured

(Luke 9:28–36)

Just the Facts

A detective's job is to look at clues to find the answer to a question. Read the account of Jesus' transfiguration in Luke 9:28–36. Fill in the clues to determine what Jesus is teaching His disciples and us through His transfiguration.

The Setting

Read Luke 9:28. Where does this event take place?

What also occurred in these similar locations? (Exodus 19:20)

(1 Kings 19:11–12)

The Events

In Luke 9:29–33, how did Jesus' appearance change?

Why was this important according to John 1:14?

The Voice

What command is given in Luke 9:35?

At what other time in Jesus' life have we heard similar words (see Matthew 3:16–17)?

The Environment

In Luke 9:34–35, what filled the mountaintop?

Read Exodus 13:21. Where else have we seen this?

Who does it signify?

REVIEW

transfiguration:_____

altered: _____

The Witnesses

One of the key characters in the transfiguration is Peter. The other disciples witness the events, but Peter is the one to speak up once again. Sometimes we can be bold speakers like Peter.

Do the disciples fully understand what they are witnessing? _____

Let's look at the facts. Choose the best answer for each question:

V. 32

1. In verse 32, the disciples were invited to pray on the mountain but instead they
   - o. build tents.
   - e. fall asleep.
   - p. write the Bible.

V. 33

2. In verse 33, Peter wants to build three _____ so they can stay on the mountain.
   - u. tents
   - s. altars
   - e. bridges

V. 34

3. In verse 34, when the disciples enter the cloud, they feel
   - m. excited.
   - t. sorry.
   - s. scared.

V. 36

4. When the disciples descended from the mountain, whom did they tell about Jesus' transfiguration?
   - r. Priests
   - e. Everyone
   - j. No one

Using the numbers listed above, fill in the blanks with the letters that correspond to your answers:

> **Who returns from the mountaintop to help the disciples continue their work?**
>
> ___ ___ ___ ___ ___
> 4   1   3   2   3

Case Closed

Jesus uses His transfiguration to give the disciples and us a glimpse of His glory. He shows us His power, yet He encourages the disciples by returning down the mountain with them. At times we, too, may feel alone and overwhelmed with the task at hand, to live as God's people. But like the disciples returning from the mountaintop, we know that Jesus is always with us.

REMEMBER 💙

Unscramble the following words and rewrite the Bible verse to make sense:
And a voice came out of the cloud, saying, "*Chosen My Son, Him! to This One; is My listen*" (**Luke 9:35**)

_____

_____

Jesus Feeds the Crowd

(John 6:1–14)

Reading Riddles

1. I am the disciple whom Jesus tested by asking, "Where are we to buy bread, so that these people may eat?" Who am I?

2. I am the disciple who brought the young boy and his lunch to Jesus. Who am I?

3. I am the sea that Jesus crossed to escape the great crowds. What am I?

4. I am the type of bread that was shared with the crowd. What am I?

5. I am the number of leftover baskets collected from the crowds. What am I?

6. I am the feast of the Jews that would be celebrated soon. What am I?

7. I am the name that tells what people hoped Jesus would become for them after He fed the crowd. What am I?

REVIEW

Choose the correct definition to match the following words. Circle the correct answer below each word.

1. Used in our earthly life
   A. temporal B. eternal C. prophetic

2. Used for an infinite time
   A. temporal B. eternal C. prophetic

3. Divinely inspired, such as a revelation
   A. temporal B. eternal C. prophetic

Food for a Crowd

When Jesus arrived at the Sea of Galilee, He was expecting to rest and spend time with His disciples. Instead, He was surprised to see a large crowd of people following Him.

How many men were in the crowd (John 6:10)?

_____

Why was it so difficult to feed the crowd?

_____

_____

Why was it necessary to feed the crowd?

_____

_____

_____

Jesus uses the resources available to Him to perform the miracle. At the wedding at Cana, Jesus uses the water available to create the wine. Here, He uses the loaves and fishes, a common boy's lunch, to feed a large crowd.

Besides objects, God also works through people to perform miracles. Read the same account of this event in Luke 9:10–17. In Luke 9:16, who actually distributes the food to the crowd?

_____

The Lord Blesses Me

Jesus shares His blessings with us through people. It may be someone you know, or even a stranger. Just imagine the food on your table. God uses a variety of people to get that food to you. First, there is the farmer who plants the seed, the worker who transports it to the factory, where it is cleaned, packaged, and shipped to the store. Then the store employees receive and stack the food on the shelves. Next, your parents, who work for the money to buy the food, travel to the store, purchase the products, and transport them home to prepare them for you. And we didn't even mention the inventors of the cooking utensils your parents use, the gas station employee who sells gasoline to the transporters, and so on. You get the idea.

Using the same idea, create a blessings chain by drawing arrows to show the means God uses to bless His people.

farmer   transporter   factory   store worker   parents   you

REMEMBER

You cause the grass to grow for the livestock and plants for man to cultivate, that he may bring forth food from the earth. **(Psalm 104:14)**

Jesus Feeds the Crowd

(John 6:1–14)

Crown Him

The human resources department in any company has an important job. They must find the best person to work in every position. When a company is looking for a new employee, they must first determine the exact job description for the type of employee they are seeking. For example, a computer programmer must have experience using certain computer programs. Then the job is advertised and potential employees can apply for it if the job fits their skills.

Take a look at the following want ad. Who could apply for this job?

Wanted:

Technology Instructor for local Lutheran school. Must have a BA in education and at least ten years experience. Working with computers a must. Salary and benefits are included. Send résumé including references.

Now imagine that you are living in biblical times. Countries are still ruled by royalty. Write a want ad for a king. Be sure to include a description of the job, the benefits offered, and the country's expectations.

_____
_____
_____
_____
_____
_____

Jesus' Résumé

Other Names: Bread of Life (John 6:48); Son of Man (John 6:27); Holy One of God (John 6:68)

Parents: Mary and Joseph, God the Father (John 6:27)

Experience: Turns water into wine (John 2:11); heals the sick, feeds the 5,000 (John 6:11); teacher

Offers to Believers: forgiveness, eternal life (John 6:54), support when tempted (Hebrews 2:18); food of eternal life (John 6:27)

Objective: that everyone believe and be baptized to be saved.

REVIEW

sanctification _____

An Unexpected King

Does Jesus' résumé fit your expectations of an earthly king? After Jesus fed the crowd, many people wanted Him to be their King (John 6:15). The more the people interacted with Him, the more they realized He was not offering what they wanted. He would not just give them military protection or money or material goods.

1. In John 6:66, when the crowds realized Jesus was not the earthly king they were seeking, what did many of Jesus' followers do?

_____

2. Peter confirms the greatest gift Jesus could provide in John 6:68. What is that blessing?

_____

The crowds did not understand the true blessings Christ was offering to them. He would meet their spiritual needs in a way that earthly kings could not.

A Job Well Done

Think about Jesus as true God and true man and all of the things that qualify Him to be your Savior. Write a job description for Jesus. Explain what He has done for you. Share this description with those who don't know Jesus.

_____
_____
_____
_____

REMEMBER

To the King of ages, immortal, invisible, the only God, be honor and glory forever and ever. Amen. **(1 Timothy 1:17)**

Jesus Walks on Water

(John 6:16–24)

A Picture of That Night

Jesus had sent His disciples away in a boat. They were sailing to the other side of the Sea of Galilee. Then Jesus spent time with His heavenly Father in prayer. Suppose the disciples kept a scrapbook page of the events recorded in John 6:16–21. What might its pages have looked like? Draw pictures in the boxes to show the events of that night's adventure.

Disciples Go

Winds Blow

Jesus Shows

Peace They Know

REVIEW

deliverer _____

peace _____

The Winds in Our Lives

The winds of sin and Satan blow storms into our lives just as they did for the disciples. Satan would love nothing more than to see us drown in the seas of unbelief, worry, sorrow, and sin. He blows different winds our way, but the same Jesus who rescued the disciples comes walking to us and says, "It is I; do not be afraid." Our Savior rescues us as well.

_____ _____

- What clothes should I wear?
- Who should I sit by at lunch?
- What will I do after school?

_____

_____

_____ _____

- An argument with someone
- A headache, stomachache, or cold
- A bad grade on an assignment or test

_____

_____

_____ _____ _____

- Serious sickness of yourself or someone you love
- Someone being mean to you on a regular basis

_____

_____

_____ _____ _____

- Death of someone we love
- Divorce of parents
- A move to a new placc

_____

_____

A Prayer for Deliverance

Jesus promises to hear our prayers for help—wherever and whenever we need Him. Write a prayer asking God for His help and deliverance with a problem that you are facing today. Be confident in knowing that Jesus hears your prayer and will be with you as you face that problem. What He said to the disciples, He says to you: "It is I; do not be afraid."

REMEMBER

You are my help and my deliverer; do not delay, O my God! **(Psalm 40:17b)**

We Experience Wind and Waves Too!

When the disciples were in the boat, they experienced the winds and the waves, tossing the boat in the darkness. Then the disciples thought they saw someone walking on the water. They were afraid, but they did not need to fear because it was Jesus coming to them. We live in a world where we are tossed about by the winds and waves of sin—our sins and the sins of others. We do not need to despair and lose hope. We thank God that He comes to us when our boat is shaking and tells us not to be afraid—He is with us.

It Is I; Do Not Be Afraid

Jesus is also true God. When Jesus tells His followers not to be afraid for He is with them, we can take those words to heart and be encouraged because Jesus is God. Circle each phrase below that explains why we need not be afraid.

God punishes sin.

God is love.

God sent His Son to save us.

God sees everything we do.

God knows all of our thoughts.

God forgives our sins for Jesus' sake.

REVIEW

_____ is a name meaning "The Lord saves."

_____ is another word for characteristic.

God Loves and Cares for Me

Jesus loves me! This I know,
For the Bible tells me so.
Little ones to Him belong;
They are weak, but He is strong.
Yes, Jesus loves me!
Yes, Jesus loves me!
Yes, Jesus loves me!
The Bible tells me so. (LSB 588)

These simple words may have been one of the first songs you learned about Jesus. The song is so simple, but the message is powerful. The God who created the heavens and the earth, who is omnipresent, omnipotent, and omniscient, loves and cares about me.

A Prayer of Thanks and Praise

Imagine the conversation the disciples had with Jesus when they reached the other shore. The disciples probably could not stop sharing their story about how scared they were and how thankful they were to have Jesus get into the boat with them.

Let's thank God for being in the boat of our lives with us by finishing the words of this prayer of thanks and praise to God for His amazing love and protection.

Dear heavenly Father,
Thank You for blessing me with

_____ .

Thank You for taking care of me when

_____ .

You have given me

_____ .

You are_____and _____.

    I am so glad that You love me and care for me.

    In Jesus' name.

    Amen.

REMEMBER

> [Jesus said,] "In the world you will have tribulation. But take heart; I have overcome the world." **(John 16:33)**

The Parable of the Rich Fool

(Luke 12:13–21)

He Focused on Himself

Wow! Look at my abundance of crops. Where shall I store them all?

I'll tear down my old barns and build bigger and better ones.

Then I'll kick back and relax—eat, drink, and be merry! Life is good.

And Look What He Got!

That night the man died. He didn't get to enjoy his wealth.

THE RICH FOOL

What is the man's problem?_____

_____

REVIEW

greed abundance priorities

Fill in the missing words.

God has given us an _____ of blessings. He wants us to use those blessings to give

glory to Him and to share the message of His love with others. In our _____ , we

sometimes make those blessings more important than God. We can ask God for His forgiveness

and help in setting our _____ on things that honor our heavenly Father.

Where Is Our Focus?

As God's blessed children, we know that God cares for us and loves us. We know in our hearts and minds that following Jesus should be the number one priority in our lives. However, we do not always put God first. The devil puts so many other temptations in front of us. They look great, and when we fill our lives with them, there is no room for Jesus. We may want to live our life for Jesus, but we do not always reflect Jesus in our thoughts, words, and actions.

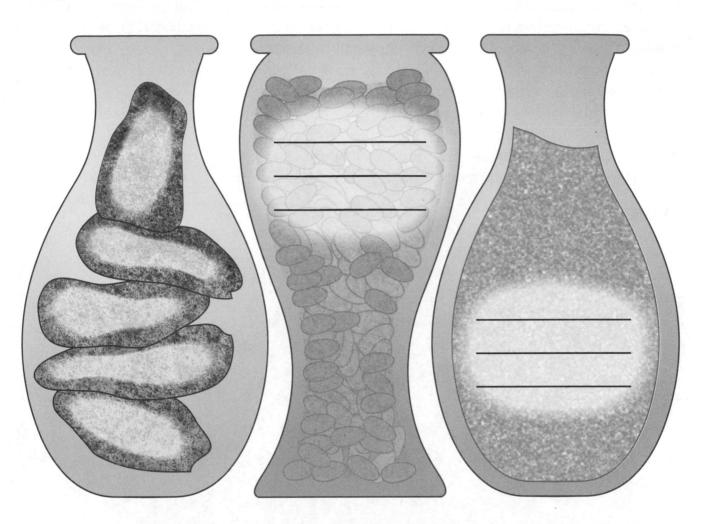

Dear Jesus, Please Help Me Put First Things First!

If our lives are going to be focused on God, then through the help of the Holy Spirit, we need to put the big rocks into the jar of our life first.

Directions: Label the rocks, the jar of pebbles, and the jar of sand with the words your teacher gives you.

REMEMBER

But seek first the kingdom of God and His righteousness, and all these things will be added to you. **(Matthew 6:33)**

The Parable of the Rich Fool

(Luke 12:13–21)

A Web of Worry

After Jesus tells the parable of the rich fool, He immediately goes on to talk to His disciples about worry. They have left their jobs, their families, and their homes. They will not have the opportunity to store up earthly riches as they follow Christ, but the eternal benefits are much greater. He does not want them to worry about any of their physical needs. They will be taken care of according to God's abundant blessings.

A spider spins its web in hopes of catching some unsuspecting prey to be its next meal. Satan often sets a web of worry for us. He hopes to trap us in this web—leading us to trust in ourselves and what we can do about the problems we are facing rather than trusting in God. We are Satan's unsuspecting prey.

What are some things you worry about? What are some things your friends worry about? What are some things your family members worry about? Write those worries on the web.

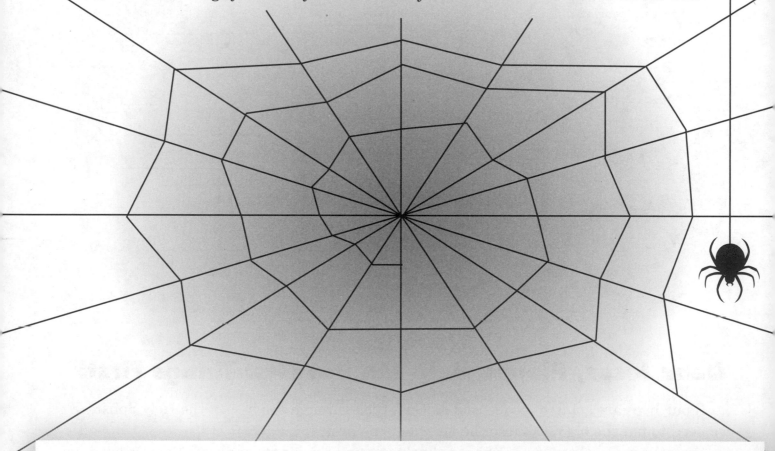

REVIEW

trust _____

worry _____

166

God Is Trustworthy

Jesus is trustworthy. God has promised that because we know and believe in Jesus as our Savior, we are His children and He will always care for us. No person or thing will ever be able to snatch us out of God's hand.

Use your finger to "write" your name in the palm of your hand. God holds you in His hands. Look back at the web of worry that you made before. Give those worries to the Lord by "writing" them on you hand as well. As you "write" each one, quietly ask God to help you trust Him to help you with the problem rather than worry about it.

Staying Connected

Trust is an easy word to say, but sometimes it is a difficult word to do. It becomes easier to trust someone when you know and spend time with him or her. The more time we spend with Jesus, the easier it is to trust Him as well. He also gives us His Holy Spirit to help us place our trust in Him. Cross off all the X's in the lines below and highlight the other letters to show ways we are connected to Jesus and how we learn to trust Him. Write those ways on the lines.

XXXXXCXXXXXXXHXXXXXXUXXXXXXXXXRXXXXXXXXCXXXXXHX_____

XXXXPXXXXXXXXRXXXXXXXAXXXXXXXYXXXXXXXEXXXXXRXXXX_____

XRXXXEXXXAXXDXXIXXXNXXGXXTXXXHXXXEXXBXXIXXBXXLXE_____

_____

Asking God to Help Us Trust

Dear heavenly Father, I know sometimes I worry about things that are bothering me. These things weigh heavy on my heart. Forgive me for worrying about them. Help me to trust You in all circumstances. You are my Good Shepherd who gives me eternal life. I thank You that no one can ever snatch me out of Your hand. In Jesus' name. Amen.

REMEMBER

To You, O Lord, I lift up my soul. O my God, in You I trust. **(Psalm 25:1–2a)**

167

The Lost Sheep

(Luke 15:1–7)

Draw a picture of something you lost. Write a "lost and found" ad below the picture.

LOST

_____

_____

_____

_____

REVIEW

Draw a straight line from the words to their definitions.

righteous	turning away from sin
repentance	God's love for us even though we don't deserve it
grace	being perfect in God's eyes
rejoice	to show that you're very happy

Write a sentence with one of the review words that shows its meaning.

_____

_____

From Lost to Found

G
R
A
C
E

_____
_____
_____
_____
_____
_____
_____
_____
_____
_____

When Found

Reflect about a time when you found someone or something that was lost or when you were found after being lost.

How did you feel? What comfort does God give us when we are found?

Use your Bible to make a small poster or card that might help someone who feels lost in his or her faith—someone who feels separated from God. Use the space to the left to make a miniature poster or card.

 **REMEMBER**

The Son of Man came to seek and to save the lost. **(Luke 19:10)**

The Good Shepherd
(John 10:1–18, 27–29)

Read John 10:7–18. Draw a line from each phrase to the correct picture.

Is the door

Thieves and robbers

Comes to steal and kill

Comes to destroy

Comes to give life

Leaves the sheep

Knows the sheep

Lays down life

Sheep know

Sheep listen to

REVIEW

Write the definition for **shepherd**.

_____

_____

My Shepherd

Read John 10:27.

1. How do we hear God's voice?

_____

_____

_____

_____

2. How do we follow Him?

_____

_____

_____

_____

3. Which came first—hearing or following?

_____

_____

Did you know *pastor* means "shepherd"? Read John 10:28.

1. Fill in the blank. "I_____ them eternal life."

2. What does it say we have to do to get eternal life?

_____

_____

Read John 10:29.

1. Are you ever afraid that you will lose your faith?

2. In verses 1–12, Jesus says wolves, thieves, and robbers come to steal, or snatch, the sheep. In verse 29, He says no one is able to snatch us from God the Father. Can you explain that?

REMEMBER

I give them eternal life, and they will never perish, and no one will snatch them out of My hand. **(John 10:28)**

Jesus Raises Lazarus

(John 11:1–45)

Powerful Feelings

Since Adam and Eve and their children, the very first family, the sting of death has been a painful part of life. During Jesus' earthly life, He saw and felt the sting of death too. Death can make us feel overwhelmed and powerless, but it can't do that to Jesus. His life, death, and resurrection have forever changed the power death once held.

How might this family be feeling? Write some likely feelings in the thought bubbles below. Have you ever felt those emotions because of the death of someone you loved?

REVIEW

Names can have important meanings. Unscramble the meanings of these names from today's lesson.

Jesus—VISORA _____

Lazarus—HWOM OGD PSELH _____

172

A Powerful Savior

Death causes us to feel strong emotions. In today's Bible reading, watch for the strong feelings of the disciples, Jesus, Mary, Martha, and the Jews.

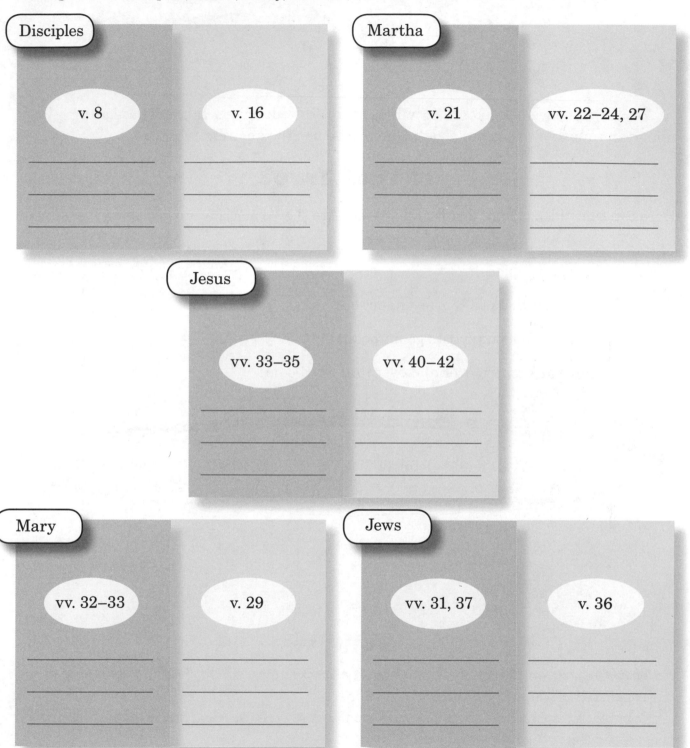

Disciples

v. 8

_____
_____
_____

v. 16

_____
_____
_____

Martha

v. 21

_____
_____
_____

vv. 22–24, 27

_____
_____
_____

Jesus

vv. 33–35

_____
_____
_____

vv. 40–42

_____
_____
_____

Mary

vv. 32–33

_____
_____
_____

v. 29

_____
_____
_____

Jews

vv. 31, 37

_____
_____
_____

v. 36

_____
_____
_____

REMEMBER

[Jesus said,] "Because I live, you also will live." **(John 14:19)**

Jesus Raises Lazarus

(John 11:1–45)

What will heaven be like? Who will be there? How do we get there? These are important questions to think about. God's Word has the answers!

Is That True?

Here are some ideas about death and heaven. Are they true? How do you know?

T or F 1. Heaven is a place.

T or F 2. Only our spirits go to heaven, not our bodies.

T or F 3. When we die, our spirits go immediately to heaven.

T or F 4. People are reborn over and over into new bodies.

Hebrews 9:27–28   John 14:2–3   Luke 23:43   John 5:28–29

REVIEW

Perishable means something can die or decay. The prefix *im* means "not." Add the prefix and you get *imperishable*, something that cannot die or decay.

These apples look alike, but they are very different. One is perishable and one is imperishable. Label them according to the information given.

This apple came from the plastic fruit bowl on Grandma's dining table.

_____

This apple came from the produce section of the grocery store.

_____

What Could You Say?

With a partner, choose a situation to act out. Select a verse to help you decide what you could say in that situation. Use the verse to help express confidence in going to heaven someday.

A disciple is telling about Jesus. A Pharisee threatens to stone the disciple if he or she doesn't stop.

A child worries about dying. Mom or Dad reassures the child.

A person is upset about the death of a grandparent. A friend offers comfort.

A pastor explains to a mom or dad why the Baptism of a baby is so important.

A doctor tells a patient the illness is not curable. The doctor is surprised by the patient's reaction.

John 11:25–26: "Jesus said to her, 'I am the resurrection and the life. Whoever believes in Me, though he die, yet shall he live, and everyone who believes in Me shall never die. Do you believe this?'"

John 3:36: "Whoever believes in the Son has eternal life; whoever does not obey the Son shall not see life, but the wrath of God remains on him."

Romans 8:18: "For I consider the sufferings of this present time are not worth comparing with the glory that is to be revealed to us."

Romans 8:38–39: "For I am sure that neither death nor life, nor angels nor rulers, nor things present nor things to come, nor powers, nor height nor depth, nor anything else in all creation, will be able to separate us from the love of God in Christ Jesus our Lord."

REMEMBER

In My Father's house are many rooms. If it were not so, would I have told you that I go to prepare a place for you? **(John 14:2)**

The Parable of the Great Banquet

(Luke 14:12–24)

The Ruler's Guest List

The Pharisees were frequent critics of Jesus. Still, one Sabbath, Jesus went to dine at the house of a ruler of the Pharisees. We may wonder which other Pharisees may have gathered to eat with Jesus. Very few Pharisees are named in Scripture. Surprisingly, Jairus, who expressed great faith in Jesus and whose daughter Jesus healed (Mark 5:22–23, 35–42), was a Pharisee. So was Nicodemus (John 3:1). They probably were not at this dinner with Jesus, but they are the type of people who would have been on the guest list—influential people in the area and from the ruling council of the local synagogue.

With His radical hospitality, God is persistent in inviting people to His banquet table.

Jesus' Guest List

_____

_____

_____

_____

_____

_____

_____

Jesus' Guest List

Whom did Jesus suggest should be invited to a banquet? To find out, read Luke 14:13, 21, 23. Write the answers you find on the note pad to the left.

REVIEW

Directions: Find the definitions of the following words in the glossary and write them on the lines below.

invitation:_____

response:_____

guest:_____

Jesus' Invitation

Study these Bible passages: Luke 14:12–24; Matthew 11:28; 1 Timothy 2:4; Song of Solomon 2:4; Psalm 34:8. Is there anyone who should not receive an invitation? Now complete Jesus' invitation, inviting people to His great feast.

Greetings, _____ ,

The honor of your presence is requested at my continuous banquet feast. Serving begins immediately.

The Water of Life will be served (John 4:10; Revelation 22:17).
Received at your Baptism _____.
(date)

Nutritious appetizers served at school during religion class
_____.
(time)

Main course served at worship services
_____.
(times)

Extra helpings available at the Lord's Table.

Exercise at Christian education activities
_____.
(insert activity)

Snacks available at any time
_____.
(times of daily devotions)

I urge you to join Me at this great feast (Matthew 11:28; 22:4).
-Jesus

An Invitation for Eternity

Parties are a lot of fun. There are many parties on earth, but they only last a little while. Believers in Christ enjoy a party that will never end. He calls it "the Marriage Supper of the Lamb" (Revelation 19:9) because He is celebrating having in His family all those who trust Him for their salvation. He has invited you!

REMEMBER

Behold, I stand at the door and knock. If anyone hears My voice and opens the door, I will come in to him and eat with him, and he with Me. **(Revelation 3:20)**

The Parable of the Great Banquet

(Luke 14:12–24)

The Banquet

Maybe you have been with a lot of people talking and visiting and having fun when all of a sudden someone says something worth remembering, something wise and worth thinking about, such as

Hunger never saw bad bread. Benjamin Franklin
"I am the bread of life." Jesus (John 6:48)
When the pupil is ready, the teacher will come. Chinese proverb

A wise statement occurred between the two parables Jesus taught when He was having dinner with the ruler of the synagogue. Write the man's words from Luke 14:15 on the line below.

_____

Eating in the Kingdom

When do we "eat bread in the kingdom of God?" In other words, when does God feed us? Write any ideas you have about this question here.

_____

_____

Now munch on these Bible verses and a reading. Then add some more ideas about when God feeds us: John 20:31; 2 Timothy 3:15; and Romans 10:17.

_____

_____

_____

REVIEW

Directions: Use all three of these review words in one sentence that summarizes the main idea in this lesson: **blessing**, **bread**, **Scriptures**.

_____

_____

Feasting in the Kingdom

If we want a quick bite to eat, we might head for a fast food restaurant. If we want a little variety in our meal, we might head for a family restaurant. If we're celebrating a special occasion, we'd probably head for a fine restaurant.

God has a really fine meal for His people. It's called the Lord's Supper. In this meal He serves His finest blessings. Look at these Bible passages: Matthew 26:28 and 1 Corinthians 11:23–26. Then list the blessings God gives to those receiving this meal.

_____

_____

Do You Agree?

The man at the banquet said that everyone who will eat bread in God's kingdom would be blessed (Luke 14:15). Do you agree? See John 6:48–51. Are you blessed by your eating at the Lord's banquet? Explain your ideas below.

_____

_____

_____

REMEMBER

Blessed is everyone who will eat bread in the kingdom of God! **(Luke 14:15b)**

179

Jesus Clears the Temple

(Luke 19:45–48)

Why Jesus Was Angry

On the lines below, describe what Jesus thought would be the proper use of the temple.

prayer, teaching.

_____

_____

Did Jesus have a right to be angry in the temple? Explain your thinking.

_____

_____

_____

REVIEW

Give the meaning for each of the following words:

temple:_____

anger:_____

worship:_____

Worshiping Rightly

[handwritten: togo to church]

1. What is the difference between attending and participating in worship?

[handwritten: God actually worshiping]

_____

_____

_____

2. To meditate on God's Word means that I think about how a part of God's Word applies to me. After you read Joshua 1:8, write your own meditation response and prayer based on this verse of Scripture.

_____

_____

_____

3. Read Colossians 3:16. Then write your own meditation response and prayer based on this text.

_____

_____

_____

_____

4. What are some things I can do to worship rightly?

[handwritten:]
- listen what the pastar says
- pray to God
- siny Gods song
- read the bible.

_____

My Worship Prayer

As I pray, dear Jesus, hear me;
Let Your words in me take root.
May Your Spirit e'er be near me
That I bear abundant fruit.
May I daily sing Your praise,

From my heart glad anthems raise,
Till my highest praise is given
In the endless joy of heaven.
　　Anna Sophia von Hessen-Darmstadt
　　(*LSB* 589:4)

REMEMBER

But He said, "Blessed rather are those who hear the word of God and keep it!"
(Luke 11:28)

Jesus Clears the Temple

(Luke 19:45–48)

Jesus Teaches about Prayer

Jesus became so frustrated with what was happening in the temple that He turned tables over and chased money-changers out! He said, "My house shall be a house of prayer" (Luke 19:46). What did Jesus teach about prayer? Read each of the following Bible passages and briefly summarize what Jesus taught.

Matthew 5:44

_____

_____

_____

Luke 18:1

to al always
pray and
not to
lose heart

Matthew 21:22

_____

_____

_____

Luke 11:13

_____

_____

_____

A Right Attitude toward Worship and the Things of God

Jesus cleansed the temple of the improper activities taking place there. Draw a line through each of the following activities that take focus away from the worship of God. Circle those that show a right attitude toward worship and the things of God.

Merchants were turning God's house into a marketplace with their buying and selling.

People were not participating in worship.

People were hanging on Jesus' words.

REVIEW

Write a definition for each word.

prayer:_____

petition:_____

collect:_____

Let's Talk about It

God's people value worship and the house of worship because of God's salvation and the Savior they gather there to worship. But the devil continues to use every opportunity to turn people's attention away from God and the proper worship of Him. Consider each of the following examples. Tell how each could either help or detract from our worship of God.

1. Amy can't wait to go to church every Sunday to see her friends.
2. Mac marks in his Bible during church.
3. Jamal takes money with him to church.

For Grace to Receive God's Word

For centuries people in the Church have used a special form for prayer called the *Collect*. Look at the collect below and the parts of it that are labeled. Match the parts of the prayer on the left with their lables on the right. Then write a short collect using this form.

Blessed Lord, ○	○ Reason (why we are praying to God)
You have caused all Holy Scriptures to be written for our learning. ○	○ Amen. (It shall be as God thinks right.)
Grant that we may so hear them, read, mark, learn, and inwardly digest them that, ○	○ Conclusion (shows we depend on God's promises)
by patience and comfort of Your holy Word, we may embrace and ever hold fast the blessed hope of everlasting life; ○	○ Result (the desired outcome of the petition)
through Jesus Christ, our Lord. ○	○ The Address (a name for God or a person of the Trinity)
Amen. ○	○ Petition (the request; what we want God to do)

(*LSB* p. 308)

My Collect: _____

_____

_____

_____

_____

_____

REMEMBER

Let the words of my mouth and the meditation of my heart be acceptable in Your sight, O LORD, my rock and my redeemer. **(Psalm 19:14)**

The Lord's Supper

(Luke 22:7–23)

A Gift Like No Other

With your classmates, read Luke 22:7–23. These events all happened on Thursday of Holy Week, which we call Maundy Thursday. As you read these verses, pay special attention to the gift that God gave us on Maundy Thursday evening. At this time, Jesus first gave the gift of the Lord's Supper. In this account He also called it the New Covenant. Look at the picture below. What do people receive when they go to the Lord's Supper?

REVIEW

Passover:_____

_____

sacrifice:_____

_____

covenant:_____

_____

God's Special Gift

What makes any gift special?

_____

_____

_____

What is the greatest gift you have ever received?

_____

What is the greatest gift you have ever given?

_____

What makes the Lord's Supper such a great gift? Before you answer, read the section of *Luther's Small Catechism with Explanation*, "The Benefit of the Sacrament of the Altar," beginning on page 237. Then write your answer on the lines below.

_____

_____

_____

_____

_____

_____

Thanks for the Gift

First say, then sing this hymn as a prayer of thanks for the gifts God gives to us in the Lord's Supper.

O living Bread from heaven,
How well You feed Your guest!
The gifts that You have given
Have filled my heart with rest.
Oh, wondrous food of blessing,
Oh, cup that heals our woes!
My heart, this gift possessing,
With praises overflows.
(*LSB* 642:1)

REMEMBER

This is My _**blood**_ of the covenant, which is _**poured**_ out for many for the forgiveness of _**sins**_. (Matthew 26:28)

LESSON 90

The Lord's Supper

(Luke 22:7–38)

Helps for Remembering

In each box below is a picture of something people do to help remember things. Tell how what is pictured helps a person remember.

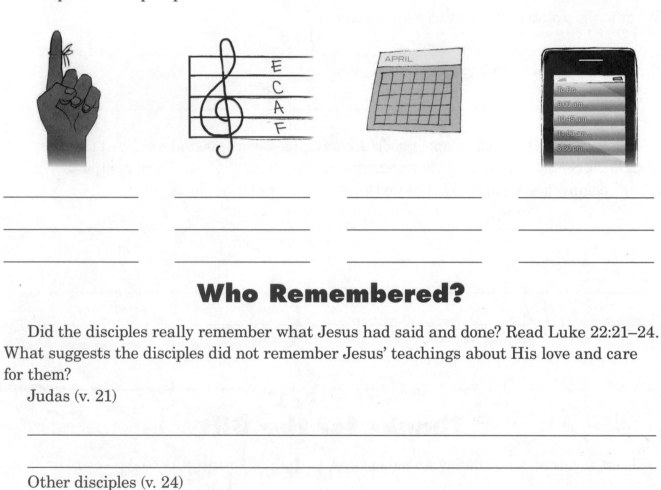

_____   _____   _____   _____

_____   _____   _____   _____

_____   _____   _____   _____

Who Remembered?

Did the disciples really remember what Jesus had said and done? Read Luke 22:21–24. What suggests the disciples did not remember Jesus' teachings about His love and care for them?

Judas (v. 21)

_____

_____

Other disciples (v. 24)

_____

_____

REVIEW

Match the following words to the correct definition:

_____1. recline   a. to work against someone who trusts you

_____2. remembrance   b. to lie back or down

_____3. betray   c. the act or process of recalling information

Remembering Jesus

When people go to the Lord's Table to receive the bread and the wine, they also receive Christ's true body and blood in a mysterious way. When Jesus gave this meal to His disciples, He asked that His followers for all time to eat and drink this special meal in remembrance of Him. "For as often as you eat this bread and drink the cup, you proclaim the Lord's death until He comes" (1 Corinthians 11:26).

What does it mean to remember Jesus? We remember Jesus when in faith we believe that Jesus' death takes away our sin. When we remember Jesus, we examine ourselves to see if we plan, with the help of the Holy Spirit, to change our sinful life. It does not mean we look to see if we have lived a good enough life to receive the Sacrament.

Questions to Help Me Remember Jesus

1. Am I sorry for my sins?

_____

2. Do I believe Jesus is my Savior and that in the
   Sacrament I receive forgiveness for my sin?

_____

3. With the help of the Holy Spirit, do I plan
   to amend my sinful life?

_____

You can read more about these questions in *Luther's Small Catechism with Explanation*, Question 303.

REMEMBER

Blessed are those whose lawless deeds are forgiven, and whose sins are covered. **(Romans 4:7)**

Jesus in Gethsemane

(Luke 22:39–46)

Jesus' Plans

Throughout His earthly ministry, Jesus was dedicated to carrying out God's plan to save us. On the planning pages below, write things that Jesus did to carry out that plan.

GOALS
To show that He was true God:
To show God's forgiveness:
To show God's love and care:

God's will for Jesus also meant that He had to rescue us from having to suffer punishment for our sins. Jesus knew the suffering and agony He would face in our place on the cross. Jesus prepared for what was to come by taking time to pray to His Father in an olive garden called Gethsemane.

God's Will

God's will is "that His Word be taught correctly and that sinners be brought to faith in Christ and lead godly lives" (*Luther's Small Catechism with Explanation*, Question 215).

When Jesus prayed in the garden, for what did He ask His Father (Luke 22:42)?

Remove this cup.

With what words does Jesus end His prayer (Luke 22:42)?

"not my will but Yours, be done"

What was God's will for Jesus?

God's will was that Jesus would suffer and die in our place for our sins.

REVIEW

agony:

temptation:

God's Will for Me

What is God's will for your life? Read each of the Bible passages below. Then, in each circle, summarize His will for you.

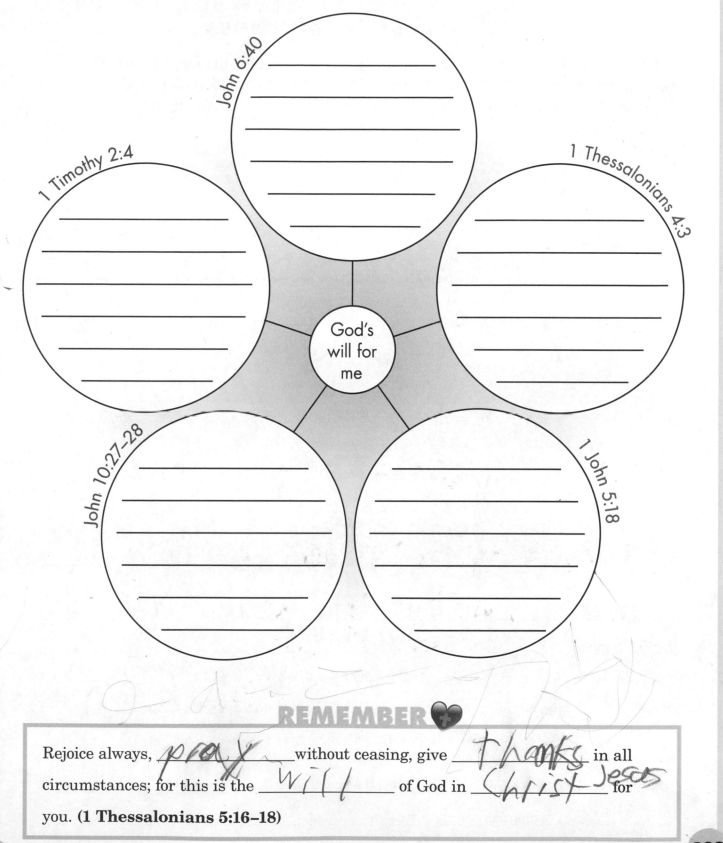

REMEMBER

Rejoice always, _pray_ without ceasing, give _thanks_ in all circumstances; for this is the _will_ of God in _Christ Jesus_ for you. **(1 Thessalonians 5:16–18)**

Jesus in Gethsemane (Jesus Taken, Peter Tested)

(Luke 22:47–62)

All about Forgiveness

The day before Jesus' death had begun. Soon Jesus would surrender Himself to be taken before the council. He was determined to earn God's forgiveness for us.

Briefly describe Jesus' activities on Maundy Thursday on the timeline below.

Jesus prepares Passover — Luke 22:8–13

Jesus eats next meal — Luke 22:14–20

Jesus predicts betrayal — Luke 22:21–23

Jesus predicts Peter denial — Luke 22:31–34

Jesus prays to disciples sleep — Luke 22:39–46

Judas betrays Jesus — Luke 22:47–48

disciples take Jesus as a servants ear — Luke 22:49–53

Jesus heals — Luke 22:54

Jesus taken to high priest house — Luke 22:55–62

Peter denies Jesus 3 times

Daytime   **Sundown**   **Evening**   **Late night**

REVIEW

Circle the number of the correct definition for each word below.

forgiveness: 1. the removal of our sins by God because of Jesus' sacrifice for us

  2. the removal of our sins by God because of our good works

grace: 1. receiving God's riches because we keep God's Law on our own

  2. receiving God's riches because of what Jesus has done for us as our Savior

Repentance and Forgiveness

Directions: Under each box, write a caption that summarizes the Scripture and describes the scene.

Luke 22:54–62

1 John 1:8–9

John 21:15–17

_____

_____

_____

_____

_____

_____

_____

_____

_____

_____

_____

_____

_____

_____

_____

REMEMBER

And with His _____striped_____ we are _____healed_____ (Isaiah 53:5)

Jesus Dies to Save Us

(Luke 23:26–49)

Jesus' Acts

The Second Article of the Apostles' Creed tells the story of what Jesus has done for us as our Savior. Recite the Second Article. Then write the ten verbs from the article that describe the saving works Jesus performed or allowed.

[He] was _concived_ by the Holy Spirit, _born_ of the Virgin Mary, _sufferd_ under Pontius Pilate, was _cracied_, _died_ and was _burved_. He _deciend_ into hell. The third day He _rose_ again from the dead. He _acended_ into heaven. . . . From thence He will come to _Judge_ the living and the dead.

Salvation Timeline: Good Friday

| Luke 23:8–9 | Luke 23:25 | Luke 23:26 | Luke 23:33 | Luke 23:34 | Luke 23:36 | Luke 23:43 | Luke 23:44 | Luke 23:45 | Luke 23:46 |

| 6:00 a.m.–9:00 a.m. | 9:00 a.m.–Noon | 3:00 p.m. |

REVIEW

crucifixion:_____

salvation:_____

The Greatest Pardon

Heads of states and nations have the ability to grant *pardons* to individuals who have been convicted of crimes. A *pardon* frees someone from a punishment or penalty. Another word for *pardon* is "forgiveness." A person who is pardoned doesn't get the punishment he deserves.

Our salvation is given us by the greatest pardon ever. Carefully examine the four cases described below. Study the Bible passages associated with each one. Based on the Bible evidence, write the crime and punishment deserved for each case.

Cases to Consider	Crimes Committed	Deserved Punishment
Case 1: Adam	Genesis 3:3–6	Genesis 3:17–19, 22–23
Case 2: Criminal #2 on the cross	Luke 23:41a	Luke 23:39–41a
Case 3: Jesus	2 Corinthians 5:21	Luke 23:41b
Case 4: You	Romans 3:23 and 5:12	Romans 6:23a

. . . but the free gift of God is eternal life in Christ Jesus our Lord (Romans 6:23b).

REMEMBER ❤

The three underlined words in the Bible verse below are not where they belong. Place them in the correct place by crossing out each word and writing it in the correct place.

For the word of the ~~saved~~ *cross* is folly to those who are perishing, but to us who are being ~~power~~ *saved* it is the ~~cross~~ *power* of God. (**1 Corinthians 1:18**)

Jesus Is Buried

(Luke 23:50–56)

On Good Friday, Jesus was buried quickly. His close friends planned to give Him a better burial after Passover. Use the chart below to compare the burial practices of today with those of Jesus' friends.

Burial Today

- The body is sent to a funeral home.
- The body is cleaned and prepared for burial.
- The body is dressed in clothing selected by the family and placed in a casket.
- Generally after the funeral service, the casket is taken to the cemetery to be buried in a plot selected by the family.
- The pastor usually will conduct a graveside service. The grave is then filled with dirt.
- Grass is planted on the area, and a gravestone or a grave marker is placed at the head of the grave for identification.

Jesus' Burial

- Who prepared Jesus' body for burial (Luke 23:50 and John 19:38–39)?

  Joeshph or Arimathea Nicademos

- How was Jesus' body prepared (John 19:39–40)?

  used 75 pounds of myrah, aloes, and spices

- How was Jesus' body dressed for burial (Luke 23:53; John 19:40; and Luke 23:34)?

  bound in linen clouths (shourd)

- Where was Jesus' body buried (Luke 23:53; John 19:41; and Mark 15:46)?

  in a tomb in a garden (cut out of rock)

- Why did Jesus' body have to be buried so quickly (Luke 23:54 and Exodus 35:2)?

  burriing the body could not be done on the sabbath

REVIEW

Use the glossary to find the definition for these words. Write the definition on the line.

redemption:_____

redeemer: _____

Redeemed

Deshawn loved to build radio-controlled airplanes with his dad. On Saturday, they went out to a field near their house to fly their latest creation. Up, up, up in the air it went. Deshawn used the plane's controller to make the craft loop around and around the field.

Suddenly, a strong gust of wind picked up the small airplane and carried it over the trees at the edge of the field and out of sight. Deshawn and his dad ran after the plane. After searching for hours, the plane was nowhere to be found.

Several days later, Deshawn and his dad were walking in front of the hobby store on their town's main street. In the store window sat a model plane that looked exactly like the one they had lost. Once inside, Deshawn and his dad carefully examined the

plane. It was the plane they had built! Deshawn told the store manager that the plane in the window was the one he and his dad had made.

The store manager told them someone who lived about five miles outside of town had found the plane in his front yard and had brought it in that morning. If they wanted the plane, they would have to buy it for $50.00 like anyone else. Deshawn's dad opened his wallet and handed the manager the money to make the purchase. As Deshawn and his dad walked out of the store, Deshawn held up the airplane and said, "Dad, this plane is really special because it's twice ours. First we made it and now we bought it back."

Look back at the meaning of the word *redemption*. How is this story an example that explains the meaning of this word? How does this story mirror what Jesus has done for you through His suffering and death?

One of the names the Bible uses for Jesus is *Redeemer*. Jesus redeemed us with "His holy, precious blood and with His innocent suffering and death" (*Luther's Small Catechism*, p. 119). Why did Jesus redeem us? Before you answer, read Ephesians 1:7.

REMEMBER

> Christ redeemed us from the curse of the law by becoming a curse for us—for it is written, "Cursed is everyone who is hanged on a tree." **(Galatians 3:13)**

Jesus Rises from the Dead

(Matthew 28:1–10)

Powerful Truth

After reading Matthew 28:1–10, carefully examine these statements and compare them to the Scripture. Put a + by each true statement. If a statement is false, rewrite it so that it is true.

F 1. On the first day of the week, Mary Magdalene, the other Mary, ~~and Jesus' eleven disciples~~ went to see Jesus' tomb.

T 2. An angel of the Lord had rolled the stone away from the entrance of Jesus' tomb.

F 3. The angel ~~killed~~ *shoked* the guards who were there at Jesus' tomb.

T 4. The angel invited the women inside the tomb to see the place where Jesus' body had been.

F 5. The women ~~stayed at the tomb for a while before they~~ *quickly left* to share the news.

T 6. On their way to the disciples, the women saw Jesus and worshiped Him.

F 7. Jesus would meet His disciples in ~~Samaria~~ *Galiee*.

REVIEW

Circle the letter of the best definition for each word below.

1. resurrection: a. the rising of one from the dead
   b. rising into heaven
   c. the act of waking up after sleeping

2. omnipotent: a. all-knowing
   b. present everywhere
   c. almighty and all-powerful

Powerful Hope

Believing that Jesus died to save us from our sins and that He rose again (was *resurrected*) from the dead, is what saves us. If Jesus did not come alive again after He died, our faith in Him would be meaningless. Jesus' resurrection proves that He is the true, omnipotent God. It is powerful evidence that Jesus has conquering power over all things, including sin, death, and Satan.

When is it especially important and comforting to know that Jesus is omnipotent? Name several of these times below.

The butterfly is a symbol of Jesus' resurrection. Inside a dead-looking cocoon, a caterpillar transforms into a butterfly and breaks free as a new creature. Jesus, once dead, burst out of the tomb on that first Easter day, and now is alive forever.

Carefully examine the drawing of the butterfly below. Within it, find and circle these five symbols that show Jesus' power: Chi-Rho, an anchor cross, a burning candle, three nails, and a rock in front of an empty tomb. Then look up the Scripture references below in your Bible. Write the name of the symbol on the line next to the Bible verse that describes it.

John 17:3

_____

John 8:12

_____

Hebrews 6:19

_____

John 20:25

_____

1 Corinthians 10:4

_____

_____

Through God's Word and through the Sacraments, the Holy Spirit works in us to strengthen our faith in Jesus and His power. The Holy Spirit gives us the power and courage to share the Good News of Jesus with others. How might you use the butterfly drawing to share the message of salvation through Jesus with someone who does not yet know Him?

REMEMBER 💙

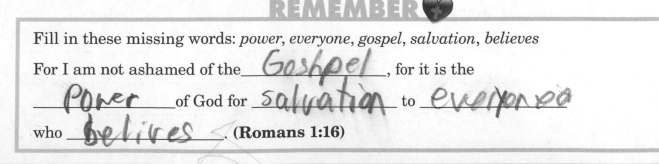

Fill in these missing words: *power, everyone, gospel, salvation, believes*

For I am not ashamed of the ___Goshpel___, for it is the

___Power___ of God for ___salvation___ to ___everyone___

who ___belives___. **(Romans 1:16)**

Jesus Appears to Mary

(John 20:11–18)

What Does Jesus' Death and Resurrection Mean to You?

Directions: Answer this question in seventy-five words or fewer.

I was sad the disiple's any the wrong ordre was be trayd by Judas

Mary's Journal

Read about Mary's encounter with Jesus at the empty tomb in John 20:11–18. If Mary kept a journal, what might she have written about her early morning surprise?

I was sad because someone took Jesus away but he appeared in front of me and told me to go tell his diciples that He is risen.

REVIEW

Use the glossary to find the definitions of the following words. Then write the definitions.

conquer:_____

victory: _____

Why are you also a victorious conqueror over sin, death, and Satan? _____

_____

V-I-C-T-O-R-Y

Leader: Jesus is risen from the dead and lives forever!

Students: V-I-C-T-O-R-Y! Our Lord Jesus is alive!

Leader: "Who shall separate us from the love of Christ? Shall tribulation, or distress, or persecution, or famine, or nakedness, or danger, or sword? . . . No, in all these things <u>we are more than conquerors through Him</u> who loved us" (Romans 8:35, 37).

Students: V-I-C-T-O-R-Y! Christ is with us, by our side!

Leader: "For if we have been united with Him in a death like His, we shall certainly be united <u>with Him</u> in a resurrection like His. We know that our old self was crucified <u>with Him</u> in order that the body of sin might be brought to nothing, so that we would no longer be enslaved to sin. Now if we have died <u>with Christ</u>, we believe that we will also live <u>with Him</u>" (Romans 6:5–6, 8).

Students: V-I-C-T-O-R-Y! Satan's plans have been denied!

Leader: "Jesus said to her, 'I am the resurrection and the life. <u>Whoever believes in Me</u>, though he die, yet shall he live, and <u>everyone who lives and believes in Me</u> shall never die'" (John 11:25–26).

Students: V-I-C-T-O-R-Y! With faith in Christ we will not die!

Leader: "Therefore, <u>if anyone is in Christ</u>, he is a new creation. The old has passed away; behold, the new has come" (2 Corinthians 5:17).

Students: V-I-C-T-O-R-Y! New life is God's greatest prize!

REMEMBER

> If Christ has not been raised, your faith is futile and you are still in your sins.
> **(1 Corinthians 15:17)**

The Ascension

(Acts 1:1–11)

Cheers and Tears!

Excitement swirled around them as the crowds roared their congratulations for the amazing tournament victory! Being first in the state was truly outstanding, but deep down the players were crying. Tears of sadness welled up as they realized their beloved coach was leaving. They had depended on him to guide them and lead them, and now he was moving away. They worried that they would never see him again. The disciples had a similar experience shortly after Jesus' great Easter victory. Read Acts 1:1–11 to find out the details.

Where? (Acts 1:12)

When? (Acts 1:3)

What happened? (Acts 1:9)

Mountaintop Moments

Fill in your reporter's notebook to the right to describe this momentous event.

Me at the Mountain

Imagine yourself on the mountaintop beside your newly risen Savior, Jesus. Tell (or dramatize) what you would see and what you would hear.

_____

How would you feel?

_____

REVIEW

Draw a line from each word in the first column to the word in the second column to which it most closely relates. Then explain your choices to a friend.

prophet	sacrifice
priest	king
ruler	foretell
judge	Last Day

You Will Be My Witnesses

Jesus did not leave His disciples alone. He gave them a Helper and He gave them a task. He said, "But you, _____, will receive power when the Holy Spirit has come upon you, and you will be [one of] My witnesses in Jerusalem and in all Judea and Samaria, and to the end of the earth" (Acts 1:8).

Insert your name in the blank above. Jesus chose you to receive His salvation and to share the Good News with others!

God's Spirit helps you to tell others about Jesus and His free gift of salvation. How can you witness to people who live in your "Jerusalem"—your neighborhood or community?

_____

_____

in your "Judea"—your region or state?

_____

_____

in your "Samaria"—your country or area beyond your region or state?

_____

_____

somewhere at the end of the earth—in a far country?

_____

_____

IDEA: Put names of missionaries or other people you are praying for on a globe or world map as a reminder.

REMEMBER

God chose to make known how great among the Gentiles are the riches of the glory of this mystery, which is Christ in you, the hope of glory. **(Colossians 1:27)**

The Ascension

(Acts 1:1–11)

Your Own Special Place!

A popular television show called *Extreme Makeover* featured people who were burdened with many problems. Then a home was prepared just for them, designed to meet their needs and give them happiness. Read John 14:1–19 to discover God's loving plans to prepare an eternal home for you.

Loaded with Promises

Jesus knew His ministry on earth would be short. With loving promises, Jesus prepared His friends for life after His ascension. Highlight or underline four or more of Jesus' promises in this Bible reading that seem important to you. Chat about your choices with a friend. Together decide which promise of Jesus could comfort these questioners.

Can I be sure I will rise from the dead? (John 14:19)

because I live you also u live

Will Jesus answer my prayers? (John 14:14)

What will heaven be like? (John 14:2)

Many rooms

Will Jesus come again? (John 14:3)

yes

REVIEW

Match these words to the corresponding parts of Jesus' life.

incarnation	returned to heaven
crucifixion	rose from the dead
resurrection	died on the cross
ascension	sits at God's right hand
exaltation	birth

Picturing Heaven!

Many years after Jesus ascended into heaven, God gave the apostle John a picture of what heaven would be like. John recorded this *vision*, or picture, in the last book of the Bible, the Book of Revelation. Look up selected verses from Revelation and supply the words missing from the following portions of God's Word that tell us about heaven.

"Behold the dwelling place of God is with man. He will dwell with them, and they will be His people, and God Himself will be with them as their God. He will wipe away every tear from their eyes, and _____ shall be no more, neither shall there be _____, nor _____, nor _____ anymore, for the former things have passed away" (Revelation 21:3–4).

"No longer will there be anything _____, but the throne of God and of the Lamb will be in it, and His servants will worship Him. They will see His face, and His name will be on their foreheads. And _____ will be no more. They will need no light of lamp or sun, for the Lord God will be their light, and they will reign forever and ever" (Revelation 22:3–5).

REMEMBER

And if I go and prepare a place for you, I will come again and will take you to Myself, that where I am you may be also. **(John 14:3)**

Pentecost

(Acts 2:1–21)

Are You Plugged In?

 Many others before Thomas Edison invented versions of the light bulb. But Edison invented a better incandescent light bulb in 1879 and also a direct-current electrical distribution system, now commonly known as electricity.

Today, we're reading about Jesus' followers—His disciples and others. They had spent nearly three years following Jesus, hearing Him preach and teach and watching Him heal others. But they couldn't tell anyone about their Savior. They were not _____ _____ to power!

Jesus told them to wait for power. What kind of power (Acts 1:8)? The _____ _____ . They were like incandescent light bulbs without electricity.

What about you? Are you plugged in? How do you keep your Holy Spirit power "juiced up"? Through _____ _____.

The disciples and other followers of Jesus—including His mother, Mary—were huddled behind closed doors in the city of Jerusalem, praying and waiting for the "power from on high" (Luke 24:49) that had been promised. Have you ever had to wait for an answer to prayer? Imagine waiting two, six, even ten days!

Then . . . POW! Imagine a freight train coming straight through your house! That's what the mighty wind surely sounded like—God rushing through the house as wind. How cool is that?

REVIEW

Circle the correct answer(s) (in bold) for each sentence.

1. Jerusalem is the capital of (choose one) **Israel, Palestine, Poland**. It was conquered for the Jewish people by **Moses, David, Peter**. Jesus visited Jerusalem **often, never, only as a child**.
2. The Holy Spirit is the **First, Second, Third** Person of the Trinity. The Holy Spirit was present at **creation, Jesus' Baptism, Pentecost**, . The Holy Spirit gives us **singing talent, good thoughts, faith-filled power**.
3. Pentecost means **fifty cents, fifty days, fifty weeks**. Pentecost comes **after, before, during** Easter.

Empowered to Share God's Word

The disciples and other followers of Christ on Pentecost were given the power to speak in the languages of the people in Jerusalem—Jewish people who had come from many places in the world.

1. Look at the numbers to the left of the globe. How many languages do you think are spoken in the world today? Circle one.

2. How many has the Bible been translated into? Circle the answer on the right.

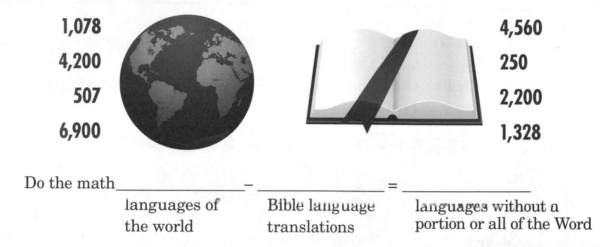

1,078		4,560
4,200		250
507		2,200
6,900		1,328

Do the math _____ – _____ = _____

languages of the world   Bible language translations   languages without a portion or all of the Word

By the way, the number of people speaking languages into which the Bible has not been translated? The Lutheran Bible Translators organization estimates it is about 350 million people!

Remember Christ's missionary command to the disciples (and us)? It's called the *Great Commission* (Matthew 28:19). How important is it to take the Gospel to people through God's Word in their own language? **Sort of, somewhat, very**

Missionaries today use every means possible to bring the Good News to others, including those who are poor, who live in remote areas, or who don't understand Christianity and can't get to a church.

What types of people can share the Good News with others? (Acts 2:18–19)

_____

My personal Gospel message:

_____

_____

_____

_____

REMEMBER 💙

No one can say "Jesus is Lord" except in the Holy Spirit. **(1 Corinthians 12:3)**

Pentecost

(Acts 2:22–47)

Together around God's Word

In some Christian churches in Africa, such as Grace Lutheran in Mbarara, Uganda, the joy of being together in the Lord is so awesome and joyous that a Sunday worship service that can last for hours.

Is that how Sunday is for you? Or is Sunday church just another duty to "get through" like homework, piano practice, and walking the dog? Glad hearts. Awe and wonder. Praise and joy. That's how the first Christians describe church. In Acts 2, we read first about the coming of the Holy Spirit at Pentecost.

Together as God's People

"Repent! The end is near!"

There's probably nobody like the man on the left carrying a similar sign in your neighborhood, but the message is real. Sin. It's a problem for every one of us all the time.

Sin. We all have the same problem. We all have the same solution: repent. In our worship service, we repent. We ask forgiveness both for sins we committed and those other sins—what we should have done but didn't. Take a few minutes and write your confession.

Rejoice! We are forgiven. Jesus died for our sin, so that we might live with Him forever. Write a note, thanking God for saving your life.

FORGIVEN

REVIEW

Circle the correct answer.

repent: feel really bad, apologize, turn away from sin

Church: fellowship of believers, a building where people gather, group of people who do not sin

David: psalm writer, king of Israel, ancestor of Jesus

Keep on Plugging!

Acts records that at Pentecost, Peter preached a powerful sermon. God worked in the hearts of the listeners, and three thousand people were baptized and added to the number of believers. After coming to faith, the early Christians organized into groups of believers, forming congregations, or churches. Acts 2:42 says, "And they devoted themselves to the apostles' teaching and the fellowship, to the breaking of bread and the prayers." Read the sentences below, then read Acts 2:42 again. For each sentence below, choose one of the four activities of the early Christians that most closely matches the sentence. Write it on the blank next to that sentence.

_____ 1. The confirmation class members of St. Stephen's Church listened intently to the pastor's sermon, taking notes.

P_____ 2. After the sermon, the pastor asked God to heal those in the congregation who were sick, including Becky's grandmother, who was in the hospital.

b_____ 3. Kneeling before the altar, men and women received Jesus' body and blood in the Sacrament of Holy Communion.

_____ 4. At Holy Cross's congregational annual picnic, people of all ages had fun and played games.

_____ 5. Fifteen people attended the Sunday School teachers' banquet.

REMEMBER 💙

The Spirit of the LORD speaks by me; His word is on my tongue. **(2 Samuel 23:2)**

Peter and John Heal the Lame Man

(Acts 3:1–16)

More Precious than Gold and Silver

Narrator: It is 3:00 p.m.—prayer time at the great temple of Jerusalem. You see the men and women of the community coming to the temple of Herod to pray. This is also the time of day they offer sacrifices. The ones coming now are poor and have only grain offerings. After they place their gifts on the altar, they will separate, as men and women do not sit together in the temple. The poor and handicapped who must beg for charity will soon show up at the gates of the temple. Today, a crippled beggar is about to have a life-changing experience. And so the story begins.
(Enter two students supporting their crippled friend as he walks, helping him position himself on the floor at the Beautiful Gate, the door of the temple. They hand him his bowl for collecting alms. They exit. Enter four students, two boys and two girls, walking quietly into the temple with sheaves of wheat [spaghetti noodles] in their hands. Their heads are lowered.)

Crippled Beggar: Alms for the poor. Have mercy on this poor cripple! *(The crippled beggar holds up his alms bowl. As the four students pass the him, each one tosses one to two coins in his alms bowl.)* God will reward you and bless you for your kindness!
(The boys go to one side of a table, the girls the other. They put their harvest offerings on the table, bow, then walk to opposite spots of the table to pray. They can either kneel on cushions or sit. Quietly, they bow their heads in prayer.)

Jewish Worshipers: *(Quietly pray Psalm 121)* "I lift up my eyes to the hills. From where does my help come? My help comes from the LORD, who made heaven and earth. He will not let your foot be moved; He who keeps you will not slumber. Behold, He who keeps Israel will neither slumber nor sleep. The LORD is your keeper; the LORD is your shade on your right hand. The sun shall not strike you by day, nor the moon by night. The LORD will keep you from all evil; He will keep your life. The LORD will keep your going out and your coming in from this time forth and forevermore" (Psalm 121:1–8).
(John and Peter walk to the gate.)

Crippled Beggar: Help me, you men of Galilee, be kind. *(He looks up at Peter and John*

REVIEW

Place a check mark before each correct group of words below.

Nazareth:
_____Name of the crippled man Jesus healed
_____Town where Peter was born
_____Jewish holiday
_____Town where Jesus grew up

alms:
_____Almond-flavored cakes given to the poor
_____Medicine used for the crippled
_____Money given to the poor
_____Gate where the crippled man begged

ransom:
_____Money given to the poor
_____Price paid to redeem someone
_____A town in Judah
_____Dice used to cast lots

imploringly, holding out his alms bowl.) Have pity on me, a poor cripple.

Peter and John: *(Looking directly at beggar)* Look at us!

Crippled Beggar: I am looking! What do you have for me, a poor beggar? A cripple since birth! *(Again, he holds out his alms bowl.)*

Peter: I have no silver or gold. But what I do have, I give to you. *(Louder and with authority)* In the name of Jesus Christ of Nazareth, rise up and walk! *(Peter takes the beggar by his right hand and raises him up.)*

Narrator: Look, Peter speaks the name above all names—Jesus—and the beggar is completely healed! His feet and ankles are strong. He's full of joy and well; he's loud, praising God, leaping. Soon he has everyone's attention! *(The crippled beggar leaps and walks, following Peter and John into the temple.)*

Crippled Beggar: Hallelujah! God be praised. God of Abraham, Isaac, and Jacob be praised! Jesus of Nazareth be praised! Lord and King. Hallelujah! I'm healed! *(The praying Jews look up and run to the three men as they enter the temple.)*

Praying Jewish Girl 1: I know this man—he's the cripple who sat at the Beautiful Gate, begging.

Praying Jewish Girl 2: You're right. I've seen him there for years. I just gave him some alms this morning!

Praying Jewish Boy 1: My parents told me he was born crippled. How can he be walking?

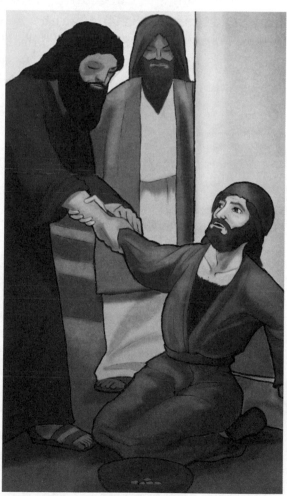

Praying Jewish Boy 2: It looks like his feet and ankles are as strong as mine! I believe those Galileans over there *(points to Peter and John)* healed him.

Praying Jewish Girl 1: Amazing!

Narrator: Peter told the astonished crowd that it was not their own "power or piety" that healed the man, but the God of Abraham, Isaac, and Jacob. He reminded them of Jesus' crucifixion and resurrection, telling them Jesus is the Messiah promised by the prophets. Jesus is the author of life.

Peter: *(Turning to face the crowd)* "And His name— by faith in His name—has made this man strong whom you see and know, and the faith that is through Jesus has given the man this perfect health in the presence of you all" (Acts 3:16).

REMEMBER 💙

You were ransomed . . . not with perishable things such as silver or gold, but with the precious blood of Christ. **(1 Peter 1:18–19)**

Peter and John Heal the Lame Man

(Acts 3:1–16)

Healing in the Name of Jesus

"In the Name of Jesus Christ of Nazareth, rise up and walk!" (Acts 3:6).

Peter healed the crippled beggar with great power: Jesus' power! That same power, the awesome life-giving power of Jesus Christ, Lord and Messiah, is ours every day. His power erases our sins and gives us life everlasting.

Consider the following statements as you review the events of the healing of the lame man. If a statement is true, write *true* in the blank before it. If a statement is false, write *false* in the blank before it. Then correct the false statement to make it true.

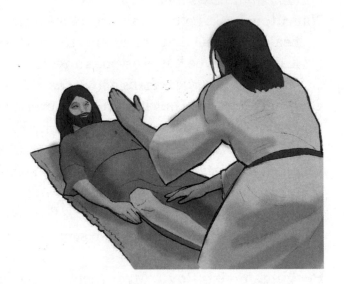

_____1. Peter and John went to the temple at the hour of prayer, the ninth hour (Acts 3:1).

_____2. A lame man, who had been lame since an accident, came to the temple gate to ask alms of those entering the temple (v. 2).

_____3. Peter said, "In the name of Jesus Christ of Nazareth, rise up and walk!" (v. 6).

_____4. The man's feet and ankles became strong and he leaped to his feet (v. 7).

_____5. The healed man ran home, walking and leaping and praising God (v. 8).

REVIEW

Words: Jerusalem, temple, Jesus Christ of Nazareth, Christ, Messiah

1. Peter and John worshiped and prayed in the _____ . It was located in the city of _____ where it had been built by King Herod.

2. The crippled man in Acts 2 could walk again through the name_____ _____ _____ _____.

3. The name _____ means Anointed One. Jesus is the promised _____ .

Jesus, the Great Physician

The Gospels tell us how, during the years leading up to His death on the cross, Jesus healed people who were sick, deaf, blind, or who suffered from conditions involving muscles and bones. A simple touch or word from Jesus brought complete physical healing. But Jesus provided a greater gift of healing for all people when He died on the cross. All people need this kind of healing because all people suffer from the sickness of sin.

All healing that happens is God's gift. And for a world made sick by sin, we know there is only one who can work healing for our sinful condition; His name is Jesus. The healing Jesus provides for spiritual and physical sicknesses did not stop when Jesus left the earth to go to heaven. Just as Jesus brought healing to the lame man through Peter and John, Jesus brings it to people today through the work of others.

Today, the healing power of Jesus is still at work in the world. First through the sharing of the Good News by Christians and missionaries around the world and also through the medical knowledge, skills, and medicines God has given in our day. On the prescription pads below, write the ways you have received God's gift of healing, either from physical or spiritual sicknesses.

R͞X Spiritual Healing
_____
_____
_____
_____
_____
_____

R͞X Physical Healing
_____
_____
_____
_____
_____
_____

Jesus Power!

The powerful name of Jesus gives us healing. What are some things we can do to continue to receive a regular dose of His name in our daily lives?

_____
_____
_____
_____

REMEMBER

He heals the brokenhearted and binds up their wounds. **(Psalm 147:3)**

Philip and the Ethiopian

(Acts 8:26–40)

Webs from the Word

The Bible gives us many details of the two men in this story. Use your Bible to complete the webs by identifying some facts about and actions of each character. Add more arrows, if needed.

_____   _____

_____   _____

(Philip)

_____   _____

_____   _____

_____   _____

_____   _____

(Ethiopian)

_____   _____

_____   _____

REVIEW

What are the means, or ways, by which the Holy Spirit creates faith? Complete the puzzle by filling in the boxes using the following clues:

1. God's way of talking to us

2a. Gift of God with a visible element

2b. Washes away sins

MEANS OF GRACE

Water, Word, and Work of the Holy Spirit

Who creates and keeps us in faith to believe that Jesus Christ is Lord and Savior?

Finish the illustration of Philip and the Ethiopian to explain how the Holy Spirit works faith. Draw and label the Word (scroll) and water, which connects with the Word in Baptism.

REMEMBER

So faith comes from hearing, and hearing through the word of Christ. **(Romans 10:17)**

Philip and the Ethiopian

(Acts 8:26–40)

Go and Make Disciples

God told Philip where to go and what to do in order to spread the Good News to the world. Read the account of Philip and the Ethiopian, and follow their paths on the map below as you read.

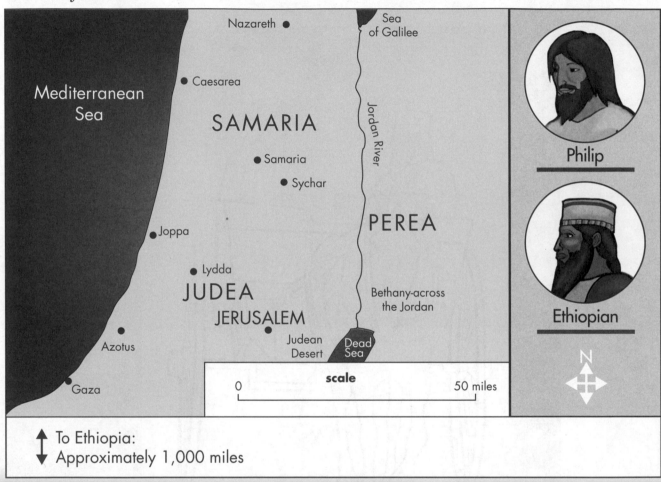

To Ethiopia: Approximately 1,000 miles

REVIEW

If you know the definition of the word *evangel*, you can figure out the meaning of many other words. Study the definition for *evangel*, and write the word *evangel* on each wavy line to make three new words. Use the part of speech as a clue to help you figure out the definition of each new word.

evangel: (noun) the Gospel of Jesus Christ, Good News

_____ ize (verb) _____

_____ ist (noun) _____

_____ ical (adj.) _____

_____

All Nations

The Ethiopian was an international traveler. His journey took him from his home in the kingdom of Ethiopia to Jerusalem and then back again. It was on his return journey, while reading God's Word, that he met Philip, came to believe in Jesus as his Savior, and, having been baptized, went on his way rejoicing. Consider the map of the world below. In the time in which this story took place, travelers might average twenty miles per day. If the Ethiopian traveled for seventy-five days at the average speed, what would have been the approximate distance from Jerusalem to his home? (Note: At the time of this story, Ethiopia also included portions of present-day Sudan. We do not know the exact location of the Ethiopian's home.)

_____miles

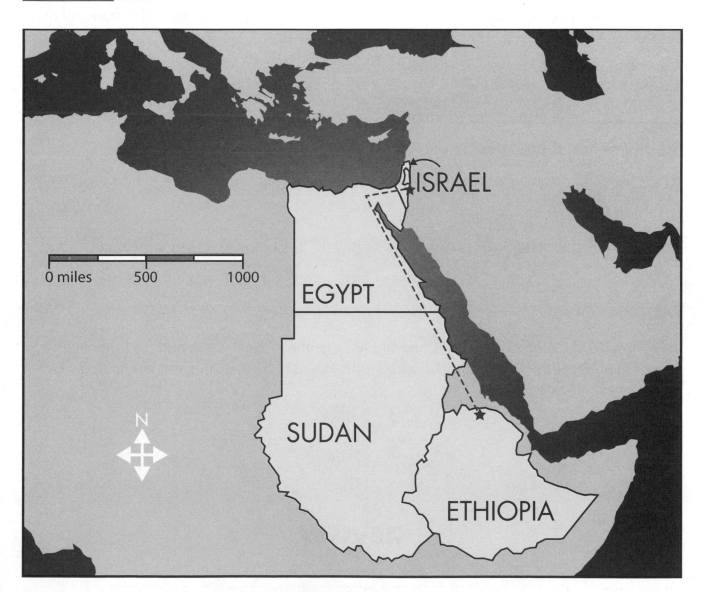

REMEMBER

I have no pleasure in the death of the wicked, but that the wicked turn from his way and live. (Ezekiel 33:11)

Paul's Nephew Saves Paul's Life

(Acts 23:10–24)

Getting the Facts Straight!

Everything happened so quickly! Paul, the great Christian missionary, had been arrested and was in big trouble. One minute Paul was in the temple and the next minute an angry mob was dragging him to prison! In fact, there was so much noise and commotion that Paul didn't even know why they were arresting him. In the days that followed, Paul experienced many amazing events. Read the following list of activities. Give each a number from one to seven, according to the order in which they really happened. As you use your detective skills, you will see that the marked letters will be your clues to discovering a special theme throughout this Bible story.

____	Jews: We are bo**u**nd by an oath to kill him before his trial.
____	Paul: Take him to the tribune. He h**a**s something to say.
____	Tribune: If I don't send him to the barra**c**ks, they will tear him to pieces!
____	Paul's Nephew: Uncle Paul, I overhea**r**d some people saying they want to kill you!
____	God: Take c**o**urage!
____	Paul's Nephew: Some people want to **g**o and kill Paul even before his trial.
○	Tribune: Don't tell anyone that you have informed me of th**e**se things.

What gift did God give to Paul and to Paul's nephew? Look back and find the bold letter clues. Place each letter in the blank with the matching number below to find the answer to this question.

___ ___ ___ ___ ___ ___ ___
1   2   3   4   5   6   7

REVIEW

Look up the following words in the dictionary and write their meanings below. Discuss them as a class.

oath—_____

conspiracy—_____

elders—_____

Pinpointing the Evidence

God has given you the courage to stand up for what is right! This is not always easy to do—especially if it is not a popular choice or your friends are not on your side. But Jesus, our Savior, remains by our side. He provides us with the courage we need in order to do the right thing as we serve Him.

Read the two lists below and draw a line to connect each problem with a possible solution.

Problems

1. Your friends are all saying mean things about the new kid.

2. The students in your class all know Mark stole the field trip money from your teacher's drawer.

3. You know you shouldn't have looked at someone else's paper during the test, but it was only for one answer.

4. You see bruises on David's arms and legs nearly every day, and now he keeps holding his side.

5. Your friend from across the street asks you if you want to try some beer she found in her parents' refrigerator.

Solutions

1. You decide to tell the teacher—even if it means getting an F.

2. During a private conversation, you make the teacher aware of the injuries.

3. You say no to your friend and encourage her to talk to her parents about what happened.

4. You do not join in and you try to be nice to him.

5. During a private conversation, you tell the teacher who took the money.

REMEMBER

Let no one despise you for your _____, but set the believers an example in _____, in conduct, in _____, in faith, in _____. **(1 Timothy 4:12)**

Paul Is Shipwrecked

(Acts 27:1–28:10)

Dive Right In!

Paul found himself traveling to Rome to stand trial because of his preaching about Jesus. Paul's voyage to Italy as a prisoner turned out to be far longer and more dangerous than anyone expected. In fact, Paul traveled to so many places and experienced such a variety of activities that it is difficult to keep the events of this Bible story straight! Dive into the facts and be an editor for the *High Seas Herald* by reading the list of events below and placing a check mark next to each event that is true according to Acts 27:1–28:10. If the event is false, explain why in the space provided.

High Seas Herald

1. _____ Paul and some other prisoners were sailing toward Italy.

_____

2. _____ Paul suggested that the crew should not sail to Phoenix, and they listened.

_____

3. _____ A southeaster caught the ship and blew it off course.

_____

4. _____ An angel visited Paul and told him that there would be no loss of life during their voyage.

_____

5. _____ The ship remained safe in the storm.

_____

6. _____ When needing to swim to shore, the soldiers killed the prisoners so they couldn't escape.

_____

7. _____ When Paul was bitten by a viper, he saved himself by quickly shaking the viper into the fire.

_____

8. _____ The Malta islanders thought Paul's misfortune of being bitten was because he was a murderer.

_____

9. _____ When Paul didn't die, they thought he was a magician doing a trick.

_____

10. _____ Paul healed Publius's father and many other people on the island in the name of the Lord.

_____

REVIEW

Write the meanings of each of the words below.

tempestuous—_____

fathom—_____

reef—_____

Stay Afloat!

At times, we all have storms in our lives. God always knows our needs and promises to protect us according to His good plan for our lives. Even when our sinful selves are afraid, God's forgiveness and protecting love are with us forever.

Pair up with another student and trade books. Interview each other about a time when you or someone you know experienced God's protection. As you talk, be sure to record the reporting essentials—who, what, when, where, why, and how—in each other's books for your records. If time permits, share your reports with the class.

Witnessing Protection Report

Interview Of: _____ Interview By: _____
      (Name of Person Being Interviewed)   (Name of Interviewer)

A Witnessing Protection Story: _____
          (Title)

Who: _____ What: _____

When: _____ Where: _____

Why: _____ How: _____

Additional Comments/Reactions:

_____

_____

Step on Shore!

God's protection is with us every day of our lives. What a wonderful gift! Write a prayer on the lines below, thanking God for being the lifesaver for your body and the "life Savior" of your soul!

Dear Lord, our Savior,

Thank You for_____

_____

_____

In Your redeeming name we pray. Amen.

REMEMBER

For He will hide me in His shelter in the day of _____; He will conceal me under the _____ of His tent; He will lift me high upon a _____. **(Psalm 27:5)**

Paul and Timothy

(Acts 16:1–5; 2 Timothy 1:1–14)

Legacy of Faith

Write a question that is answered by each of the words on the left. The first one is done for you as an example.

Lois—Who was Timothy's grandmother?

Eunice—_____

_____

Paul—_____

_____

Timothy—_____

_____

REVIEW

Define each of the following.

disciple—_____

ancestors—_____

My Personal Faith Journey

Spiritual mentors are people who give of their time and efforts to teach you God's Word and help you to apply it in your life. Timothy's spiritual mentors included his mother Eunice and his grandmother Lois. Similarly, God uses the spiritual mentors in your life to support and encourage you as you grow in faith.

Add the names of people who have mentored you in your faith journey in the blank spaces on the map.

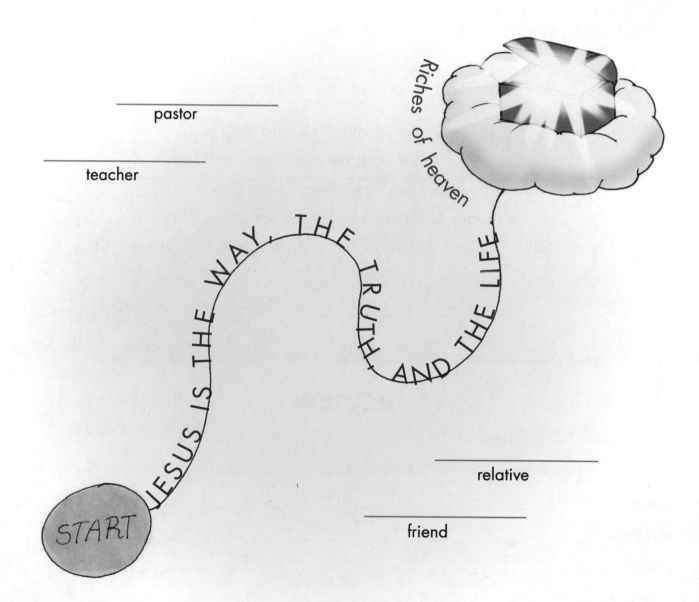

_____ pastor

_____ teacher

Riches of heaven

JESUS IS THE WAY, THE TRUTH AND THE LIFE

START

_____ relative

_____ friend

REMEMBER

And I am sure of this, that He who began a good work in you will bring it to completion at the day of Jesus Christ. **(Philippians 1:6)**

Paul and Timothy

(Acts 16:1–5; 2 Timothy 1:1–14)

BE BOLD!

Read 2 Timothy 1:1–14. Read the "Boldness in Witness" prayer on page 33 of *AGPS*.

In the "Boldness in Witness" prayer, we ask for forgiveness, humbleness, trust in God's grace and mercy. We ask God to make us bold too: bold to live by serving, bold to speak God's Word, and bold to be known as Christians.

Find and highlight the verses in this text where Paul tells Timothy that he is

- remembering Timothy's sincere faith (v. 5).
- mindful of the Spirit we have received from God (v. 7).
- remembering that God gives us His grace (v. 9).
- aware of all Jesus has done for us (v. 10).
- remembering that the Holy Spirit enables us to be bold (v. 14).

REVIEW

"Fan into flame" (2 Timothy 1:6)

Write the correct definition to each vocabulary word.

grace—_____

manifest—_____

power—_____

testimony—_____

How do these vocabulary words apply to spreading the Gospel message?

_____

_____

_____

Who Am I? I Am a Christian!

Paul wrote to Timothy a letter of encouragement. He begins the letter, identifying himself as "Paul, an apostle of Christ Jesus" (2 Timothy 1:1). Write a bold faith statement, beginning with your identity as a Christian. In this statement, include the phrases *by God's purpose and grace* and *God gave us a spirit of power, love, and self-control.*

BRAVELY GO TELL the WORLD about Jesus!

_____, "a Christian by the will of God according to the
(your name)

promise of the life that is in Christ Jesus" (2 Timothy 1:1).

_____

_____

_____

_____

_____

_____

_____

The Holy Spirit lives in me, so that I can boldly sign this statement,

_____, a Christian!

REMEMBER

For this reason I remind you to fan into flame the gift of God, which is in you through the laying on of my hands, for God gave us a spirit not of fear but of power and love and self-control. **(2 Timothy 1:6–7)**

APPENDIX

Table of Contents

abundance Having plenty, more than enough.

accuse To call to account; to charge with a fault or offense.

adoption The act of taking on and claiming as one's own.

adoration Praise.

adultery Something that has been made impure. The term usually refers to having a sexual relationship outside of marriage. Antonym: purity.

adversary Enemy; opponent.

adversity An instance or condition of serious or continued misfortune.

agony Extreme pain and suffering.

alms Money given to the poor.

altered Made different without being changed into something else.

ancestors People in our family who have come before us.

anger A strong feeling of displeasure.

anointed Specially chosen by God.

apostle A person who was with Jesus and preached the Gospel.

ark of the covenant A special wooden chest that was covered with gold. The ark showed the people that God was with them; it was placed in the Most Holy Place in the temple.

arrogant Believing you are better than others.

attribute A characteristic.

Baptism Sacred act to wash away sins.

barrier Something that blocks the way. Sin created a barrier between God and man.

betray To give aid or information to an enemy.

bitterness A strong feeling of cynicism, severe grief or regret, or hatred.

bless To give good things to. Antonym: curse.

blessing Something that brings happiness or welfare. Antonyms: curse, condemnation.

boast To brag.

bread A basic food consisting mostly of baked flour. Bread baked without yeast is used in the Sacrament of Holy Communion. Christians receive forgiveness together with Christ's body and blood through the bread and wine of the Lord's Supper.

bulrush Tall grasses growing along rivers.

casting lots Method often used in Bible times to decide something.

ceremonial washing Washing required by Old Testament laws.

Chaldeans Another name for Babylonians.

chariots Wheeled, horse-drawn carts.

Christ The official title of Jesus, meaning "the Anointed One." It is a Greek word, and it means the same as the Hebrew word *Messiah*.

church (1) Fellowship of believers. (2) A building where people gather. (3) All people who believe in the one true God.

cleanse To make clean or remove something bad.

coat of mail A coat-like armor made of interlocking metal rings.

Collect A prayer that follows a special format.

commander A leader who is in charge of a military unit.

commandment An order or expectation.

condemn To find guilty and deserving of punishment.

confession An admission to God or to another person of our sin and desire to turn from the sin and to make amends.

conflict The opposition of incompatible forces. Antonym: peace.

conquer To gain or acquire by force of arms.

consecrate To set aside for a special activity, especially for serving Yahweh (God); may be done after confession and absolution for a sin.

conspiracy An agreement or plot between two or more people, usually to harm someone, do something illegal, or take over as ruler.

content Satisfied with what you have. Antonym: unhappy.

covenant (1) An agreement between God and His people. (2) A statement describing the relationship between two people or parties. (3) A promise.

covet To sinfully desire to possess what belongs to someone else.

creation The act of bringing into being; in the case of the *creation* of the world, the act of making something from nothing.

credit (1) Reputation for honesty or integrity. (2) A source of honor.

crucifixion The method whereby Jesus died to save us.

curse Insult or condemn.

cycle Something that repeats itself or goes around.

David Psalm writer who was the king of Israel and ancestor of Jesus.

deceive To mislead or give a false impression.

deliverer One who rescues or sets free.

despise To look down on with contempt; to hate.

determined Having reached a decision.

disciple Follower of Christ.

dishonor To cause disgrace; to shame; to cause a loss of good reputation.

divine Godly.

divine nature Everything about Jesus that shows He is God.

dream Thoughts, images, or emotion occurring during sleep. God sometimes spoke to His people through dreams.

elders (1) The older men of a town or nation who were the leaders of their community and made all the important decisions; each town had its own groups of elders. After the people of Judah returned from exile to Babylon, the elders made up the Sanhedrin, their ruling council. (2) The leaders of the church, often specifically pastors.

Emmanuel Name for Jesus, meaning "God with us." (Sometimes spelled *Immanuel*.)

enmity Hatred.

eternal Used for or lasting an infinite time.

evangelical Being in agreement with or loyal to the Good News/Gospel.

evangelist A person who shares the Gospel/Good News.

evangelize To preach (or share, tell, etc.) the Gospel/Good News of Jesus Christ.

exalt To elevate by praise or in estimation.

exodus (1) Movement of a large group of people from one place to another. (2) A book in the Bible that tells the story of how God rescued His people from slavery in Egypt.

faithfulness Firm dedication and obedience.

false witness Sinful words; lies.

fathoms A unit of length equal to six feet, used especially for measuring the depth of water.

favorite Especially liked.

fickle Likely to change frequently without good reason.

fluctuate To be constantly changing.

forerunner A person who goes before others to prepare the way.

foretell To tell beforehand.

forgiveness The removal of our sins by God because of Jesus' sacrifice for us.

friend A person who cares for another.

friendship The close relationship one person has with another.

fulfill To carry out or finish something.

Galilee Northern part of Israel; it includes the cities of Cana, Nazareth, and Capernaum.

genesis (1) Origin. (2) The first book of the Bible, it includes the story of the creation of the world.

gentle Mild; not harsh, stern, or rough.

glorious (1) Wonderful, exciting, delightful. (2) Full of glory. (3) Spectacularly beautiful or splendid.

glory (1) Divine power. (2) Honor and praise.

Godly Pious; devout.

God's will God's desire or purpose.

grace (1) God's love for us when we don't deserve it. (2) The state of having received something you don't deserve.

gracious Showing undeserved kindness and forgiveness.

greed Selfish desire for more money or possessions than one needs.

griefs Pain or sorrows.

guests People attending a special occasion at the invitation of another.

hatred A strong dislike of someone or something.

heal To restore to health.

heaven (1) The place where God lives. (2) The expanse of sky over the earth.

herald An official who announces important information.

hesitate (1) To stop or pause because of uncertainty or indecision. (2) To be unwilling.

Holy Spirit The Third Person of the Trinity; the Holy Spirit brings us to faith in Jesus and keeps us in this faith.

human nature Everything about Jesus that is like us.

humility The state of being content, gentle, or modest.

idol A false and powerless object of worship and devotion.

idolatry Worshiping someone or something other than the true God.

image A form designed to represent an object or person.

imperishable Unable to die or decay.

incarnation (1) The appearance of God in an earthly form. (2) The union of divine and human natures in Jesus Christ.

incense A mixture of spices from plants; when burned, it makes a sweet smell. Incense was burned on the golden altar to worship God.

inhabitant One who lives in a particular place.

inspire (1) To breathe. (2) To fill with a message. (3) To spur to action.

insolent (1) Disrespectful or rude in speech or conduct. (2) Showing boldness or rudeness.

integrity The act of doing what is right and blameless in every situation.

invitation A request made to someone to attend an event.

javelin A light spear thrown as a weapon of war or in hunting.

jealous A strong, often sinful, desire over a person and his or her possessions.

jealousy The act of strongly desiring a person or what the person has.

Jerusalem The political and religious center of Judah.

Jesus A name for God's Son, meaning "The Lord saves"; our Savior.

Judea Southern part of Israel; it includes the cities of Jerusalem and Bethlehem.

judge A leader God chose to deliver His people from their enemies.

judgment (1) A decision or opinion. (2) A decision of guilt or innocence made by a judge in a court of law; punishment decided by a court. (3) A decision from God, especially the final judgment when God will reward those who believe in Him and condemn all others to hell.

justified Made righteous by Jesus' death on the cross.

kill To take the life of another person.

king A male monarch of a major territorial unit.

Last Day Another name for the final day on earth, when Jesus will return to take His people to heaven.

Lazarus (1) A name meaning "whom God helps." (2) The brother of Mary and Martha and friend of Jesus (see John 11).

leprosy A skin disease.

lie To make an untrue statement with intent to deceive.

limp (1) To walk lamely. (2) To go slowly or with difficulty.

Magi Member of the priestly class among ancient Medes and Persians.

malice A desire to harm someone.

manifest Make apparent; obvious understanding.

marvel To wonder at with a sense of awe.

matzah A flat, unleavened bread Hebrews ate while they were slaves in Egypt; they took this type of bread with them when they fled Egypt.

merciful Providing relief.

mercy Compassion, especially for those who do not deserve it.

merit Conduct deserving of a reward; a praiseworthy quality.

Messiah One who saves.

miracle A supernatural act.

mission A specific goal or task, such as to share the Good News.

modest (1) Having a limited and not overly high opinion of oneself and one's abilities. (2) Not boastful.

Nazareth Town where Jesus grew up.

Nazirite An Israelite consecrated to God.

neighbor (1) Anyone we may know or relate to in any way. (2) All people.

oath A promise in which one asks God to witness that something is true.

obey To follow God's commands.

offspring Descendants.

omni- A prefix meaning *all*.

omnipotent All-powerful.

omnipresent Present everywhere at once.

omniscient All-knowing.

original sin The total corruption of our human nature, which we have inherited from Adam through our parents—the natural desire to do wrong with which we were born.

overthrow Overturn, upset; to cause the downfall of.

pagan One who follows many gods with primitive spiritual understandings.

parable Story with a spiritual meaning; Jesus told many parables.

Passover The religious celebration commemorating God saving the firstborn children in Israelite families by passing over homes that had the blood of a lamb painted on the door posts.

peace Calmness, lack of strife.

Pentecost (1) In the Old Testament, a feast to celebrate the fiftieth day after Passover. (2) The fiftieth day after Easter; often called the birthday of the Church. (3) Today, celebrated as the day when the Holy Spirit came to dwell with Christ's followers.

perishable Able to die or decay.

perished Died.

petition A request.

Pharaoh Royal title for the ruler over Egypt.

pillar A firm structural support such as that provided by a sturdy column.

plague (1) A disease that kills many people, such as the plague of boils. (2) An event that causes much suffering or loss, especially a trouble in which there is a great number of offending agents, such as the plague of locusts.

prayer Speaking to God in words and thoughts.

power Having might and authority.

pride Arrogance; thinking more of yourself than you ought.

priest A religious leader in the temple.

priesthood People dedicated to serving God.

priorities Things that are given or deserve attention before other things.

promise To tell someone that you will do something for him or her at a later time.

prophecy Prediction about the future.

prophet A person chosen to speak for God, especially about the future.

prophetic Divinely inspired.

provide To supply, make available, or meet a need.

providence God's power guiding and caring for humanity.

provisions Things that are needed.

ransom Price paid to redeem someone.

rebellion Disobedience and turning against those in authority.

recline To lie back or down.

reconcile To bring peace between God and man.

redeemed Bought back; paid for through someone else's sacrifice, as in Christ's sacrifice for us on the cross.

redeemer (1) One who redeems. (2) Jesus Christ, who paid for our sins when He died on the cross for the forgiveness of our sins.

redemption Salvation from sin through Christ's sacrifice.

reef A chain of rocks or coral or a ridge of sand at or near the surface of water.

regenerate To revive and to produce anew.

reigns Rules over.

reject To turn away from, to say no more, to cancel a promise.

rejoice To show that you're very happy.

rely To trust, depend, or count on someone to keep a promise.

remembrance The act or process of recalling information.

renew To restore, replenish, or re-establish.

repair To restore to a good condition after decay or damage.

repent To be truly sorry for the wrong things we have done and to express a desire to not repeat those wrong things.

repentance Turning away from sin.

rescue To save or deliver from harm and danger.

response How a person reacts to something (e.g., to an invitation).

resolute Firmly determined.

restoration Bringing back to a former position or condition.

restore To bring back to a former condition.

resurrection Coming alive again after death.

reverence A feeling of deep love and respect.

righteous Being perfect in God's eyes.

ruler One who rules or governs; sovereign.

sacrament Gift of God with a visible element.

sacrifice To give up or offer to God.

salvation The state of being saved from punishment for our sins through Jesus Christ.

Samaria Central part of Israel; it includes the city of Samaria.

sanctification The continued, ongoing work of the Holy Spirit in our hearts. Our *sanctification* begins when we become Christians. By faith in Christ, we are holy, forgiven for all sins. In a narrower sense, it means that the Holy Spirit enables us to do good (holy) works.

sanctified Receiving the work of the Holy Spirit to change our lives to be pleasing to God.

sanctify To make holy.

Savior A name for Jesus that means He saves His people from sin.

scepter A rod or stick held by a king or queen as a sign of royal power and authority.

Scripture All or part of the Bible. When the Bible uses this word, it usually means the Old Testament, since the New Testament had not yet been written. Today, we call the Old and New Testaments the Bible or Holy Scripture.

scroll A roll of paper or parchment for writing a document.

seder (1) A service commemorating God's saving of His people during the night of the death of the firstborn in Egypt. (2) The meal eaten in remembrance of the event, which follows a prescribed order of serving the meal components.

Sheol Name used in Bible times for the place of the dead.

shepherd A person assigned to care for, guide, and protect sheep.

shield-bearer A person who carries a soldier's shield.

shofar An Old Testament "trumpet" made from a ram's horn; it has important uses to the people of Israel.

sin Every thought, word, and deed contrary to God's Law. Antonym: virtue.

slave A person who works for someone else without any pay. He or she may be owned by that person.

sling A projectile weapon typically used to throw a blunt object, such as a stone.

solace Relief.

sower (1) Person who plants or throws seeds. (2) Focus of a parable told by Jesus.

Spirit of the Lord The Holy Spirit.

staff A stick or pole to assist with walking; sometimes used as a weapon.

successor The person who continues your work after you.

supplication A humble and earnest request.

synagogue A place of worship, teaching, and meeting for the Jewish people.

tabernacle Special tent where God's people went to worship and give praise to God.

tempestuous Of, relating to, or resembling a tempest; violent, stormy.

temple Special place in Jerusalem where God's people went to worship and give praise to God.

temporal Used in our earthly life, not lasting.

temptation (1) Something that lures us away from God and His ways. (2) Something that lures us to do something wrong, against the Law of God.

testimony Open declaration of faith.

thanksgiving Gratefulness.

transfiguration (1) When Jesus' appearance changed from His earthly appearance to His heavenly appearance. (2) Change of appearance; a bright and glorious spiritual change.

treachery Evil behavior.

triumph (1) The act, fact, or condition of being victorious. (2) A noteworthy or remarkable success. (3) The feeling of joy victory brings.

trust Confidence in God—a way to overcome fear.

unswerving Not turning aside; steady, unfaltering.

unwavering Steady, sound.

usurp To take over by force.

vacillate To hesitate between courses or opinion; be unable to choose.

victory The overcoming of an enemy or antagonist.

Word God's way of talking to us.

worry To feel anxious and uneasy.

worship (1) To honor, respect, or deem worthy. (2) To express reverence or devotion. (3) Anything a person does to show love and respect. Solomon built the temple to *worship* the one true God.

Aaron Brother of Moses; spokesman for Moses before Pharaoh; Israel's first high priest.

Abednego Young Judean brought by King Nebuchadnezzar into captivity in Babylon; one of four young men chosen by the king to be educated according to Babylonian ways so that they could serve in his palace. Abednego's Judean name was Azariah.

Abel Second son of Adam and Eve; murdered by his older brother, Cain.

Abigail Beautiful wife of Nabal who rescued her cruel and foolish husband. After Nabal's death, she became the wife of David.

Abijah (1) Son and successor of King Rehoboam who reigned for three years. (2) Second son of Samuel. (3) Son of Jeroboam I, king of Israel; only member of his family to go to his grave in peace.

Abimelech Name of more than one of the Philistine kings.

Abinadab Son of Jesse; second of seven sons who were passed over before David was anointed the next king of Israel.

Abner Son of Ner; commander of King David's army.

Abraham (Abram) Father of the Hebrew people; promised by God that his children would make a mighty nation; Sarah's husband; Isaac's father.

Absalom Son of David; murdered his half-brother Amnon; plotted to take over David's throne.

Achan Israelite who kept riches from the battle of Jericho; as a result of his theft, he and his family were stoned to death.

Common jobs in Bible times: farmer (Genesis 4:2); herdsman (Genesis 4:20); fisherman (Matthew 4:18); shepherd (1 Samuel 17:15); hunter (Genesis 10:9); merchant (Proverbs 31:18); winemaker (Matthew 21:33); olive oil maker (Exodus 27:20); baker (Genesis 40:2); cook (1 Samuel 9:24); potter (Isaiah 29:16); seamstress (Proverbs 31:22); engraver, embroiderer, weaver (Exodus 35:35); importer/exporter (2 Chronicles 1:17); priest (Exodus 28:1); Levite (2 Chronicles 13:10); musician (Genesis 4:21; Psalm 68:25); wife, husband, parent; landowner (1 Kings 16:24); carpenter (Isaiah 44:13); woodcutter (Joshua 9:21); builder (1 Kings 5:18); craftsman (Exodus 35:10); silversmith (Acts 19:24); goldsmith (Isaiah 46:6); metalworker (Genesis 4:22); brickmaker (Exodus 5:14); mason, stonecutter (2 Kings 12:12); jeweler (Exodus 28:11); government official (John 4:46; Acts 24:1); tax collector (Luke 5:27); mourner (Luke 8:52); judge (Luke 18:1); soldier (Acts 10:7); slave (Philemon 15–16); banker (Matthew 25:27); expert in the Law (Matthew 22:35)); physician (Colossians 4:14); preacher (1 Timothy 2:7); teacher (Ephesians 4:11); writer (1 Corinthians 16:21).

Adam First man God created; sinned by disobeying God, thereby bringing all people under the curse of sin.

Agrippa I See Herod Agrippa I.

Ahab Wicked king of Israel; together with his wife, Jezebel, caused Israel to worship Baal rather than God.

Ahijah Prophet of Shiloh who told Jeroboam that he would be the ruler over ten tribes of Israel.

Amos Prophet sent to announce God's judgment to the Northern Kingdom (Israelites); worked with flocks and sycamore-fig groves; author of the Book of Amos.

Ananias (1) Husband of Sapphira who was struck dead for lying to God. (2) Disciple who baptized Saul. (3) High priest before whom Paul was tried.

Andrew One of Jesus' twelve disciples; an apostle; witness to Jesus' resurrection; from Bethsaida (John 1:44); first a disciple of John the Baptist, he

brought to Jesus his brother Peter, who also became one of the Twelve (John 1:35–42); fished on Sea of Galilee with brother Peter (Mark 1:16–20). Church history says Andrew died for the faith in Greece, crucified on an X-shaped cross.

Anna Prophetess from the tribe of Asher; widow who never left the temple, where she worshiped day and night.

Antipas See Herod Antipas.

Antipater II Firstborn son of Herod the Great, made first heir in Herod's

will. Lived 46–4 BC. Found guilty by a Roman court of trying to kill his father; executed by order of Caesar Augustus.

Apollos Jewish leader in the Early Christian Church; taught by Priscilla and Aquila.

Apostles Original twelve disciples who followed Jesus during His ministry and saw and heard Him (Matthew 10:2–4; Mark 3:16–19; Luke 6:13–16; Acts 1:13). All but Judas were witnesses of Jesus' resurrection from the dead. Jesus sent them out as missionaries to tell the world about Him. Matthias, who replaced Judas, and St. Paul are also called apostles because they too were witnesses to Jesus' resurrection. The New Testament tells what the apostles saw, heard, and wrote down under the guidance (inspiration) of the Holy Spirit.

Aquila Jew who met Paul in Corinth. He and wife Priscilla were leaders and teachers in the Early Christian Church.

Archelaus See **Herod Archelaus.**

Aristobulus IV Son of Herod the Great and Mariamne, the last of the Jewish line of Hasmoneans. Herod the Great ordered him killed in 7 BC.

Artaxerxes King of Persia who permitted the Israelites to return to Jerusalem after their captivity in Babylon.

Asa Son of Abijah and third of Judah's kings; worked to rid the land of heathenism.

Asher Eighth son of Jacob; born to Zilpah, Leah's handmaid.

Athaliah Wicked daughter of Ahab and Jezebel; married Jehoram, king of Judah, and introduced Baal worship into Judah. Athaliah later killed her own grandchildren and usurped the kingdom.

Augustus Caesar See Caesar Augustus.

Baal Name of many false gods in Canaan; each section of Canaan had its own Baal.

Balaam Seer who tried to curse Israel during their journey to the Promised Land, but God would not allow it.

Balak Son of Zippor, king of Moab; wanted Balaam to curse the Israelites so that they could not cross through Moab.

Barabbas A robber who had committed murder during an insurrection; he was released instead of Jesus by Pilate at the will of the people.

Barak Military commander who was led by Deborah, a prophetess of Ephraim, under God's hand, to deliver Israel from its enemies at Jezreel.

Barnabas Apostle and evangelist; co-worker with Paul on his first missionary journey.

Bartholomew One of Jesus' twelve disciples; an apostle; witness to Jesus' resurrection; also known as Nathanael; brought to Jesus by Philip (John 1:45–51); known for his simple, forthright character; he died for his faith.

Bartimaeus A blind beggar of Jericho who appealed to Jesus and was healed by Him.

Bathsheba Wife of Uriah; committed adultery with David and later became his wife and the mother of Solomon.

Belteshazzar Babylonian name that the king gave to Daniel when the Judeans were taken captive by the Babylonians.

Benjamin Twelfth son of Jacob; Rachel was his mother; younger brother of Joseph.

Bernice Oldest daughter of Herod Agrippa I, who first married her uncle Herod and after his death lived with her brother Agrippa II.

Bethuel Son of Nahor, nephew of Abraham, and father of Rebekah and Laban.

Boaz Husband of Ruth; father of Obed; ancestor of King David and Jesus.

Caesar Title used by the emperors of Rome from 300 BC to about AD 300; a title used by other countries for their king or emperor.

Caesar Augustus First ruler of the Roman Empire; lived 63 BC–AD 14; ruled when Jesus was born; also called Octavian. After Caesar's assassination in 44 BC, Augustus joined forces with Mark Antony and Marcus Aemilius Lepidus in a military dictatorship known as the Second Triumvirate. When this partnership failed, Augustus restored the Roman Republic with power vested in the Roman senate. In practice, he retained power as a dictator. By law, he held a collection of powers granted to him for life by the senate. Augustus expanded the Roman Empire, secured its boundaries, and ruled in relative peace. After his death, the senate declared him a god to be worshiped by the Romans. The month of August is named in his honor.

Caiaphas High priest of the Jews during the time of Jesus' public ministry, death, and resurrection.

Cain Adam and Eve's firstborn son; murdered his brother Abel.

Caleb One of twelve men sent to spy in Canaan; only he and Joshua encouraged Israelites to take possession of Canaan.

Candace Name applied to a dynasty of Ethiopian queens.

Chilion Son of Naomi and Elimelech; husband of Orpah.

Christ Name for Jesus, God's Son. This is a Greek word that means "Messiah" or "Anointed One."

Cleopas One of the two disciples who traveled from Jerusalem to Emmaus on the day of the resurrection.

Cornelius Roman centurion to whom God sent Peter to preach the Gospel; was one of the first Gentiles to become Christian.

Cyrus King of Persia; helped the Judeans return to the Promised Land, giving them gold and silver that King Nebuchadnezzar had taken from them in captivity.

Daniel Young Judean brought by King Nebuchadnezzar into captivity in Babylon; one of four young men chosen by the king to be educated according to Babylonian ways so that they could serve in his palace. Daniel's Babylonian name was Belteshazzar.

Darius King of Persia who wrote a decree that allowed the Judeans to rebuild the temple in Jerusalem.

David Son of Jesse; anointed as young boy to become king of Israel; after Saul's death, became king; author of a portion of Psalms.

Deborah Prophetess and judge who led Israel to victory over the Canaanites.

Delilah Lover of Samson who, after constant pleading, got him to tell her the secret of his great strength.

Demetrius Silversmith from Ephesus; made silver idols; accused Paul of destroying business because Paul preached of the one true God.

devil An evil spirit, an angel who rebelled against God and was cast out of heaven. There are many devils or demons. "The devil" sometimes refers to a specific evil spirit, also called Satan, Lucifer, the evil one.

Dinah Daughter of Jacob and Leah.

Eli High priest of Israel; Samuel spent the early years of his life living in the temple with Eli.

Eliezer Abraham's chief servant who journeyed to the home of Bethuel to secure a wife for Isaac.

Elijah Prophet of the Lord during the reign of Ahab; taken to heaven in a whirlwind and later appeared with Moses at the transfiguration of Jesus.

Elimelech Husband of Naomi; moved from Bethlehem to Moab because of a famine. After Elimelech and his sons died, Naomi and daughter-in-law Ruth returned to Bethlehem.

Elisha Prophet who succeeded Elijah when he was taken up to heaven.

Elizabeth Wife of Zechariah who miraculously became the mother of John the Baptist at an advanced age.

Elkanah Zuphite from Ephraim; Hannah's husband and father of Samuel.

Enoch Man who "walked with God"; later in life was taken to heaven by God without dying.

Ephraim Second son of Joseph by Leah.

Esau Firstborn son of Isaac and Rebekah and twin of Jacob; sold his birthright to Jacob for a pot of stew; was tricked out of his blessing by Jacob; later in life, he and Jacob met and were reconciled.

Esther Beautiful Jewish woman from Persia; King Xerxes chose her out of many women to be his queen.

Eunice God-fearing mother of Timothy.

Eutychus A youth at Troas who, having fallen asleep during Paul's sermon and out of a window to his death, was brought back to life by Paul.

Eve First woman God created. Her name means "mother of all the living."

Ezra Priest and teacher of the Law; led a group of exiles back to Judah and helped them rebuild the temple in Jerusalem.

Felix Roman governor who heard the complaints of the Jews against Paul and then heard Paul's explanation.

Gabriel Archangel who appeared to Mary to tell her she would become the mother of the Savior of the world.

Gamaliel Most famous Jewish teacher of his time; was president of the Sanhedrin (the Jewish Council); Saul of Tarsus was one of his students.

Gideon Youngest son of Joash of an undistinguished family; nicknamed Jerubbaal, which means "let Baal contend against him"; fifth and greatest judge of Israel; tested God with a woolen fleece.

Goliath Famous Philistine giant who may have been nine or ten feet tall; slain by David in the power of God.

Hagar Egyptian handmaid of Sarah; mother of Ishmael (Abraham's son).

Haggai Prophet who encouraged the Israelites to rebuild the temple after they returned from exile in Babylon; author of the Book of Haggai.

Ham One of Noah's three sons.

Haman Enemy of the Jews who was a leader in the court of the king of Persia; was hanged on the gallows he had built for Mordecai the Jew.

Hannah Wife of Elkanah; prayed for a son, after which God gave her Samuel.

Hasmoneans The ruling family of the Kingdom of Israel (Northern Kingdom) from 140–37 BC; established under leadership of Simon Maccabaeus two decades after his brother Judas defeated the Seleucid army (Greek-speaking people from Alexander the Great's kingdom). Intertestamental Apocryphal books 1 and 2 Maccabees provide some of their history. Roman leaders Mark Antony and Octavian stopped a brief Hasmonean uprising that resulted in Herod the Great becoming king in 37 BC and ended Hasmonean rule.

Herod Family name of five kings who ruled Palestine under the Roman emperor: Herod the Great (Matthew 2:1–8, 16); Herod Antipas (Mark 6:14–29); Herod Philip (Matthew 14:3); Herod Agrippa I (Acts 12:1–4, 19–23); Herod Agrippa II (Acts 23:35; 25:13–26:32).

Herod the Great Also called King Herod; ruled Judea for Rome from 37–4 BC; called "the Great" because he built many large and impressive structures, including the third temple in Jerusalem, sometimes called Herod's Temple. He was known as a ruthless man who killed his favorite wife, his own sons, many rabbis, and others who got in his way. His land was divided between his three sons after his death.

Herod Agrippa I Grandson of Herod the Great, eaten by worms for defying God (Acts 12:20–23).

Herod Agrippa II Great-grandson of Herod the Great; called Herod in the report in the Book of Acts of St. Paul's trial before Agrippa before being sent to Rome. Agrippa ruled without a Roman procurator, the only king of the time to do so except for Herod the Great.

Herod Antipas Son of Herod the Great; ruled as a tetrarch over Galilee and Perea (the east side of the Jordan River) after his father's death; ordered the death of John the Baptist. Jesus called him "that fox" to indicate his sneakiness (Luke 13:32). After Jesus' arrest, Pontius Pilate sent Him to be tried by Herod Antipas, but he sent Jesus back to Pilate.

Herod Archelaus Son of Herod the Great; ruled Judea, Idumaea, and Samaria as an ethnarch (not king) after his father's death.

Herod Philip Son of Herod the Great who ruled the region beyond the Sea of Galilee and to Bashan after his father's death.

Hezekiah King of Judah who restored the temple, reinstituted proper worship, and sought the Lord's help against the Assyrians.

high priest The main priest who served God in the Israelite tabernacle and temples.

Hilkiah High priest during the reign of Josiah.

Hophni One of Eli's wicked sons; died in battle in fulfillment of the Lord's prophecy.

Hosea First of the minor prophets; wrote the Book of Hosea.

Huldah Prophetess during the time of King Josiah.

Ichabod Son of Phinehas and grandson of Eli; born shortly after the death of both.

Isaac Promised son of Abraham and Sarah; offered as a sacrifice by Abraham; married Rebekah; father of Jacob and Esau.

Isaiah Prophet called by God to prophesy to Judah; many of his prophecies were about the coming Messiah.

Ishbosheth Youngest of Saul's sons and his likely successor.

Ishmael Son of Abraham by Hagar the Egyptian, born when Abraham was 86 years old.

Jacob (Israel) Second son of Isaac and Rebekah; twin brother of Esau; bought Esau's birthright with a pot of stew; later tricked Isaac into giving him the blessing that belonged to Esau; wrestled with God, and his name was changed to Israel; had twelve sons, all of whom eventually went to Egypt during a famine; settled in Egypt; buried by his son Joseph in Canaan, the Promised Land.

Jael Woman who killed Israel's enemy Sisera by driving a tent stake into his head.

Jairus Official who asked Jesus to come and make his sick daughter well. Jesus raised her from the dead.

James One of Jesus' half brothers, a son of Mary and Joseph, along with Joseph, Judas, and Simon (Matthew 12:46; 13:55; Mark 6:3); did not believe in Jesus as the Messiah until after witnessing Jesus' resurrection (1 Corinthians 15:7); leader in the Jerusalem Church (Acts 12:17; 15:1–21; 21:17–18; Galatians 1:18–19; 2:9–12); author of the Book of James; died by stoning for his faith in Christ.

James the Greater
One of Jesus' twelve disciples; an apostle; witness to Jesus' resurrection; son of Zebedee and Mary, also called Salome (Matthew 27:56);  fished with his brother John (also one of the Twelve) and father on the Sea of Galilee (Mark 1:19–20); Jesus called the brothers "Sons of Thunder" (Mark 3:17); one of Jesus' trusted inner circle along with Peter and John (Matthew 17:1; Mark 5:37; 13:3; 14:33). James was the first of the remaining eleven disciples to die for believing in Jesus, killed by sword at the command of King Herod Agrippa I in Jerusalem (Acts 12:1–2). Shells in his shield refer to his travels.

James the Lesser
One of Jesus' twelve disciples; an apostle; witness to Jesus' resurrection; son of Alphaeus; died for his faith in Christ.

Japheth Youngest of Noah's three sons.

Jason A friend of the apostle Paul.

Jehoahaz King of Judah after his father Josiah's death; became king when he was twenty-three years old and reigned for only three months; did evil in the eyes of the Lord.

Jehoiachin King of Judah; became king when he was eighteen years old and reigned for only three months and ten days; did evil in the eyes of the Lord.

Jehoiakim King of Judah after Jehoahaz's death; became king when he was twenty-five years old and reigned for eleven years; did evil in the eyes of the Lord.

Jehoshaphat King of Judah; son of Asa who began to reign when he was thirty-five years old and reigned for twenty-five years.

Jehu King of Israel; known for driving like a madman (2 Kings 9:20).

Jephthah Judge of Israel whose foolish pledge resulted in the loss of his daughter.

Jeremiah Prophet called by God to prophesy to Judah; often referred to as the "prophet of gloom" because he prophesied the destruction of Judah; also told about the coming of the Savior, Jesus Christ.

Jeroboam Official in Solomon's court; rebelled and became king of the northern Kingdom of Israel.

Jesse Father of David; all of his sons were looked at by Samuel, but only the last and youngest, David, was chosen to be the king of Israel.

Jesus God's only begotten Son, Second Person of the Trinity, true God and true man; our Savior from sin who lived without sinning and died on the cross to pay for our sins, who rose from the grave, ascended into heaven, and promises to return to earth on the last day. *Jesus* means "the Lord saves." Other forms of the name are *Joshua* and *Jeshua*. Jesus' life in the flesh is told about in the Gospels, the first four books of the New Testament—Matthew, Mark, Luke, and John.

Jethro (Reuel) Priest of Midian; father-in-law of Moses who offered Moses good advice on leadership.

Jezebel Sidonian wife of King Ahab who promoted the worship of Baal in Israel.

Joab Nephew of David; general in David's army.

Joash (1) Son and successor of Israel's king Jehoahaz. (2) Father of Gideon.

Job God-fearing wealthy man of Uz who lost and regained much, yet remained faithful to the one true God throughout his life's experiences.

Jochebed Wife of Amram and mother of Moses and Aaron.

John One of Jesus' twelve disciples; an apostle; witness to Jesus' resurrection; son of Zebedee and Mary, also called Salome (Matthew 27:56); fished with his brother James (also one of the Twelve) and father on the Sea of Galilee (Mark 1:19–20); Jesus called the brothers "Sons of Thunder" (Mark 3:17); one of Jesus' trusted inner circle along with Peter and James (Matthew 17:1; Mark 5:37; 13:3; 14:33). Church history says that enemies tried to kill John by poisoning his drink, but the Lord spared him. John was the only one of the Twelve to die a natural death, around the age of ninety-four in AD 100. He is the author of the Gospel of John; 1, 2, and 3 John; and Revelation.

John the Baptist Son of Zechariah and Elizabeth; preached in the desert, preparing the people for Jesus; baptized Jesus in the Jordan River; was arrested and executed by Herod.

Jonah Reluctant prophet sent to Nineveh; God caused him to be swallowed by a big fish.

Jonathan Son of King Saul; David's best friend; always tried to keep David out of trouble.

Joseph (1) Son of Jacob and Rachel; sold by brothers into slavery but in turn of events became ruler of Egypt; instrumental in saving God's people by bringing them to Egypt during a time of severe famine. (2) Mary's husband; Jesus' earthly father. (3)

(of Arimathea) Follower of Jesus; provided his tomb as the burial place for the body of Jesus. (4) One of Jesus' half brothers, a son of Mary and Joseph, along with James, Judas, and Simon (Matthew 12:46; 13:55; Mark 6:3).

Joshua Moses' aide and successor; led the people into Canaan and in the battle of Jericho.

Josiah King of Judah; became king when he was eight years old and reigned for thirty-one years; did what was right in the eyes of the Lord.

Judah Fourth son of Jacob by Leah; ancestor of King David and ultimately of Christ.

Judas One of Jesus' half brothers, a son of Mary and Joseph, along with James, Joseph, and Simon (Matthew 12:46; 13:55; Mark 6:3).

Judas Iscariot One of Jesus' twelve disciples; held the money bag for Jesus and the disciples, and was a thief (John 12:6; 13:29); conspired with the chief priests to betray Jesus with a kiss in the Garden of Gethsemane (Matthew 26:14–16, 47–50); received thirty pieces of silver for betraying Jesus; killed Himself soon after Jesus was crucified (Matthew 27:3–10).

Jude One of Jesus' twelve disciples; an apostle; witness to Jesus' resurrection; also called Judas and Thaddaeus (Matthew 10:2–4;

Mark 3:16–19). Church history says he traveled many places to share the Gospel, accompanied by the apostle Simon; a ship on his shield reminds us of his travels.

Julius Roman centurion charged with taking Paul from Caesarea to Rome.

Keturah Married Abraham after Sarah's death; she bore him six children.

Kish Father of King Saul.

Korah Son of Izhar; Levite who rebelled against Moses and Aaron; he and his followers and family went to their graves alive when the earth swallowed them.

Laban Brother of Rebekah and father of Rachel and Leah; tricked Jacob into marrying both Leah and Rachel.

Lamech Father of Noah.

Lazarus Brother of Martha and Mary whom Jesus brought back from the dead.

Leah First wife of Jacob; had six sons and one daughter.

Levi Third son of Jacob by Leah; his descendants formed the priestly line among God's people.

Levite A man from the tribe of Levi; Levites served God's tabernacle and temple as priests, musicians, singers, cleaners, guards, and builders, as well as in other functions.

Lois Godly grandmother of Timothy.

Lot Nephew of Abraham; chose the richer lands near the wicked cities of Sodom and Gomorrah when he and Abraham separated.

Luke Author of the Gospel of Luke and the Acts of the Apostles; physician; co-worker and traveling companion of St. Paul; work as an evangelist is shown by a winged calf, which reminds us of the sacrificial death of our Lord Jesus.

Lydia First European convert of St. Paul, whom she hosted in her home in Philippi.

Maccabees A Jewish family group who led a revolt against the Seleucid king and obtained a 25-year freedom from Roman rule from 167–142 BC; ruled Israel in the first century BC. See **Hasmonean.**

Magi Name used for the people who brought gifts to the baby Jesus; the Wise Men.

Mahlon First husband of Ruth; son of Naomi and Elimelech.

Malachi Last prophet of the Old Testament; name means "my messenger"; author of the Book of Malachi.

Mark Author of the Gospel of Mark; his work as an evangelist is often shown by a winged eagle, which reminds us of the grace of the Holy Spirit, which was always with Jesus, or of Jesus' ascension. (Sometimes Mark is represented by a lion and John is represented by an eagle.)

Martha Sister of Mary and Lazarus; hostess who showed concern for Jesus' comfort while He taught at her home.

Mary (1) Mother of Jesus. (2) (Magdalene) Woman whom Jesus freed from demons; became faithful follower of Jesus and His ministry. Among the first to whom Jesus appeared after His resurrection. (3) Sister of Martha and Lazarus, faithful followers of Jesus. (4) (Salome) Mother of James and John, traveled with Jesus and the disciples, witnessed the resurrection.

Matthew One of Jesus' twelve disciples; an apostle; witness to Jesus' resurrection; a tax collector and son of Alphaeus (Matthew 9:9–13; Mark 2:13–17); also called Levi (Mark 2:14); author of the Gospel of Matthew; his work as an evangelist is shown as a winged man, which reminds us of the human nature of the Lord Jesus or his incarnation, or by moneybags to show his first profession. Church history says Matthew died for his faith by crucifixion in Ethiopia.

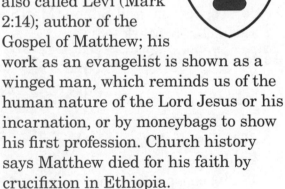

Matthias Apostle elected to replace Judas after Jesus' ascension.

Mephibosheth Son of Jonathan; born lame in both feet; King David showed him kindness for Jonathan's sake.

Meshach Young Judean brought by King Nebuchadnezzar into captivity in Babylon; one of four young men chosen by the king to be educated according to Babylonian ways so that they could serve in his palace. Meshach's Judean name was Mishael.

Methuselah Son of Enoch; sixth in descent from Seth, the son of Adam; father of Lamech; lived 969 years, the oldest man in recorded history.

Micaiah Faithful prophet of God in Samaria.

Michael Archangel; described in Daniel as the "prince" of Israel.

Michal Daughter of King Saul and wife of David; helped David escape when Saul sought to kill him; ridiculed David for dancing before the Lord.

Miriam Sister of Moses who watched him when, as a baby, he floated in the Nile; later led Israel in praising God for delivering them from Egypt at the time of the exodus.

Mordecai Uncle of Esther who raised her; contributed to saving the life of the king.

Moses Hebrew slave adopted by an Egyptian princess; later killed an Egyptian who was abusing a Hebrew slave; fled to Midian, where he herded sheep; chosen by God to be leader of Israelites in their journey out of Egypt and across the desert to the Promised Land.

Naaman Commander of the army of the king of Aram; healed of leprosy by the prophet Elisha.

Nabal Foolish and cruel husband of Abigail who showed disrespect to David and therefore to the Lord.

Naboth Jezreelite who owned a vineyard in Jezreel; would not sell his vineyard to King Ahab because it was the inheritance of his fathers, so Ahab had him killed.

Naomi Wife of Elimelech; moved from Bethlehem because of a famine. After her husband and both sons died, she returned with daughter-in-law Ruth to Bethlehem, where Ruth married Boaz, a relative of Elimelech's.

Nathan Prophet during the reign of kings David and Solomon; pointed out David's sin when he committed adultery.

Nathanael See **Bartholomew.**

Nebuchadnezzar King of Babylon; brought the people of Judah into captivity in Babylon.

Nehemiah Cupbearer to King Artaxerxes of Persia; author of Book of Nehemiah.

Nicodemus Pharisee who visited Jesus at night and learned about being born again; prepared Jesus' body for burial with Joseph of Arimathea.

Noah "A righteous man" in early Bible times; built an ark as God commanded him; God made a covenant with him never again to cover the entire earth with a flood.

Obadiah (1) Believer in the Lord; in charge of King Ahab's palace; sheltered a hundred of the Lord's prophets from Jezebel when she wished to have them killed. (2) Prophet who wrote the Book of Obadiah.

Obed Son of Ruth and Boaz; ancestor of King David.

Og King of Bashan; one of the last of the giant race of Rephaim.

Omri King of Israel; became king after Tibni son of Ginath died; did evil in the eyes of the Lord.

Onesimus Runaway slave of Philemon who was a believer in Christ; was sent back to his master by Paul.

Orpah Moabite woman who married Chilion, son of Naomi and Elimelech; sister-in-law to Ruth.

Paul Missionary and apostle of the Early Church; met the risen Christ on the road to Damascus, where he intended to arrest Christians on authority of the Jewish leaders in Jerusalem; took three missionary trips recorded in the Book of Acts, and possibly others; arrested by Romans in Jerusalem and eventually taken to Rome to plead his case to Caesar. The Book of Acts ends with Paul under house arrest in Rome. Church tradition says he was released from prison in Rome and traveled to Spain before being once again imprisoned in Rome, where he died for his faith in AD 68 during Nero's persecution of Christians. Paul suffered much for Christ, enduring flogging, jail, stoning, hunger, and other trials.

Peleg Ancestor of Christ; born 101 years after the flood. His name is associated with a dividing.

Peter One of Jesus' twelve disciples; an apostle; witness to Jesus' resurrection; from Bethsaida (John 1:44); also called Simon (Matthew 4:18; 10:2), Simon Peter (Luke  5:8; John 1:40; 13:6) and Cephas (John 1:42; 1 Corinthians 1:12; 3:22; 9:5; 15:5; Galatians 1:18; 2:9, 11, 14); fished with brother Andrew (also one of the Twelve) on the Sea of Galilee (Mark 1:16–20); one of a trusted inner circle along with James and John (Matthew 17:1; Mark 5:37; 13:3; 14:33); considered the leader of the Early Church; imprisoned by Herod Agrippa I in Jerusalem, but set free by an angel (Acts 12:1–19). Church history says Peter died for his faith in Rome in AD 68 during Nero's persecution of Christians, crucified upside down because he said he wasn't good enough to die as Jesus did.

Pharisee A religious leader during the time of Jesus; demanded rigid adherence to God's Law.

Philemon Slave-owning believer who received a letter from Paul asking him to welcome back his runaway slave Onesimus.

Philip One of Jesus' twelve disciples; an apostle; witness to Jesus' resurrection; from Bethsaida (John 1:44); brought Nathanael to Jesus (John 1:45–51);  ministered in Samaria after Pentecost (Acts 8:5–13); baptized the Ethiopian eunuch (Acts 8:26–39); bread in his shield refers to his part of the feeding of the 5,000 (John 6:1–14). Church tradition says Philip died for his faith in Christ by stoning and crucifixion.

Philip (Herod) See Herod Philip.

Phinehas Wicked son of Eli who, together with his brother Hophni, died in battle in fulfillment of God's words to Samuel.

Phoebe Important early Christian referred to in Romans 16.

Pompey Roman general who conquered Judea in 63 BC.

Pontius Pilate Roman governor of Judea; questioned Jesus and sent Him to Herod; finally consented to Jesus' crucifixion when crowds chose Barabbas rather than Jesus.

Potiphar Egyptian captain of Pharaoh's guard; owner of Joseph.

priest A man from the tribe of Levi; served in the temple, offering sacrifices to God.

Rachel Daughter of Laban; Jacob's second but favorite wife; mother of Joseph and Benjamin.

Rahab Prostitute who hid Israelite spies before the battle of Jericho.

Rebekah Sister of Laban; wife of Isaac; mother of Esau and Jacob. With her encouragement, Jacob tricked his father into giving him the blessing that normally would be given to the oldest son, Esau.

Rehoboam Son of Solomon; reigned during and after the division of the kingdom; reigned seventeen years as king of Judah.

Reuben Firstborn son of Jacob and Leah.

Rhoda Servant girl who failed to open the door for Peter in her excitement at knowing he was freed from prison.

Ruth Moabite woman who married Mahlon, a son of Naomi and Elimelech; traveled with Naomi to Bethlehem after Mahlon's death; met Boaz and later married him; ancestor of King David and Jesus.

Sadducee Jewish religious group of priests who opposed the Pharisees from the second century BC. Ceased to exist sometime after the destruction of the temple in Jerusalem in AD 70.

Salome Daughter of Herodias; was granted her request for the head of John the Baptist after dancing for Herod Antipas on his birthday.

Samaritan A person from the area of Samaria. Samaritans and Jews were related. When the Assyrians took Israel into captivity, they repopulated the area with people from other lands. Those people intermarried with the small remnant of Israelites left behind. Though they retained some aspects of their faith in the one true God, they did not worship God in Jerusalem. Because of this, the Jews considered them outcasts and traitors to the faith.

Samson Judge of Israel; his mother was told of his birth by an angel; granted great strength from the Lord.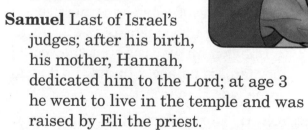

Samuel Last of Israel's judges; after his birth, his mother, Hannah, dedicated him to the Lord; at age 3 he went to live in the temple and was raised by Eli the priest.

Sanhedrin Jewish Council of seventy religious leaders plus the high priest; responsible for the temple and the worship and religious life of the Jews; sometimes called the Supreme Court of Israel. During early New Testament times, the Sanhedrin met in the Hall of Hewn Stones in the temple in Jerusalem.

Sapphira Wife of Ananias; was struck down for lying to God.

Sarah (Sarai) Wife of Abraham; laughed at the word from God that she would bear a son in her advanced age; mother of Isaac.

Satan Another name for the devil.

Saul (1) First king of Israel; disobeyed God; David's father-in-law. (2) Jewish name of the apostle Paul; persecuted those who believed in God; was called by Jesus to be His disciple; apostle and missionary to the Early Church. See **Paul**.

Scribe Person who learned the Jewish Law and copied it onto scrolls by hand. During New Testament times, scribes were often very wealthy and agreed with the Pharisees about many things.

Sennacherib Enemy of Israel; the angel of the Lord killed 185,000 of his soldiers when they marched against the people of God.

Seth Son of Adam and Eve; born after Cain killed Abel; ancestor of Jesus.

Shadrach Young Judean brought by King Nebuchadnezzar into captivity in Babylon; one of four young men chosen by the king to be educated according to Babylonian ways so that they could serve in his palace. Shadrach's Judean name was Hananiah.

Shaphan Court secretary to King Josiah; read the Book of the Law when it was found in the presence of the king.

Shem One of Noah's three sons; ancestor of Jesus.

Sihon King of the Amorites when Israel arrived at the Promised Land.

Silas Prophet who was a co-worker with Paul on his second missionary journey.

Simeon Servant of the Lord; in the temple when Jesus was presented.

Simon (1) Peter's given name; see **Peter**. (2) (of Cyrene) Man whom the guards forced to carry the cross of Jesus at His crucifixion. (3) One of Jesus' half brothers, a son of Mary and Joseph, along with James, Joseph, and Judas (Matthew 12:46; 13:55; Mark 6:3).

Simon the Zealot One of Jesus' twelve disciples; an apostle; witness to Jesus' resurrection; died for his faith in Christ; church history says he traveled many places to share his faith in Christ, along with the apostle Jude.

Sisera Commander of King Jabin of Canaan who reigned in Hazor; his army was defeated and he fled to the tent of Jael, who killed him there with a tent stake and a hammer.

Solomon Son of David and Bathsheba who became king when David died; known for his great wisdom and for building the temple in Jerusalem.

Stephen Leader in the Early Church who was arrested and put on trial; after a rousing speech before the Council (Sanhedrin), he was stoned to death.

Tabitha (Dorcas) Godly and generous woman; raised from the dead by Peter.

Terah Father of Abraham who worshiped idols.

Tertullus Orator who accused Paul before Felix.

Thaddaeus See Jude.

Thomas One of Jesus' twelve disciples; an apostle; witness to Jesus' resurrection, yet doubted it until he put his hands in Jesus' wounds (John 20:24–29; 21:1–14); a twin (John 11:16).

Timothy Fellow traveler and official representative of the apostle Paul; his mother and grandmother believed in God; joined Paul on his second missionary journey, and at one point in this journey Paul sent him to minister to the Church in Corinth; was leader in the Church at Ephesus and co-writer with Paul.

Uriah Bathsheba's husband; King David arranged for him to be killed in battle after David committed adultery with Bathsheba.

Uzziah (Azariah) King of Judah who, for most of his reign, proved a wise, godly ruler.

Vashti First queen of King Xerxes until banished from the kingdom because of disobedience, after which Esther became queen.

Xerxes King of Persia who ruled over 127 provinces stretching from India to Cush; banished his first queen, Vashti, because of her disobedience; chose Esther to be his second queen.

Zacchaeus Short tax collector who climbed a tree in order to see Jesus; upon coming to faith, promised to restore ill-gotten wealth.

Zadok Priest during the reign of David; remained faithful to David all through his reign.

zealot (1) Member of a religious group in Jesus' time who were extremely loyal to Jewish traditions and against the Roman government. (2) A person who is very excited about a certain subject.

Zebedee Fisherman and father of James and John, disciples of Jesus.

Zebulun Tenth son of Jacob and sixth of Leah. Jacob's blessing to Zebulun was that he would "dwell at the shore of the sea; he shall become a haven for ships" (Genesis 49:13).

Zechariah Elderly priest to whom John the Baptist was born.

Zedekiah (Mattaniah) Son of Josiah; last king of Judah; puppet ruler for Nebuchadnezzar, king of Babylon.

Zerubbabel Head of the tribe of Judah at the time of Israel's return from Babylonian captivity.

Ziba Servant of King Saul's household; presented Mephibosheth to David when he was looking for someone in the house of Saul to whom he could show God's kindness.

Zimri King of Israel who reigned for seven days; died when he set the palace on fire around himself after being besieged by Omri and the Israelites.

Zipporah Daughter of Jethro (Reuel) and wife of Moses.

Books of the Bible
(66 Books)

Old Testament
(39 Books)

Genesis: This is a book of beginnings: the beginning of the world, the beginning of sin, the beginning of God's promise (to Adam and Eve) to send a Savior to rescue His people from sin and death, and the beginnings of the family (of Abraham, Isaac, and Jacob) that passed on this promise from God.

Exodus: The story of God's chosen people (known as the Hebrews or Israelites) continues in the Book of Exodus, which means "to go out." The people "go out" of slavery in Egypt, led by the Lord and His appointed leader, Moses, toward the Promised Land.

Leviticus: The third of five books known as the Books of Moses, or the Books of the Law, it focuses on the worship, sacrifices, feasts, and offerings that point to the Messiah, Jesus, the perfect sacrifice to come.

Numbers: The name of this book refers to the counting of the people and their property; but it is mostly about the Israelites' wandering in the desert wilderness, as God faithfully provided for His people.

Deuteronomy: This is the retelling of God's Law—a review of what God has done and of God's will for His people, preparing them for their life in the Promised Land. God calls His people to rededicate their lives to Him.

Joshua: The section of the Bible from Joshua to Esther is called "the history section" of the Old Testament. Joshua, whose name means "the Lord is salvation," becomes the new leader, taking the people into the Promised Land (Canaan) after the death of Moses.

Judges: This tells of the continuing cycle of the people turning away from God and then being conquered by evil enemies, followed by God's call to repentance and His deliverance through His chosen leaders (such as Gideon, Deborah, and Samson).

Ruth: The story of Ruth is about a woman who was not an Israelite, but came to faith in God and became one of the ancestors of Jesus, reminding us that God's kingdom is for all people who have faith in Him.

1 and 2 Samuel: These books tell the story of Samuel, a prophet, priest, and judge. Until the time of Samuel, leaders were chosen by God to carry out His will because God Himself was the true ruler of the people. However, the people wanted a king like nations around them. The first two kings, Saul and David, were anointed by God's prophet Samuel.

1 and 2 Kings: These books continue the history from the time when David and Solomon ruled over a united kingdom, through the times of the divided kingdom, with Israel to the north and Judah in the south. The northern Kingdom of Israel never had a king who was faithful to God; the southern Kingdom of Judah was mostly unfaithful too, though occasionally it was ruled by God-fearing kings who tried to lead the people back to the Lord.

Eventually, both kingdoms were taken into captivity.

1 and 2 Chronicles: These books focus on the reigns of King David and his son Solomon (who built the temple), and continue the history of this royal family in the southern Kingdom of Judah. The family line of David carried the promise of the Messiah, who came centuries later in Christ Jesus.

Ezra: The Books of Ezra, Nehemiah, and Esther continue the story of God's people who had been in captivity in Babylon for seventy years and finally began to see their need for hope in the true God. Ezra was part of a group that returned to Jerusalem to complete the rebuilding of the temple.

Nehemiah: Without the protection of city walls, the people who had returned to Jerusalem from captivity were in constant danger. This is the story of Nehemiah, chosen by God to guide the people to rebuild the walls (in just fifty-two days).

Esther: This book tells of Jewish people who stayed in Persia instead of returning to Judah. Again we see how God can work through ordinary people, such as Esther, to accomplish His will. This ends the historical section of the Old Testament.

Job: This begins a section of five books of poetry. These were originally written in Hebrew and do not rhyme as do poems in English. This is the story of a man who loses everything and suffers much. Job's life is a witness to others that even troubles can provide opportunities to praise God.

Psalms: This is a book of prayer and praise that gives examples of how God's people deal with both joys and sorrows.

David (as shepherd, warrior, and king) wrote about half of the psalms. There is frequent mention of the coming Messiah.

Proverbs: This is a collection of wise sayings that tell how to live a godly life. There is practical advice on many subjects such as making friends, handling money, and caring for the poor; but real wisdom is based on honoring and faithfully following God.

Ecclesiastes: The author of this book speaks of the real purpose of life and encourages us to stay away from things that are meaningless. Some things in life are empty, but life with God brings true joy and direction.

Song of Solomon: Also known as *Song of Songs*, this book tells of the relationship between a husband and wife. We can compare this to the love God has for us, which is perfect and faithful.

Isaiah: He prophesied concerning Judah and Jerusalem during the reigns of Uzziah, Jotham, Ahaz, and Hezekiah, kings of Judah. Isaiah foretold the Messiah's virgin birth and His innocent suffering and death. Isaiah was the son of Amoz.

Jeremiah: Jeremiah loved his nation enough to speak out the truth about their sin and the coming punishment. His harsh warnings often made him unpopular with his countrymen, who ridiculed him; but he remained faithful to God.

Lamentations: This is a poetic book of weeping. The author, thought to be Jeremiah, is crying over the destruction of Jerusalem—the consequence of sin, as prophesied. However, even in the middle of terrible sadness, with God there is hope.

Ezekiel: The prophet Ezekiel lived in difficult times, calling the unfaithful people to repentance. He used picture language and even acted out some of the prophecies to explain the visions he had received from the Lord.

Daniel: This book has two parts, one telling the stories of Daniel and his friends, and the other telling of prophecies and visions from God about the future. God is in charge of all history, and He directs all things for the purpose of saving His people through Christ Jesus.

Hosea: This is the first book of the twelve Minor Prophets. It tells of the prophet Hosea's relationship to his unfaithful wife, Gomer, which is a symbol of God's constant, continual love for His unfaithful people.

Joel: The prophet speaks of a swarm of locusts that destroyed the crops in Judah. Joel warns that if the people do not repent, there will be even greater destruction, caused by the swarm of an enemy's army. He says that the "day of the Lord" will come to punish sin, but those who trust in God will be saved.

Amos: Amos was a shepherd who became God's prophet to warn the people at a time when they were rich and thought things were going well. He warned the people not to trust in money or idols, but to trust in the true God.

Obadiah: Obadiah is the shortest book in the Old Testament. The prophet speaks against the people of Edom, who were glad to see Judah suffering when taken captive by Babylon. The prophet repeats God's promise to one day restore His people to their land.

Jonah: Jonah was an unwilling prophet who tried to run from God's command. He did not want God's message of repentance and forgiveness to be shared with the people of Nineveh, Israel's Assyrian enemy. God clearly wants all people to hear His Word and to come to faith—a message for us today to share with all people.

Micah: The Book of Micah explains that God hates sin but loves the sinner. Though the people would be punished for their refusal to repent of sin, the prophet also speaks a message of hope in the coming Messiah. Micah points to Bethlehem as the birthplace of the Savior who would care for His sheep and lead them like a shepherd.

Nahum: Nahum pronounced God's judgment on the nation that had taken Israel captive. Nahum said that God is slow to anger, but He brings justice on those who are guilty and is a refuge in times of trouble for those who trust in Him.

Habakkuk: This is a conversation as the prophet asks God many questions and God answers, revealing His plan. God assures us that we can hope in Him even when surrounded by troubles, because He is still in control.

Zephaniah: The book begins with sorrow over the sin of the people, but that sadness turns to joy as the prophet speaks of God's deliverance and salvation. The prophet says that when the people return to the Lord, He will bless them, and through them the whole earth will be blessed. That blessing for all the earth is the Promised Savior.

Haggai: The prophet Haggai encouraging the people returning from captivity to rebuild Jerusalem. While the rebuilt temple would not be as beautiful as Solomon's, it would have greater glory because the Savior would one day come to this new temple.

Zechariah: As Zechariah encourages the rebuilding of the temple, he gives even greater encouragement through prophecies about the Promised Savior, such as foretelling Jesus' triumphant entry into Jerusalem on Palm Sunday.

Malachi: The last Old Testament prophet, Malachi, prophesied about the messenger (John the Baptist) who would get people ready for the coming of the Messiah (Jesus). Four hundred years would pass before the Savior was born.

New Testament
(27 books)

Matthew: The four Gospels tell the stories of Jesus' life, death, and resurrected life, each from a special point of view. Matthew, writing mostly to Jewish people, emphasized that Jesus indeed is the promised Messiah, showing over and over how Jesus fulfilled the prophecies of old.

Mark: The style of the Gospel of Mark is full of action, telling what Jesus did. The primary audience was Roman Christians, who would appreciate this active style of writing, which is brief and to the point.

Luke: The author of this book, Luke, was a doctor who had a second career as a missionary and writer. Luke emphasizes Jesus' compassion for people as he tells of Jesus' parables and healing miracles.

John: John's viewpoint tends to be more philosophical than the other Gospels, focusing more on the teachings of Jesus. This would relate especially well to John's Greek audience. His constant theme is the love of Jesus for all people.

Acts: Luke wrote this book of history called the Acts of the Apostles. It tells of the early growth of the Christian Church and how the Holy Spirit worked in the lives of believers such as Stephen, Peter, Paul, Philip, Lydia, and Dorcas.

Romans: This begins the section of *epistles* (letters). Romans was written by the apostle Paul to the Christian Church in Rome around the time of the emperor Nero. It gives basic details about our Christian faith, emphasizing the grace and mercy that is a gift from God through Christ Jesus.

1 and 2 Corinthians: These epistles were written to people in the Greek seaport city of Corinth, a city known for its many idols to false gods. Paul heard that the Church in Corinth had many problems. He wrote these letters to guide them and also encourage them about salvation through Jesus.

Galatians: Some of the people in Galatia (part of modern-day Turkey) were demanding that new Christians follow old Jewish law. Paul emphasizes that faith in Jesus alone is all that is necessary for salvation, not rules or works.

Ephesians: Ephesus was a very large commercial city. As Paul writes to the Church in Ephesus, he is telling us today too, that the Church is not a building; the Church is people—believers in Christ Jesus who want to serve Him.

Philippians: Philippi was a wealthy Roman colony in Macedonia. Paul's letter is full of joy, encouraging the people to be faithful even when troubles come, knowing that in Christ they can do all things.

Colossians: Paul writes to the Church in the city of Colossae that they should be careful of false teachings. He wants them to know that human knowledge is nothing compared to the greatness of God and the saving truth He offers us.

1 and 2 Thessalonians: Thessalonica was a busy seaport. These epistles were written to Christians there who were being persecuted. Paul encourages them to continue in their faith and look forward to the hope that is theirs in Christ Jesus.

1 and 2 Timothy: Having been raised in a godly home, Timothy was led to Christ by Paul and was trained by him as he accompanied Paul on several mission trips. Paul wrote these two letters to Timothy to explain how workers in the Church should teach and live.

Titus: This letter is to Titus, a Greek church worker on the island of Crete who had traveled with Paul on some of his missionary journeys. Paul emphasizes that godly living is always motivated by God's love for us in Christ Jesus.

Philemon: This is a personal letter to Philemon, who is a slave owner. Paul asks for mercy for Philemon's runaway slave, Onesimus, offering to pay off his debts and asking that Philemon welcome him back. This is a picture of us as sinners who are slaves to sin. Jesus has paid the debt for our guilt and now welcomes us back to His family.

Hebrews: This was written to Jewish communities, who were familiar with the priesthood, to teach about the work of Jesus. It shows that not only is Jesus the great High Priest but He is also the perfect and complete sacrifice for the forgiveness of our sins.

James: James wants people to understand that works are an important sign of faith and that "faith without works" is dead. Good works do not create saving faith, but when saving faith in Jesus exists, it is always followed by Christian living.

1 and 2 Peter: Peter sends these letters to people who were being persecuted for their faith. He reminds them that Jesus understands because He suffered for us. The people are encouraged to be faithful until Christ comes again.

1, 2, and 3 John: John was an old man when he wrote these letters, and he often refers to the readers as his "dear children." He summarizes the love and mercy we have in Christ Jesus, which leads us to show love and mercy to others.

Jude: Jude reminds Christians that they are kept in their faith by Jesus. Jude challenges believers of all times and all ages to stand up for what they believe in—Christ—and to clearly protect the true faith.

Revelation: This book of prophecy uses picture language to tell about Jesus' coming on the Last Day to take us to heaven. As Genesis starts with the beginning of time, Revelation speaks of the end of time, when we will see Jesus Christ's complete victory over sin, death, and the power of the devil.

THE TEN COMMANDMENTS

The First Commandment

You shall have no other gods

What does this mean? We should fear, love, and trust in God above all things.

The Second Commandment

You shall not misuse the name of the Lord your God.

What does this mean? We should fear and love God so that we do not curse, swear, use satanic arts, lie, or deceive by His name, but call upon it in every trouble, pray, praise, and give thanks.

The Third Commandment

Remember the Sabbath day by keeping it holy.

What does this mean? We should fear and love God so that we do not despise preaching and His Word, but hold it sacred and gladly hear and learn it.

The Fourth Commandment

Honor your father and your mother.

What does this mean? We should fear and love God so that we do not despise or anger our parents and other authorities, but honor them, serve and obey them, love and cherish them.

The Fifth Commandment

You shall not murder.

What does this mean? We should fear and love God so that we do not hurt or harm our neighbor in his body, but help and support him in every physical need.

The Sixth Commandment

You shall not commit adultery.

What does this mean? We should fear and love God so that we lead a sexually pure and decent life in what we say and do, and husband and wife love and honor each other.

The Seventh Commandment

You shall not steal.

What does this mean? We should fear and love God so that we do not take our neighbor's money or possessions, or get them in any dishonest way, but help him to improve and protect his possessions and income.

The Eighth Commandment

You shall not give false testimony against your neighbor.

What does this mean? We should fear and love God so that we do not tell lies about our neighbor, betray him, slander him, or hurt his reputation, but defend him, speak well of him, and explain everything in the kindest way.

The Ninth Commandment

You shall not covet your neighbor's house.

What does this mean? We should fear and love God so that we do not scheme to get our neighbor's inheritance or house, or get it in a way which only appears right, but help and be of service to him in keeping it.

The Tenth Commandment

You shall not covet your neighbor's wife,
or his manservant or maidservant, his ox or donkey,
or anything that belongs to your neighbor.

What does this mean? We should fear and love God so that we do not entice or force away our neighbor's wife, workers, or animals, or turn them against him, but urge them to stay and do their duty.

The Close of the Commandments

What does God say about all these commandments? He says, "I, the Lord your God, am a jealous God, punishing the children for the sin of the fathers to the third and fourth generation of those who hate Me, but showing love to a thousand generations of those who love Me and keep My commandments." (Exodus 20:5–6)

What does this mean? God threatens to punish all who break these commandments. Therefore, we should fear His wrath and not do anything against them. But He promises grace and every blessing to all who keep these commandments. Therefore, we should also love and trust in Him and gladly do what He commands.

THE CREED

The First Article (*Creation*)

I believe in God, the Father Almighty, Maker of heaven and earth.

What does this mean? I believe that God has made me and all creatures; that He has given me my body and soul, eyes, ears, and all my members, my reason and all my senses, and still takes care of them.

He also gives me clothing and shoes, food and drink, house and home, wife and children, land, animals, and all I have. He richly and daily provides me with all that I need to support this body and life.

He defends me against all danger and guards and protects me from all evil.

All this He does only out of fatherly, divine goodness and mercy, without any merit or worthiness in me. For all this it is my duty to thank and praise, serve and obey Him.

This is most certainly true.

The Second Article (*Redemption*)

And in Jesus Christ, His only Son, our Lord, who was conceived by the Holy Spirit, born of the Virgin Mary, suffered under Pontius Pilate, was crucified, died and was buried. He descended into hell. The third day He rose again from the dead. He ascended into heaven and sits at the right hand of God, the Father Almighty. From thence He will come to judge the living and the dead.

What does this mean? I believe that Jesus Christ, true God, begotten of the Father from eternity, and also true man, born of the Virgin Mary, is my Lord,

who has redeemed me, a lost and condemned person, purchased and won me from all sins, from death, and from the power of the devil; not with gold or silver, but with His holy, precious blood and with His innocent suffering and death, that I may be His own and live under Him in His kingdom and serve Him in everlasting righteousness, innocence, and blessedness,

just as He is risen from the dead, lives and reigns to all eternity.

This is most certainly true.

The Third Article *(Sanctification)*

I believe in the Holy Spirit, the holy Christian church, the communion of saints, the forgiveness of sins, the resurrection of the body, and the life everlasting. Amen.

What does this mean? I believe that I cannot by my own reason or strength believe in Jesus Christ, my Lord, or come to Him; but the Holy Spirit has called me by the Gospel, enlightened me with His gifts, sanctified and kept me in the true faith.

In the same way He calls, gathers, enlightens, and sanctifies the whole Christian church on earth, and keeps it with Jesus Christ in the one true faith.

In this Christian church He daily and richly forgives all my sins and the sins of all believers.

On the Last Day He will raise me and all the dead, and give eternal life to me and all believers in Christ.

This is most certainly true.

THE LORD'S PRAYER

The Introduction
Our Father who art in heaven.

What does this mean? With these words God tenderly invites us to believe that He is our true Father and that we are His true children, so that with all boldness and confidence we may ask Him as dear children ask their dear father.

The First Petition
Hallowed be Thy name.

What does this mean? God's name is certainly holy in itself, but we pray in this petition that it may be kept holy among us also.
How is God's name kept holy? God's name is kept holy when the Word of God is taught in its truth and purity, and we, as the children of God, also lead holy lives according to it. Help us to do this, dear Father in heaven! But anyone who teaches or lives contrary to God's Word profanes the name of God among us. Protect us from this, heavenly Father!

The Second Petition
Thy kingdom come.

What does this mean? The kingdom of God certainly comes by itself without our prayer, but we pray in this petition that it may come to us also.
How does God's kingdom come? God's kingdom comes when our heavenly Father gives us His Holy Spirit, so that by His grace we believe His holy Word and lead godly lives here in time and there in eternity.

The Third Petition
Thy will be done on earth as it is in heaven.

What does this mean? The good and gracious will of God is done even without our prayer, but we pray in this petition that it may be done among us also.
How is God's will done? God's will is done when He breaks and hinders every evil plan and purpose of the devil, the world, and our sinful nature,

which do not want us to hallow God's name or let His kingdom come;

and when He strengthens and keeps us firm in His Word and faith until we die.

This is His good and gracious will.

The Fourth Petition
Give us this day our daily bread.

What does this mean? God certainly gives daily bread to everyone without our prayers, even to all evil people, but we pray in this petition that God would lead us to realize this and to receive our daily bread with thanksgiving.

What is meant by daily bread? Daily bread includes everything that has to do with the support and needs of the body, such as food, drink, clothing, shoes, house, home, land, animals, money, goods, a devout husband or wife, devout children, devout workers, devout and faithful rulers, good government, good weather, peace, health, self-control, good reputation, good friends, faithful neighbors, and the like.

The Fifth Petition
And forgive us our trespasses as we forgive those who trespass against us.

What does this mean? We pray in this petition that our Father in heaven would not look at our sins, or deny our prayer because of them. We are neither worthy of the things for which we pray, nor have we deserved them, but we ask that He would give them all to us by grace, for we daily sin much and surely deserve nothing but punishment. So we too will sincerely forgive and gladly do good to those who sin against us.

The Sixth Petition
And lead us not into temptation.

What does this mean? God tempts no one. We pray in this petition that God would guard and keep us so that the devil, the world, and our sinful nature may not deceive us or mislead us into false belief, despair, and other great shame and vice. Although we are attacked by these things, we pray that we may finally overcome them and win the victory.

The Seventh Petition

But deliver us from evil.

What does this mean? We pray in this petition, in summary, that our Father in heaven would rescue us from every evil of body and soul, possessions and reputation, and finally, when our last hour comes, give us a blessed end, and graciously take us from this valley of sorrow to Himself in heaven.

The Conclusion

For Thine is the kingdom and the power and the glory forever and ever. Amen.

What does this mean? This means that I should be certain that these petitions are pleasing to our Father in heaven, and are heard by Him; for He Himself has commanded us to pray in this way and has promised to hear us. Amen, amen means "yes, yes, it shall be so."

THE SACRAMENT OF HOLY BAPTISM

FIRST

What is Baptism? Baptism is not just plain water, but it is the water included in God's command and combined with God's word.

Which is that word of God? Christ our Lord says in the last chapter of Matthew: "Therefore go and make disciples of all nations, baptizing them in the name of the Father and of the Son and of the Holy Spirit." (Matthew 28:19)

SECOND

What benefits does Baptism give? It works forgiveness of sins, rescues from death and the devil, and gives eternal salvation to all who believe this, as the words and promises of God declare.

Which are these words and promises of God? Christ our Lord says in the last chapter of Mark: "Whoever believes and is baptized will be saved, but whoever does not believe will be condemned." (Mark 16:16)

THIRD

How can water do such great things? Certainly not just water, but the word of God in and with the water does these things, along with the faith which trusts this word of God in the water. For without God's word the water is plain water and no Baptism. But with the word of God it is a Baptism, that is, a life-giving water, rich in grace, and a washing of the new birth in the Holy Spirit, as St. Paul says in Titus, chapter three:

"He saved us through the washing of rebirth and renewal by the Holy Spirit, whom He poured out on us generously through Jesus Christ our Savior, so that, having been justified by His grace, we might become heirs having the hope of eternal life. This is a trustworthy saying." (Titus 3:5–8)

FOURTH

What does such baptizing with water indicate? It indicates that the Old Adam in us should by daily contrition and repentance be drowned and die with all sins and evil desires, and that a new man should daily emerge and arise to live before God in righteousness and purity forever.

Where is this written? St. Paul writes in Romans chapter six: "We were therefore buried with Him through baptism into death in order that, just as Christ was raised from the dead through the glory of the Father, we too may live a new life." (Romans 6:4)

CONFESSION

What is Confession? Confession has two parts.

First, that we confess our sins, and

second, that we receive absolution, that is, forgiveness, from the pastor as from God Himself, not doubting, but firmly believing that by it our sins are forgiven before God in heaven.

What sins should we confess? Before God we should plead guilty of all sins, even those we are not aware of, as we do in the Lord's Prayer; but before the pastor we should confess only those sins which we know and feel in our hearts.

Which are these? Consider your place in life according to the Ten Commandments: Are you a father, mother, son, daughter, husband, wife, or worker? Have you been disobedient, unfaithful, or lazy? Have you been hot-tempered, rude, or quarrelsome? Have you hurt someone by your words or deeds? Have you stolen, been negligent, wasted anything, or done any harm?

What is the Office of the Keys? The Office of the Keys is that special authority which Christ has given to His church on earth to forgive the sins of repentant sinners, but to withhold forgiveness from the unrepentant as long as they do not repent.

Where is this written? This is what St. John the Evangelist writes in chapter twenty: The Lord Jesus breathed on His disciples and said, "Receive the Holy Spirit. If you forgive anyone his sins, they are forgiven; if you do not forgive them, they are not forgiven." (John 20:22–23)

What do you believe according to these words? I believe that when the called ministers of Christ deal with us by His divine command, in particular when they exclude openly unrepentant sinners from the Christian congregation and absolve those who repent of their sins and want to do better, this is just as valid and certain, even in heaven, as if Christ our dear Lord dealt with us Himself.

THE SACRAMENT OF THE ALTAR

What is the Sacrament of the Altar? It is the true body and blood of our Lord Jesus Christ under the bread and wine, instituted by Christ Himself for us Christians to eat and to drink.

Where is this written? The holy Evangelists Matthew, Mark, Luke, and St. Paul write:

> Our Lord Jesus Christ, on the night when He was betrayed, took bread, and when He had given thanks, He broke it and gave it to the disciples and said: "Take, eat; this is My body, which is given for you. This do in remembrance of Me."
>
> In the same way also He took the cup after supper, and when He had given thanks, He gave it to them, saying, "Drink of it, all of you; this cup is the new testament in My blood, which is shed for you for the forgiveness of sins. This do, as often as you drink it, in remembrance of Me."

What is the benefit of this eating and drinking? These words, "Given and shed for you for the forgiveness of sins," show us that in the Sacrament forgiveness of sins, life, and salvation are given us through these words. For where there is forgiveness of sins, there is also life and salvation.

How can bodily eating and drinking do such great things? Certainly not just eating and drinking do these things, but the words written here: "Given and shed for you for the forgiveness of sins." These words, along with the bodily eating and drinking, are the main thing in the Sacrament. Whoever believes these words has exactly what they say: "forgiveness of sins."

Who receives this sacrament worthily? Fasting and bodily preparation are certainly fine outward training. But that person is truly worthy and well prepared who has faith in these words: "Given and shed for you for the forgiveness of sins." But anyone who does not believe these words or doubts them is unworthy and unprepared, for the words "for you" require all hearts to believe.

SECTION 2

DAILY PRAYERS

MORNING PRAYER

In the morning when you get up, make the sign of the holy cross and say:
In the name of the Father and of the Son and of the Holy Spirit. Amen.

I thank You, my heavenly Father, through Jesus Christ, Your dear Son, that You have kept me this night from all harm and danger; and I pray that You would keep me this day also from sin and every evil, that all my doings and life may please You. For into Your hands I commend myself, my body and soul, and all things. Let Your holy angel be with me, that the evil foe may have no power over me. Amen.

EVENING PRAYER

In the evening when you go to bed, make the sign of the holy cross and say:
In the name of the Father and of the Son and of the Holy Spirit. Amen.

I thank You, my heavenly Father, through Jesus Christ, Your dear Son, that You have graciously kept me this day; and I pray that You would forgive me all my sins where I have done wrong, and graciously keep me this night. For into Your hands I commend myself, my body and soul, and all things. Let Your holy angel be with me, that the evil foe may have no power over me. Amen.

ASKING A BLESSING

The eyes of all look to You, [O Lord,] and You give them their food at the proper time. You open Your hand and satisfy the desires of every living thing. (Psalm 145:15–16)

RETURNING THANKS

Give thanks to the Lord, for He is good. His love endures forever. [He] gives food to every creature. He provides food for the cattle and for the young ravens when they call. His pleasure is not in the strength of the horse, nor His delight in the legs of a man; the Lord delights in those who fear Him, who put their hope in His unfailing love. (Psalm 136:1, 25; 147:9–11)

We thank You, Lord God, heavenly Father, for all Your benefits, through Jesus Christ, our Lord, who lives and reigns with You and the Holy Spirit forever and ever. Amen.

SECTION 3

TABLE OF DUTIES

*Certain passages of Scripture for various holy orders and positions,
admonishing them about their duties and responsibilities*

To Bishops, Pastors, and Preachers

The overseer must be above reproach, the husband of but one wife,
temperate, self-controlled, respectable, hospitable, able to teach, not given
to drunkenness, not violent but gentle, not quarrelsome, not a lover of
money. He must manage his own family well and see that his children
obey him with proper respect. (1 Timothy 3:2–4)

He must not be a recent convert, or he may become conceited and fall
under the same judgment as the devil. (1 Timothy 3:6)

He must hold firmly to the trustworthy message as it has been taught,
so that he can encourage others by sound doctrine and refute those who
oppose it. (Titus 1:9)

What the Hearers Owe Their Pastors

The Lord has commanded that those who preach the gospel should receive
their living from the gospel. (1 Corinthians 9:14)

Anyone who receives instruction in the word must share all good things
with his instructor. Do not be deceived: God cannot be mocked. A man reaps
what he sows. (Galatians 6:6–7)

The elders who direct the affairs of the church well are worthy of double
honor, especially those whose work is preaching and teaching. For the
Scripture says, "Do not muzzle the ox while it is treading out the grain," and
"The worker deserves his wages." (1 Timothy 5:17–18)

We ask you, brothers, to respect those who work hard among you, who are
over you in the Lord and who admonish you. Hold them in the highest regard
in love because of their work. Live in peace with each other. (1 Thessalonians
5:12–13)

Obey your leaders and submit to their authority. They keep watch over
you as men who must give an account. Obey them so that their work will be a
joy, not a burden, for that would be of no advantage to you. (Hebrews 13:17)

Of Civil Government

Everyone must submit himself to the governing authorities, for there is no authority except that which God has established. The authorities that exist have been established by God. Consequently, he who rebels against the authority is rebelling against what God has instituted, and those who do so will bring judgment on themselves. For rulers hold no terror for those who do right, but for those who do wrong. Do you want to be free from fear of the one in authority? Then do what is right and he will commend you. For he is God's servant to do you good. But if you do wrong, be afraid, for he does not bear the sword for nothing. He is God's servant, an agent of wrath to bring punishment on the wrongdoer. (Romans 13:1–4)

Of Citizens

Give to Caesar what is Caesar's, and to God what is God's. (Matthew 22:21)

It is necessary to submit to the authorities, not only because of possible punishment but also because of conscience. This is also why you pay taxes, for the authorities are God's servants, who give their full time to governing. Give everyone what you owe him: If you owe taxes, pay taxes; if revenue, then revenue; if respect, then respect; if honor, then honor. (Romans 13:5–7)

I urge, then, first of all, that requests, prayers, intercession and thanksgiving be made for everyone—for kings and all those in authority, that we may live peaceful and quiet lives in all godliness and holiness. This is good, and pleases God our Savior. (1 Timothy 2:1–3)

Remind the people to be subject to rulers and authorities, to be obedient, to be ready to do whatever is good. (Titus 3:1)

Submit yourselves for the Lord's sake to every authority instituted among men: whether to the king, as the supreme authority, or to governors, who are sent by him to punish those who do wrong and to commend those who do right. (1 Peter 2:13–14)

To Husbands

Husbands, in the same way be considerate as you live with your wives, and treat them with respect as the weaker partner and as heirs with you of the gracious gift of life, so that nothing will hinder your prayers. (1 Peter 3:7)

Husbands, love your wives and do not be harsh with them. (Colossians 3:19)

To Wives

Wives, submit to your husbands as to the Lord. (Ephesians 5:22)

They were submissive to their own husbands, like Sarah, who obeyed Abraham and called him her master. You are her daughters if you do what is right and do not give way to fear. (1 Peter 3:5–6)

To Parents

Fathers, do not exasperate your children; instead, bring them up in the training and instruction of the Lord. (Ephesians 6:4)

To Children

Children, obey your parents in the Lord, for this is right. "Honor your father and your mother"—which is the first commandment with a promise—"that it may go well with you and that you may enjoy long life on the earth." (Ephesians 6:1–3)

To Workers of All Kinds

Slaves, obey your earthly masters with respect and fear, and with sincerity of heart, just as you would obey Christ. Obey them not only to win their favor when their eye is on you, but like slaves of Christ, doing the will of God from your heart. Serve wholeheartedly, as if you were serving the Lord, not men, because you know that the Lord will reward everyone for whatever good he does, whether he is slave or free. (Ephesians 6:5–8)

To Employers and Supervisors

Masters, treat your slaves in the same way. Do not threaten them, since you know that He who is both their Master and yours is in heaven, and there is no favoritism with Him. (Ephesians 6:9)

To Youth

Young men, in the same way be submissive to those who are older. All of you, clothe yourselves with humility toward one another, because, "God opposes the proud but gives grace to the humble." Humble yourselves, therefore, under God's mighty hand, that He may lift you up in due time. (1 Peter 5:5–6)

To Widows

The widow who is really in need and left all alone puts her hope in God and continues night and day to pray and to ask God for help. But the widow who lives for pleasure is dead even while she lives. (1 Timothy 5:5–6)

To Everyone

The commandments . . . are summed up in this one rule: "Love your neighbor as yourself." (Romans 13:9)

I urge . . . that requests, prayers, intercession and thanksgiving be made for everyone. (1 Timothy 2:1)

SECTION 4

CHRISTIAN QUESTIONS WITH THEIR ANSWERS

Prepared by Dr. Martin Luther for those who intend to go to the Sacrament.

After confession and instruction in the Ten Commandments, the Creed, the Lord's Prayer, and the Sacraments of Baptism and the Lord's Supper, the pastor may ask, or Christians may ask themselves these questions:

1. Do you believe that you are a sinner?

    Yes, I believe it. I am a sinner.

2. How do you know this?

    From the Ten Commandments, which I have not kept.

3. Are you sorry for your sins?

    Yes, I am sorry that I have sinned against God.

4. What have you deserved from God because of your sins?

    His wrath and displeasure, temporal death, and eternal damnation. See Romans 6:21, 23.

5. Do you hope to be saved?

    Yes, that is my hope.

6. In whom then do you trust?

    In my dear Lord Jesus Christ.

7. Who is Christ?

    The Son of God, true God and man.

8. How many Gods are there?

    Only one, but there are three persons: Father, Son, and Holy Spirit.

9. What has Christ done for you that you trust in Him?

    He died for me and shed His blood for me on the cross for the forgiveness of sins.

10. Did the Father also die for you?

    He did not. The Father is God only, as is the Holy Spirit; but the Son is both true God and true man. He died for me and shed His blood for me.

11. How do you know this?

    From the Holy Gospel, from the words instituting the Sacrament, and by His body and blood given me as a pledge in the Sacrament.

12. What are the Words of Institution?

    Our Lord Jesus Christ, on the night when He was betrayed, took bread, and when He had given thanks, He broke it and gave it to the disciples and said: "Take eat; this is My body, which is given for you. This do in remembrance of Me."

    In the same way also He took the cup after supper, and when He had given thanks, He gave it to them, saying: "Drink of it, all of you; this cup is the new testament in My blood, which is shed for you for the forgiveness of sins. This do, as often as you drink it, in remembrance of Me."

13. Do you believe, then, that the true body and blood of Christ are in the Sacrament?

> Yes, I believe it.

14. What convinces you to believe this?

> The word of Christ: Take, eat, this is My body; drink of it, all of you, this is My blood.

15. What should we do when we eat His body and drink His blood, and in this way receive His pledge?

> We should remember and proclaim His death and the shedding of His blood, as He taught us: This do, as often as you drink it, in remembrance of Me.

16. Why should we remember and proclaim His death?

> First, so that we may learn to believe that no creature could make satisfaction for our sins. Only Christ, true God and man, could do that. Second, so we may learn to be horrified by our sins, and to regard them as very serious. Third, so we may find joy and comfort in Christ alone, and through faith in Him be saved.

17. What motivated Christ to die and make full payment for your sins?

> His great love for His Father and for me and other sinners, as it is written in John 14; Romans 5; Galatians 2; and Ephesians 5.

18. Finally, why do you wish to go to the Sacrament?

> That I may learn to believe that Christ, out of great love, died for my sin, and also learn from Him to love God and my neighbor.

19. What should admonish and encourage a Christian to receive the Sacrament frequently?

> First, both the command and the promise of Christ the Lord. Second, his own pressing need, because of which the command, encouragement, and promise are given.

20. But what should you do if you are not aware of this need and have no hunger and thirst for the Sacrament?

> To such a person no better advice can be given than this: first, he should touch his body to see if he still has flesh and blood. Then he should believe what the Scriptures say of it in Galatians 5 and Romans 7.
>
> Second, he should look around to see whether he is still in the world, and remember that there will be no lack of sin and trouble, as the Scriptures say in John 15–16 and in 1 John 2 and 5.
>
> Third, he will certainly have the devil also around him, who with his lying and murdering day and night will let him have no peace, within or without, as the Scriptures picture him in John 8 and 16; 1 Peter 5; Ephesians 6; and 2 Timothy 2.

APOSTLES' CREED AND LORD'S PRAYER

The Apostles' Creed

I believe in God, the Father Almighty, Maker of heaven and earth.

And in Jesus Christ, His only Son, our Lord, who was conceived by the Holy Spirit, born of the Virgin Mary, suffered under Pontius Pilate, was crucified, died and was buried. He descended into hell. The third day He rose again from the dead. He ascended into heaven and sits at the right hand of God the Father Almighty. From thence He will come to judge the living and the dead.

I believe in the Holy Spirit, the holy Christian church, the communion of saints, the forgiveness of sins, the resurrection of the body, and the life everlasting. Amen.

The Lord's Prayer

Our Father who art in heaven, hallowed be Thy name, Thy kingdom come, Thy will be done on earth as it is in heaven. Give us this day our daily bread; and forgive us our trespasses as we forgive those who trespass against us; and lead us not into temptation, but deliver us from evil. For Thine is the kingdom and the power and the glory forever and ever. Amen.

UNIT PRAYERS

Unit 1

Oh give thanks to the LORD, for He is good,
for His steadfast love endures forever. Psalm 107:1

Unit 2

I will give thanks to the LORD with my whole heart;
I will recount all of Your wonderful deeds. Psalm 9:1

Unit 3

For the LORD is good; His steadfast love endures forever,
and His faithfulness to all generations. Psalm 100:5

Unit 4

The LORD is faithful in all His words and
kind in all His works. Psalm 145:13

Unit 5

Let Your steadfast love come to me, O LORD,
Your salvation according to Your promise. Psalm 119:41

Unit 6

I will bless the LORD at all times;
His praise shall continually be in my mouth. Psalm 34:1

Unit 7

The LORD is my shepherd;
I shall not want. Psalm 23:1

Unit 8

I said, "I will confess my transgressions to the LORD,"
and You forgave the iniquity of my sin. Psalm 32:5

Unit 9

Let the peoples praise You, O God;
let all the peoples praise You! Psalm 67:5

Old Testament Israel

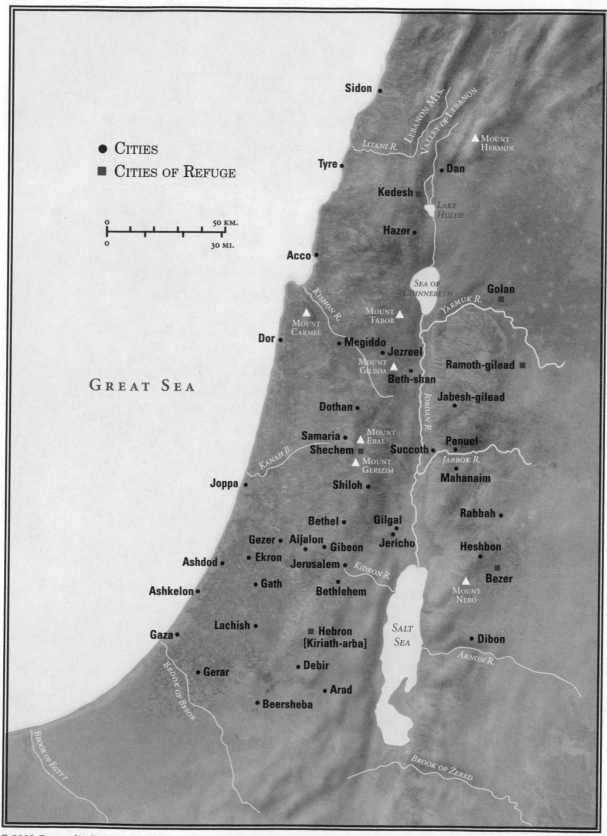

● CITIES
■ CITIES OF REFUGE

0 — 50 KM.
0 — 30 MI.

Sidon

LEBANON MTS.
VALLEY OF LEBANON
LITANI R.
Mount Hermon

Tyre
Dan
Kedesh
Lake Huleh
Hazor

Acco

Sea of Chinnereth
Golan
YARMUK R.

KISHON R.
Mount Tabor
Mount Carmel
Dor
Megiddo
Jezreel
Mount Gilboa
Ramoth-gilead
Beth-shan

GREAT SEA
Jabesh-gilead
JORDAN R.

Dothan

Samaria
Mount Ebal
Shechem
Succoth
Penuel
Mount Gerizim
JABBOK R.

KANAH B.
Mahanaim

Joppa
Shiloh

Rabbah

Bethel
Gilgal
Gezer
Aijalon
Gibeon
Jericho
Heshbon
Ashdod
Ekron
Jerusalem
KIDRON R.
Bezer
Ashkelon
Gath
Bethlehem
Mount Nebo

Lachish
Hebron [Kiriath-arba]
SALT SEA
Dibon
Gaza
ARNON R.
Gerar
Debir
Arad
Beersheba

BROOK OF BESOR
BROOK OF EGYPT
BROOK OF ZERED

Old Testament Regions

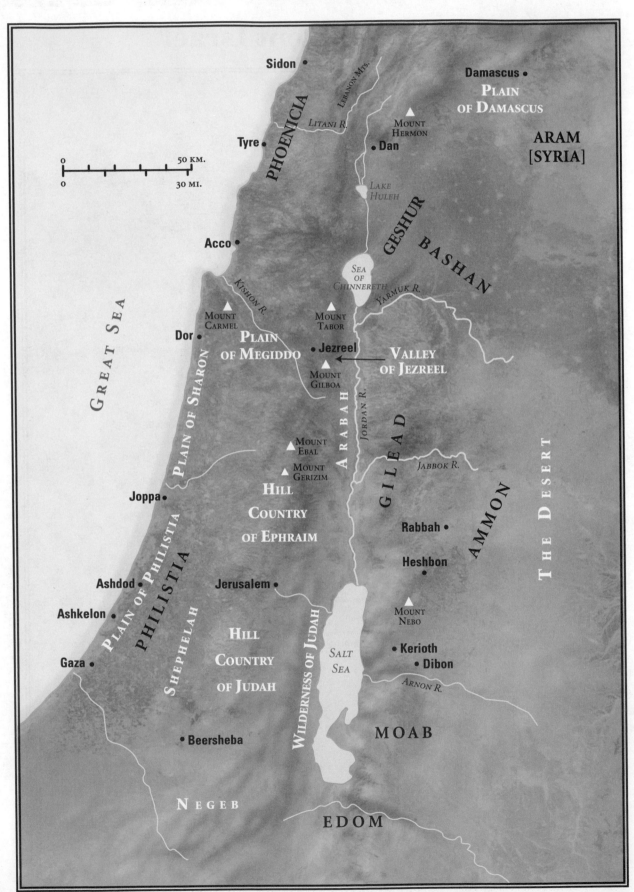

Sidon

Damascus

PLAIN
OF DAMASCUS

LEBANON MTS.

PHOENICIA

MOUNT
HERMON

ARAM
[SYRIA]

LITANI R.

Tyre

Dan

0   50 KM.

0   30 MI.

LAKE
HULEH

GESHUR

BASHAN

Acco

SEA
OF
CHINNERETH

KISHON R.

YARMUK R.

GREAT SEA

MOUNT
CARMEL

MOUNT
TABOR

PLAIN OF SHARON

Dor

PLAIN
OF MEGIDDO

Jezreel

VALLEY
OF JEZREEL

MOUNT
GILBOA

ARABAH

JORDAN R.

GILEAD

JABBOK R.

MOUNT
EBAL

THE DESERT

MOUNT
GERIZIM

HILL

Joppa

COUNTRY

AMMON

Rabbah

OF EPHRAIM

Heshbon

Ashdod

PLAIN OF PHILISTIA

Jerusalem

PHILISTIA

MOUNT
NEBO

Ashkelon

SHEPHELAH

HILL

WILDERNESS OF JUDAH

SALT
SEA

Kerioth

Dibon

Gaza

COUNTRY

OF JUDAH

ARNON R.

MOAB

Beersheba

NEGEB

EDOM

United Kingdom

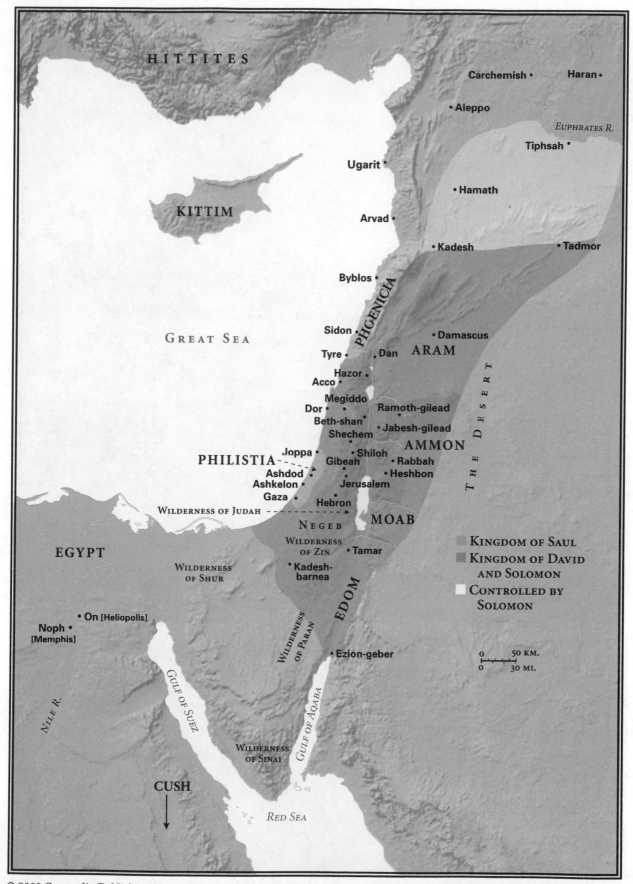

HITTITES

Carchemish •

Haran •

• Aleppo

Euphrates R.

Ugarit •

Tiphsah •

• Hamath

KITTIM

Arvad •

• Kadesh

• Tadmor

Byblos •

PHOENICIA

GREAT SEA

Sidon •

• Damascus

Tyre •

• Dan

ARAM

Hazor •

Acco •

T H E   D E S E R T

Megiddo •

Dor •

Ramoth-gilead •

Beth-shan •

• Jabesh-gilead

Shechem •

AMMON

Joppa •

• Shiloh

PHILISTIA

Gibeah •

• Rabbah

Ashdod •

• Heshbon

Ashkelon •

Jerusalem •

Gaza •

Hebron •

WILDERNESS OF JUDAH

MOAB

NEGEB

WILDERNESS
OF ZIN

• Tamar

EGYPT

WILDERNESS
OF SHUR

• Kadesh-
barnea

EDOM

• On [Heliopolis]

Noph •
[Memphis]

WILDERNESS
OF PARAN

KINGDOM OF SAUL

KINGDOM OF DAVID
AND SOLOMON

CONTROLLED BY
SOLOMON

GULF OF SUEZ

• Ezion-geber

0   50 KM.
0   30 MI.

NILE R.

GULF OF AQABA

WILDERNESS
OF SINAI

CUSH

RED SEA

New Testament Cities

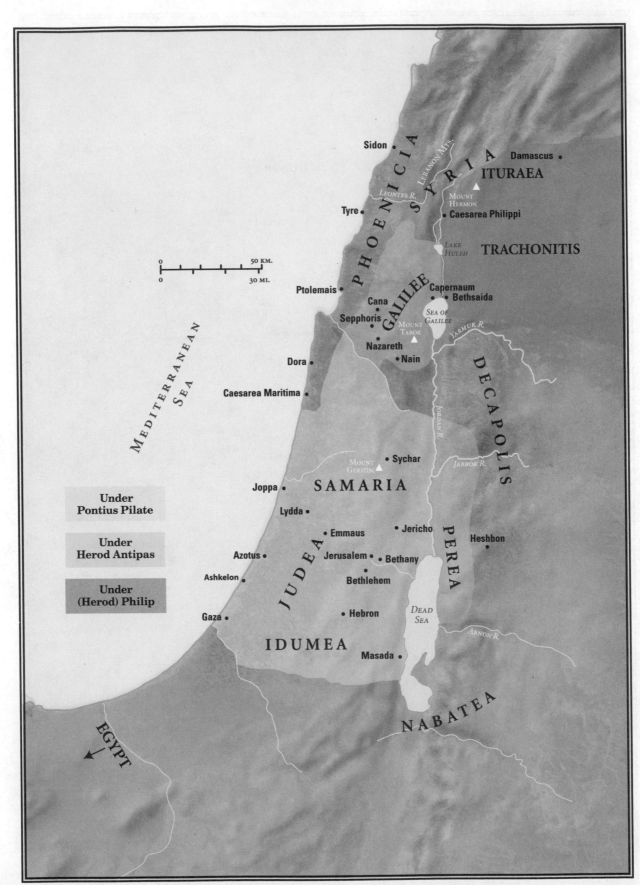

Under
Pontius Pilate

Under
Herod Antipas

Under
(Herod) Philip

MEDITERRANEAN SEA

PHOENICIA
SYRIA
ITURAEA
TRACHONITIS
GALILEE
DECAPOLIS
SAMARIA
JUDEA
PEREA
IDUMEA
NABATEA
EGYPT

Sidon
Damascus
LEBANON MTS.
LEONTES R.
MOUNT HERMON
Tyre
Caesarea Philippi
LAKE HULEH
Ptolemais
Capernaum
Bethsaida
Cana
SEA OF GALILEE
Sepphoris
MOUNT TABOR
YARMUK R.
Nazareth
Nain
Dora
Caesarea Maritima
JORDAN R.
JABBOK R.
Sychar
MOUNT GERIZIM
Joppa
Lydda
Emmaus
Jericho
Heshbon
Azotus
Jerusalem
Bethany
Ashkelon
Bethlehem
Gaza
DEAD SEA
Hebron
ARNON R.
Masada

0   50 KM.
0   30 MI.

The Twelve Tribes

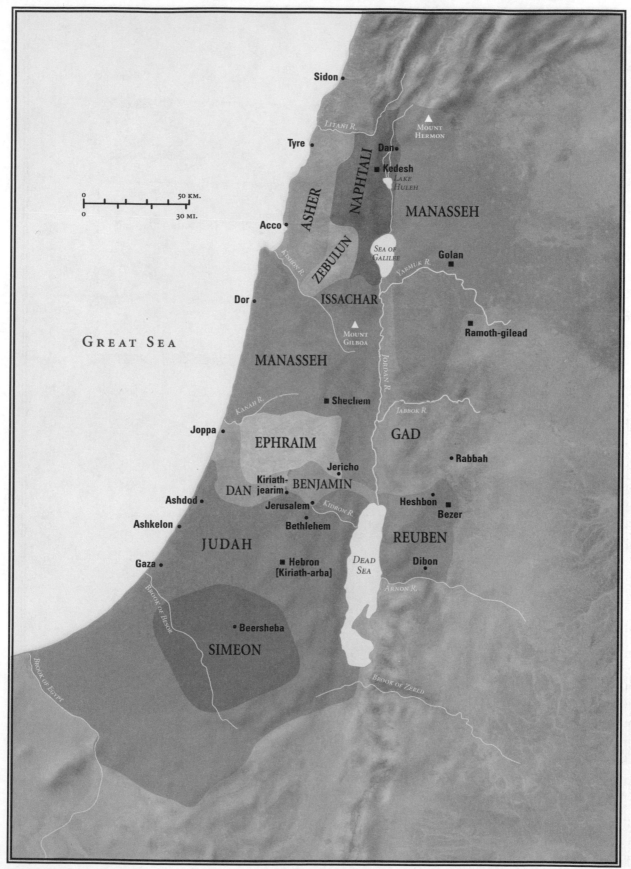

Jesus' Ministry in the Gospels

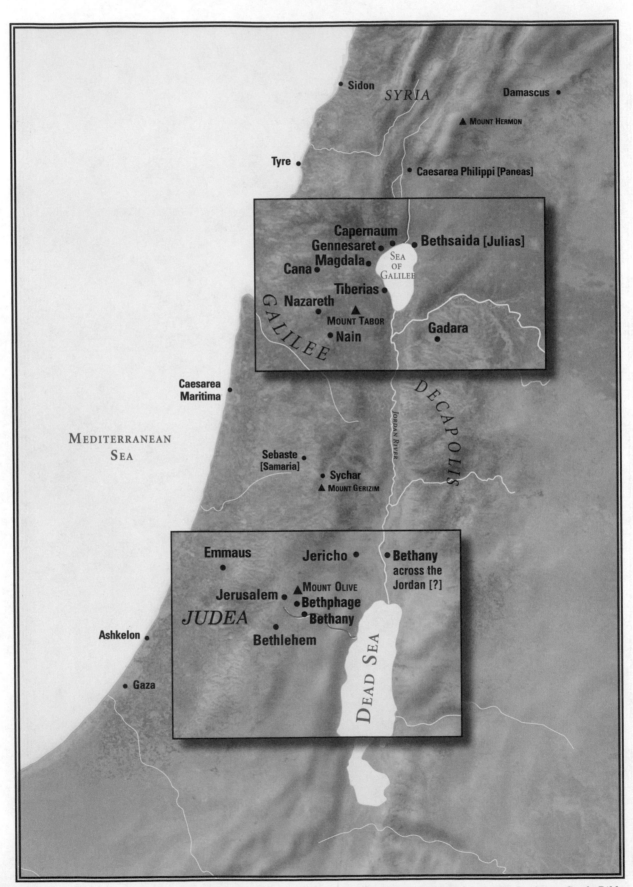

SYRIA

Sidon

Damascus •

▲ Mount Hermon

Tyre •

• Caesarea Philippi [Paneas]

Capernaum
Gennesaret
Magdala
Cana •
Bethsaida [Julias]
Sea of Galilee

Tiberias •

Nazareth •
Mount Tabor ▲
Nain •
Gadara •

GALILEE

DECAPOLIS

Caesarea Maritima •

MEDITERRANEAN SEA

Jordan River

Sebaste [Samaria] •
• Sychar
▲ Mount Gerizim

Emmaus •

Jericho •
• Bethany across the Jordan [?]

Jerusalem •
Mount Olive ▲
Bethphage •
Bethany •

JUDEA

Bethlehem •

Ashkelon •

Dead Sea

• Gaza

The Apostles' Ministry

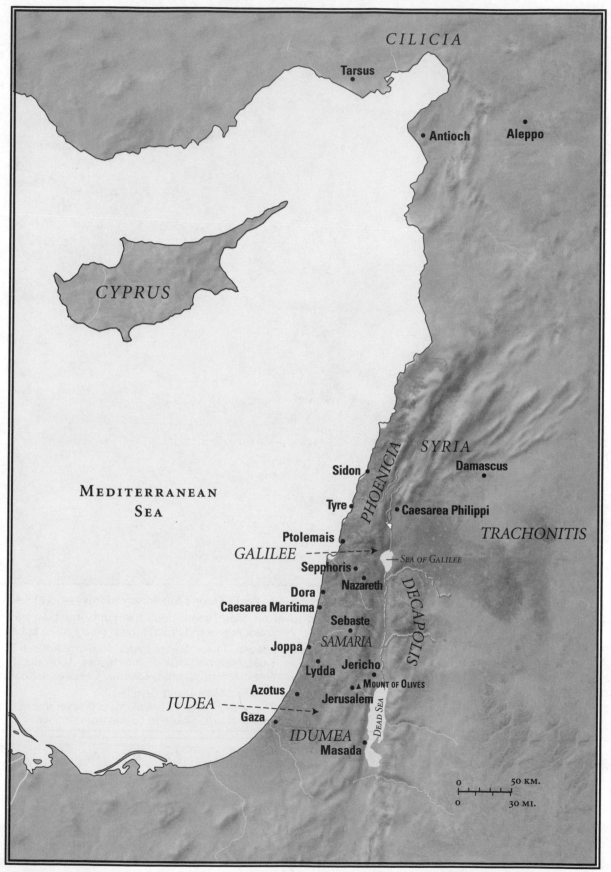

CILICIA

Tarsus

Antioch   Aleppo

CYPRUS

SYRIA

Damascus

Sidon

PHOENICIA

MEDITERRANEAN
SEA

Tyre   Caesarea Philippi

TRACHONITIS

Ptolemais

GALILEE - - - →   SEA OF GALILEE

Sepphoris

Nazareth   DECAPOLIS

Dora

Caesarea Maritima

Sebaste

Joppa   SAMARIA

Lydda   Jericho

Azotus   MOUNT OF OLIVES

JUDEA - - - →   Jerusalem

Gaza   DEAD SEA

IDUMEA

Masada

0   50 KM.

0   30 MI.

Paul's Missionary Journeys

AD 46–48—Paul's First Missionary Journey—Acts 13–14

Who— Paul, Barnabas, John Mark (leaves in Perga to return to Jerusalem)

Where— Antioch, Cyprus, Perga, Antioch in Pisidia, Iconium, Lystra, Derbe
Retrace to Perga, Attalia to Jerusalem

What— Preached to Jews first in the synagogues, then to Gentiles

AD 49/50–52—Paul's Second Missionary Journey—Acts 15:40–18:22

Who— Paul, Silas, Timothy joins them in Lystra, Luke joins them in Troas, Aquila and Priscilla travel with Paul to Ephesus

Where— Antioch, Tarsus, Derbe, Lystra, Iconium, Antioch in Pisidia, Troas, Neapolis, Philippi, Amphipolis, Apollonia, Thessalonica, Berea, Athens, Corinth, Ephesus, Caesarea, Jerusalem, Antioch

What— Preached to Jews and Gentiles
Paul wrote 1 and 2 Thessalonians Epistles from Corinth
Paul wrote the Galatians Epistle from Antioch

| 250 | BC†AD | 1 | 36 | 37 | 38 | 39 | 40 | 41 | 42 | 43 | 44 | | 48 | 4 |

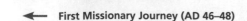 First Missionary Journey (AD 46–48)

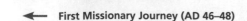 Second Missionary Journey (AD 49/50–52)

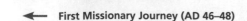 Third Missionary Journey (AD 52/53–57)

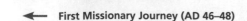 Trip to Rome (AD 59–61/62)

AD 49/50—Jerusalem Council—Acts 15

Who— Paul, Barnabas, James, Peter, Silas

Where— Jerusalem

What— Met with leaders of the entire Church, who then wrote a letter to Gentile Christians in Antioch
Paul and Silas partner; Barnabas and John Mark partner

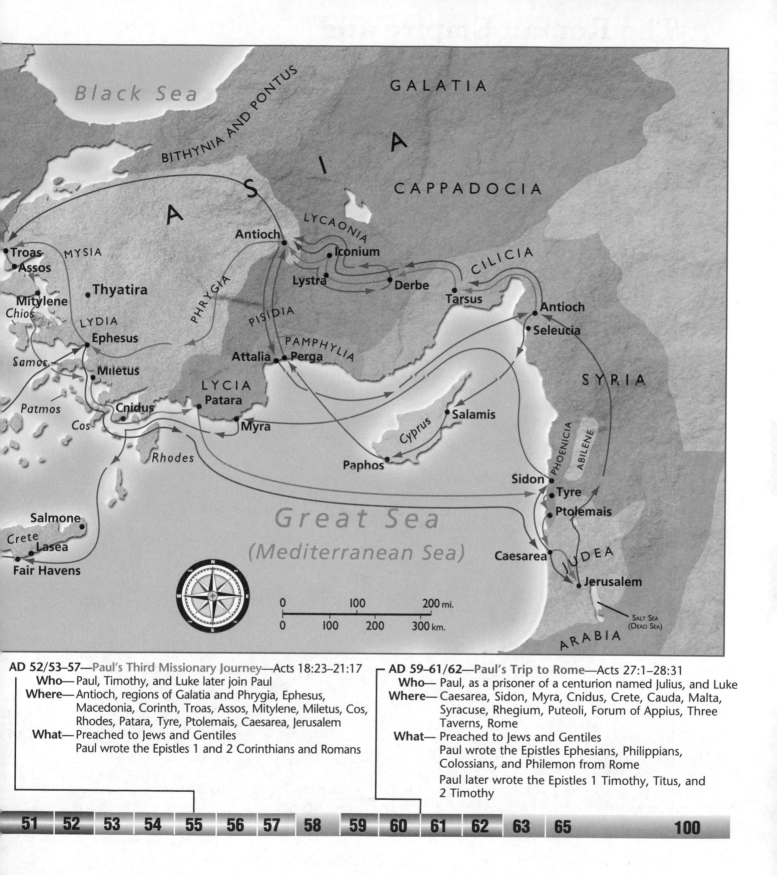

Black Sea

GALATIA

BITHYNIA AND PONTUS

A S I A

CAPPADOCIA

LYCAONIA

MYSIA

Troas
Assos
Mitylene
Chios
Thyatira
LYDIA
Ephesus
Samos
Miletus
Patmos
Cnidus
Cos
Rhodes

Antioch
Iconium
Lystra
Derbe

PHRYGIA
PISIDIA
PAMPHYLIA
Attalia   Perga
LYCIA
Patara
Myra

Tarsus

CILICIA

Antioch
Seleucia

SYRIA

Cyprus
Salamis

Paphos

PHOENICIA ABILENE

Sidon
Tyre
Ptolemais

Salmone
Crete
Lasea
Fair Havens

Great Sea
(Mediterranean Sea)

Caesarea

JUDEA

Jerusalem

SALT SEA
(DEAD SEA)

ARABIA

0   100   200 mi.
0 100 200 300 km.

AD 52/53–57—Paul's Third Missionary Journey—Acts 18:23–21:17
  Who— Paul, Timothy, and Luke later join Paul
  Where— Antioch, regions of Galatia and Phrygia, Ephesus, Macedonia, Corinth, Troas, Assos, Mitylene, Miletus, Cos, Rhodes, Patara, Tyre, Ptolemais, Caesarea, Jerusalem
  What— Preached to Jews and Gentiles
      Paul wrote the Epistles 1 and 2 Corinthians and Romans

AD 59–61/62—Paul's Trip to Rome—Acts 27:1–28:31
  Who— Paul, as a prisoner of a centurion named Julius, and Luke
  Where— Caesarea, Sidon, Myra, Cnidus, Crete, Cauda, Malta, Syracuse, Rhegium, Puteoli, Forum of Appius, Three Taverns, Rome
  What— Preached to Jews and Gentiles
      Paul wrote the Epistles Ephesians, Philippians, Colossians, and Philemon from Rome
      Paul later wrote the Epistles 1 Timothy, Titus, and 2 Timothy

| 51 | 52 | 53 | 54 | 55 | 56 | 57 | 58 | 59 | 60 | 61 | 62 | 63 | 65 | 100 |

The Roman Empire and Paul's Journey to Rome

Londinium

ATLANTIC
OCEAN

RHINE R.

Colonia Agrippina
[Cologne]

Augusta Treverorum
[Trier]

Lutetia

Augusta Vir
[Augsburg]

Burdigala

Lugdunum
[Lyon]

Cremona

Venetia

Aq

Genua

Tolosa

Pisae

Salmantica

Rome

Toletum

Puteoli
Neapoli

Corduba   Valentia

Hispalis

Caralis

Gades   Malaca

Mess

Utica
Carthage

Icosium
[Algiers]

Hippo
Regius

ME
[MA

**Paul's Journey to Rome
in AD 57–58**

Oea
[Tripoli]

0   500 MI.

0   500 KM.

282

rum

DANUBE R.

DANUBE R.

BLACK SEA

Trapezus

TIC SEA

rundisium

Philippi

Byzantium

Thessalonica

Pergamum

AEGEAN SEA

Ephesus

Tarsus

EUPHRATES R.

Rhegium

ACHAIA

Athens

Myra

Antioch

racuse

Cnidus

Sparta

CYPRUS

CRETE

Sidon

Damascus

Fair Havens

Caesarea Maritima

MEDITERRANEAN SEA

Jerusalem

Major

Alexandria

Cyrene

Petra

Aelana

Memphis

NILE R.

RED SEA

APPENDIX

Table of Contents

(repeated here for convenience)